Decentering Relational

MW00862136

Decentering Relational Theory: A Comparative Critique invites relational theorists to contemplate the influence, overlaps, and relationship between relational theory and other perspectives. Self-critique was the focus of *De-Idealizing Relational Theory*. *Decentering Relational Theory* pushes critique in a different direction by explicitly engaging the questions of theoretical and clinical overlap – and lack thereof – with writers from other psychoanalytic orientations. In part, this comparison involves critique, but in part, it does not. It addresses issues of influence, both bidirectional and unidimensional. Our authors took up this challenge in different ways.

Like our authors in *De-Idealizing*, writers who contributed to *Decentering* were asked to move beyond their own perspective without stereotyping alternate perspectives. Instead, they seek to expand our understanding of the convergences and divergences between different relational perspectives and those of other theories.

Whether to locate relational thought in a broader theoretical envelope, make links to other theories, address critiques leveled at us, or push relational thinking forward, our contributors thought outside the box. The kinds of comparisons they were asked to make were challenging. We are grateful to them for having taken up this challenge. *Decentering Relational Theory: A Comparative Critique* will appeal to psychoanalysts and psychoanalytic psychotherapists across the theoretical spectrum.

Lewis Aron, Ph.D., ABPP is the director of the New York University Postdoctoral Program in Psychotherapy and Psychoanalysis. He is the author and editor of numerous articles and books on psychotherapy and psychoanalysis and well known for his study and reading groups around the world. His most recent book, co-authored with Galit Atlas, is the Routledge title *Dramatic Dialogue: Contemporary Clinical Practice.*

Sue Grand, Ph.D., is faculty at the NYU Postdoctoral Program in Psychotherapy and Psychoanalysis. She is the author of *The Reproduction of Evil: A Clinical and Cultural Perspective* and *The Hero in the Mirror*, and has co-edited two books on the trans-generational transmission of trauma. She practices in NYC and in Teaneck, NJ.

Joyce Slochower, Ph.D., ABPP is Professor Emerita at Hunter College and Graduate Center, the City University of New York. She is on the faculty of the New York University Postdoctoral Program, the Steven Mitchell Center, the National Training Program of NIP, the Philadelphia Center for Relational Studies, and the Psychoanalytic Institute of Northern California in San Francisco. She is the author of the Routledge titles *Holding and Psychoanalysis* and *Psychoanalytic Collisions*. Second editions of both books were released in 2014. She is in private practice in New York City, where she sees individuals and couples, and runs supervision and study groups.

RELATIONAL PERSPECTIVES BOOK SERIES

LEWIS ARON, ADRIENNE HARRIS, STEVEN KUCHUCK & EYAL ROZMARIN
Series Editor

The Relational Perspectives Book Series (RPBS) publishes books that grow out of or contribute to the relational tradition in contemporary psychoanalysis. The term *relational psychoanalysis* was first used by Greenberg and Mitchell[1] to bridge the traditions of interpersonal relations, as developed within interpersonal psychoanalysis and object relations, as developed within contemporary British theory. But, under the seminal work of the late Stephen A. Mitchell, the term *relational psychoanalysis* grew and began to accrue to itself many other influences and developments. Various tributaries—interpersonal psychoanalysis, object relations theory, self psychology, empirical infancy research, and elements of contemporary Freudian and Kleinian thought—flow into this tradition, which understands relational configurations between self and others, both real and fantasied, as the primary subject of psychoanalytic investigation.

We refer to the relational tradition, rather than to a relational school, to highlight that we are identifying a trend, a tendency within contemporary psychoanalysis, not a more formally organized or coherent school or system of beliefs. Our use of the term *relational* signifies a dimension of theory and practice that has become salient across the wide spectrum of contemporary psychoanalysis. Now under the editorial supervision of Lewis Aron, Adrienne Harris, Steven Kuchuck and Eyal Rozmarin, the Relational Perspectives Book Series originated in 1990 under the editorial eye of the late Stephen A. Mitchell. Mitchell was the most prolific and influential of the originators of the relational tradition. Committed to dialogue among psychoanalysts, he abhorred the authoritarianism that dictated adherence to a rigid set of beliefs or technical restrictions. He championed open discussion, comparative and integrative approaches, and promoted new voices across the generations.

Included in the Relational Perspectives Book Series are authors and works that come from within the relational tradition, extend and develop that tradition, as well as works that critique relational approaches or compare and contrast it with alternative points of view. The series includes our most distinguished senior psychoanalysts, along with younger contributors who bring fresh vision. A full list of titles in this series is available at https://www.routledge.com/mentalhealth/series/LEARPBS

[1]   Greenberg, J. & Mitchell, S. (1983). *Object relations in psychoanalytic theory.* Cambridge, MA: Harvard University

Decentering
Relational Theory

A Comparative Critique

Edited by
Lewis Aron, Sue Grand,
and Joyce Slochower

Routledge
Taylor & Francis Group

LONDON AND NEW YORK

First published 2018
by Routledge
2 Park Square, Milton Park, Abingdon, Oxon OX14 4RN

and by Routledge
711 Third Avenue, New York, NY 10017

Routledge is an imprint of the Taylor & Francis Group, an informa business

British Library Cataloguing-in-Publication Data
A catalogue record for this book is available from the British Library

Library of Congress Cataloging-in-Publication Data
Names: Aron, Lewis, editor. | Grand, Sue, editor. | Slochower, Joyce Anne, 1950– editor.
Title: Decentering relational theory : a comparative critique / edited by Lewis Aron, Sue Grand, and Joyce Slochower.
Description: Abingdon, Oxon ; New York, NY : Routledge, 2018. | Series: Relational perspectives book series | Includes bibliographical references and index.
Identifiers: LCCN 2017060456 (print) | LCCN 2018002922 (ebook) | ISBN 9781315113609 (Master) | ISBN 9781351625531 (Web PDF) | ISBN 9781351625524 (ePub) | ISBN 9781351625517 (Mobipocket/Kindle) | ISBN 9781138080188 (hardback : alk. paper) | ISBN 9781138080201 (pbk. : alk. paper)
Subjects: LCSH: Object relations (Psychoanalysis) | Interpersonal relations. | Psychoanalysis.
Classification: LCC BF175.5.O24 (ebook) | LCC BF175.5.O24 D43 2018 (print) | DDC 150.19/5—dc23
LC record available at https://lccn.loc.gov/2017060456

ISBN: 978-1-138-08018-8 (hbk)
ISBN: 978-1-138-08020-1 (pbk)
ISBN: 978-1-315-11360-9 (ebk)

Typeset in Times New Roman and Gill Sans
by Florence Production Ltd, Stoodleigh, Devon, UK

Contents

Author biographies

Lewis Aron, Ph.D., ABPP is the Director of the New York University Postdoctoral Program in Psychotherapy and Psychoanalysis. He has served as president of the Division of Psychoanalysis (39) of the American Psychological Association; founding president of the International Association for Relational Psychoanalysis and Psychotherapy (IARPP); founding president of the Division of Psychologist-Psychoanalysts of the New York State Psychological Association. He is the cofounder and co-chair of the Sándor Ferenczi Center at the New School for Social Research; Professor, Interdisciplinary Center (IDC), Herzliya, Israel. He was one of the founders of *Psychoanalytic Dialogues* and is the series coeditor of the *Relational Perspectives* book series (Routledge). He is the editor and author of numerous clinical and scholarly journal articles and books, including *A Meeting of Minds*, and most recently, with Galit Atlas, *Dramatic Dialogue: Contemporary Clinical Practice*. He is widely known for his study/reading groups in NYC and online.

Sue Grand, Ph.D., is faculty and supervisor at the NYU Postdoctoral program in psychotherapy and psychoanalysis; faculty, the trauma program at the National Institute for the Psychotherapies; faculty, the Mitchell Center for Relational Psychoanalysis, and fellow at the Institute for Psychology and the Other. She is an associated editor of *Psychoanalytic Dialogues* and *Psychoanalysis Culture and Society*. She is the author of: *The Reproduction of Evil: A Clinical and Cultural Perspective* and *The Hero in the Mirror: From Fear to Fortitude*. She is the co-editor, with Jill Salberg, of *The Wounds of History: Repair and Resilience in the*

Trans-Generational Transmission of Trauma and *Trans-generational Transmission and the Other: Dialogues across History and Difference.* She is in private practice in NYC and Teaneck, NJ.

Joyce Slochower, Ph.D., ABPP is Professor Emerita of Psychology at Hunter College and the Graduate Center, CUNY; faculty, NYU Postdoctoral Program, Steven Mitchell Center, National Training Program of NIP, Philadelphia Center for Relational Studies and PINC in San Francisco. Second editions of her books, *Holding and Psychoanalysis: A Relational Perspective* (1996) and *Psychoanalytic Collisions* (2006) were released in 2014. She is in private practice in New York City.

Galit Atlas, Ph.D., is on the faculty at NYU Postdoctoral Program in Psychotherapy and Psychoanalysis, and faculty at the Four Year Adult and National Training Programs at NIP. She is the author of *The Enigma of Desire: Sex, Longing and Belonging in Psychoanalysis* (Routledge, 2015), and of *Dramatic Dialogue: Contemporary Clinical Practice* (co-authored with Lewis Aron. Routledge, 2017). Atlas serves on the editorial board of *Psychoanalytic Perspectives* and is the author of articles and book chapters that focus primarily on gender and sexuality. Her NYT article 'A tale of Two Twins' was the winner of 2016 Gradiva award. Atlas is a psychoanalyst and clinical supervisor in private practice in New York City.

Anthony Bass, Ph.D., is an adjunct associate professor and a supervising analyst in the Relational Orientation at the NYU Postdoctoral Program in Psychoanalysis and Psychotherapy. In addition, he teaches and supervises at the Columbia University Center for Psychoanalytic Training and Research, the NIP National Training Program, the Institute for Relational Psychoanalysis of Philadelphia, and the Stephen Mitchell Center for Relational Studies, where he serves as president of the board. He is the 2018 Visiting Professor at the Michigan Psychoanalytic Institute. He is an editor in chief of *Psychoanalytic Dialogues: the International Journal of Relational Perspectives,* and a founding board member of the International Association for Relational Psychoanalysis and Psychotherapy.

Jessica Benjamin is a supervising faculty member at the New York University Postdoctoral Psychology program in Psychotherapy and Psychoanalysis and a founding board member and faculty of the Stephen

Mitchell Relational Studies Center. She is the author of three books: *The Bonds of Love*; *Like Subjects, Love Objects*; *Shadow of the Other*. She directed The Acknowledgment Project (2004–2010), a series of dialogues between Israeli and Palestinian mental health professionals and narrated a video project on Combatants for Peace: *movingbeyondviolence.org*, available online. Her most recent book *Beyond Doer and Done to: Recognition Theory, Intersubjectivity and the Third* was published in 2017.

Sam Gerson, Ph.D., is a founder and past president of the Northern California Society for Psychoanalytic Psychology (NCSPP) and of the Psychoanalytic Institute of Northern California (PINC) where he is a training and supervising analyst. Dr. Gerson is an associate editor of *Psychoanalytic Dialogues,* and an editor for *Studies in Gender and Sexuality* and the *Psychoanalytic Quarterly.* He has written about aspects of intersubjectivity and psychopathology including the publications 'Hysteria and Humiliation' (2011, *Psychoanalytic Dialogues*) and 'The Relational Unconscious' (2004, *Psychoanalytic Quarterly*). In 2007 he received the Elise M. Hayman Award for the Study of Genocide and the Holocaust from the International Psychoanalytic Association for his paper 'When the Third is Dead: Memory, Mourning and Witnessing in the Aftermath of the Holocaust' (2009, *International Journal of Psychoanalysis*).

Adrienne Harris, Ph.D., is faculty and supervisor at New York University Postdoctoral Program in Psychotherapy and Psychoanalysis. She is on the faculty and is a supervisor at the Psychoanalytic Institute of Northern California. She is an editor at *Psychoanalytic Dialogues*, and *Studies in Gender and Sexuality*. In 2009, she, Lewis Aron, and Jeremy Safran established the Sandor Ferenczi Center at the New School University. She, Lewis Aron, Eyal Rozmarin, and Steven Kuchuck co-edit the *Relational Perspectives* book series. She has written on topics in gender and development, analytic subjectivity and self-care, and the analytic community in the shadow of the First World War. Her current work is on analytic subjectivity, on intersectional models of gender and sexuality, and on ghosts.

Donna M. Orange, Ph.D., Psy.D., is educated in philosophy, clinical psychology, and psychoanalysis. Recent books are *Thinking for Clinicians* (2010), *The Suffering Stranger: Hermeneutics for Everyday Clinical Practice* (2011), *Nourishing the Inner Life of Clinicians and Humanitarians*

(2016) And *Climate Crisis, Psychoanalysis, and Radical Ethics* (2017). She teaches at the NYU Postdoctoral Program.

Sophia Richman, Ph.D., ABPP is a psychologist and psychoanalyst licensed in New York and in New Jersey. In addition to her private practice, she is a supervisor at the New York University Postdoctoral Program in Psychotherapy and Psychoanalysis, a training analyst and supervisor at the Contemporary Center for Advanced Psychoanalytic Studies in New Jersey and faculty of the Stephen Mitchell Center for Relational Studies. Dr. Richman is a child survivor of the Nazi Holocaust and has written and lectured extensively about the long-term psychological impact of catastrophic trauma. She is the author of the award-winning memoir, *A Wolf in the Attic: The Legacy of a Hidden Child of the Holocaust* (Routledge, 2002) and *Mended by the Muse: Creative Transformations of Trauma* (Routledge, 2014).

Donnel B. Stern, Ph.D., is training and supervising analyst at the William Alanson White Institute in New York City; clinical consultant and Adjunct Clinical Professor of Psychology at the NYU Postdoctoral Program in Psychoanalysis and Psychotherapy; and faculty, New York Psychoanalytic Institute. He is founder and editor of a book series at Routledge, *Psychoanalysis in a New Key* and the former editor-in-chief of *Contemporary Psychoanalysis*. He has authored four books: *Unformulated Experience: from Dissociation to Imagination in Psychoanalysis* (1997); *Partners in Thought: Working with Unformulated Experience, Dissociation, and Enactment* (2010); and *Relational Freedom: Emergent Properties of the Interpersonal Field* (2015)); and *The Infinity of the Unsaid: Unformulated Experience, Language, and the Nonverbal* (2018). He serves on numerous journal editorial boards, has co-edited many books, has published over 100 articles, and is in private practice in New York City.

Paul L. Wachtel, Ph.D., is Distinguished Professor of psychology in the doctoral program in clinical psychology at City College and the CUNY Graduate Center. He was a cofounder of the Society for the Exploration of Psychotherapy Integration (SEPI) and is a past president of that organization. Among his books are *The Poverty of Affluence*; *Action and Insight*; *Psychoanalysis, Behavior Therapy, and the Relational World*; *Race in the Mind of America: Breaking the Vicious Circle Between Blacks* *and Whites; Relational Theory and the Practice of Psychotherapy; Inside the Session: What Really Happens in Psychotherapy; Therapeutic Communication: Knowing What to Say When*; and *Cyclical Psychodynamics and the Contextual Self: The Inner World, the Intimate World, and the World of Culture and Society.* He has been awarded the Hans H. Strupp Award for Psychoanalytic Writing, Teaching, and Research, the Distinguished Psychologist Award by Division 29 of APA, the Scholarship and Research Award by Division 39 and the Sidney J. Blatt Award for Outstanding Contributions to Psychotherapy, Scholarship, Education and Practice.

Introduction to Decentering Relational Theory

A comparative critique

Lewis Aron, Sue Grand, and Joyce Slochower

The process of evaluating a theory, its contributions and limitations, is most typically done by its critics. Their aim is almost always to find and elaborate on the theory's flaws, typically with the implicit intent of elevating the value of their own model.

This volume, *Decentering Relational Theory: A Comparative Critique,* turns that perspective on its head. Rather than examining relational theory from a critical/competitive point of entry, we invited relational theorists to contemplate the influence, overlaps, and relationship between relational theory and other perspectives.

Decentering Relational Theory is the second volume in this project. The first volume, *De-Idealizing Relational Theory: A Critique from Within,* considers the strengths and limitations of relational thinking from the inside out. Contributors were asked to engage in a loving critique of their own way of formulating analytic theory and process. In *Decentering Relational Theory,* we push that critique in the opposite direction by contemplating and elaborating on how relational theory overlaps with – and differs from – other perspectives. In part, this comparison involves critique; in part it does not; it addresses issues of influence, both bidirectional and uni-directional.

Our authors took up this challenge in different ways. Some (Atlas, Grand, Wachtel) focused on what might be missing from the Relational canon and added to it; some others (D.B. Stern, Richman, Gerson) addressed issues of influence and critique by thinkers from other schools; some traced the evolution and influences on relational thinking (Benjamin, Bass & Harris); some (Orange) picked up and further explored critiques that have been leveled at relational theory and technique. We close the volume with an essay (Aron) that addresses the meta-issue underlying both *De-Idealizing* and *Decentering*: the potential value of psychoanalytic critique.

Like our authors in *De-Idealizing*, writers who contributed to *Decentering* were tasked with the not insignificant request to step outside their own thinking. Whether to locate relational thought in a broader theoretical envelope, make links to other theories, address critiques leveled at us, or push relational thinking forward, our contributions thought outside the box. The kinds of comparisons they were asked to make were challenging. We are grateful to them for having taken up this challenge.

In the first chapter, Sue Grand offers a penetrating critique of trauma theory. It has a central place in relational thinking that has greatly enriched our understanding of human suffering and its developmental origins. Grand underscores our excessive focus on the maternal dyad and argues for a "circle of witnessing" that includes the familial, cultural, and historical dimensions of human experience. She also proposes that what is missing from contemporary trauma theory is the nature and dynamics of resilience.

Donnel Stern takes up the question of mutual influence – and the lack thereof. Relational psychoanalysis has remained somewhat isolated from the views of both European and Latin American psychoanalysis (Kleinian, Bionian, and French). They experience us as marginalizing them. And vice versa. Otherness dominates and forecloses dialogue. Stern opens this space by directly addressing what relational and interpersonal psychoanalysis can gain through thoughtful, self-reflective dialogue (rather than a defense against) the critiques leveled at us by these groups.

Sue Grand invites Jessica Benjamin to reflect on critiques of relational theory and practice. Benjamin articulates the nuances of intersubjectivity theory, arguing that the evolution of intersubjectivity is a dyadic process, one that should be grounded in the developmental phasing of attunement. Benjamin then moves to consider relational training, and argues for greater engagement with issues of aggression and unconscious fantasy.

Paul Wachtel points to the boundary the divides psychoanalytic ideas from those deriving from other therapeutic arenas. He urges us to include non-psychoanalytic approaches – cognitive-behavior therapies (specifically CBT) – *within* the relational paradigm. Wachtel voices both his objections to aspects of the CBT model *and* areas of commonality. He notes that some CBT ideas can be engaged to enhance relational work.

Sophia Richman maintains that when it comes to trauma theory, many relational thinkers have accepted and incorporated a drive theory model which is essentially incompatible with relational premises. Central to this theoretical model is the *death instinct* concept, which in Richman's view, contributes to the pathologizing tilt in our trauma theories. Richman argues for a more nuanced understanding of the holocaust's impact.

Sam Gerson's essay is a spirited rebuttal to Richman's essay. Underscoring the central role of witnessing in trauma work, Gerson argues for the power and endurance of traumatic experience among holocaust survivors. Gerson differs with Richman's perspective on Laub's (and his own) writing. In his view, he and Laub make room for both trauma and resilience in holocaust experience. While acknowledging the value of creativity in helping survivors to recover, Gerson believes (in contrast to Richman) that it is an act of denial or excess hope to believe that creativity can in fact heal victims of such massive trauma.

Galit Atlas invites us to re-conceive the relational baby. In so doing, she integrates the Freudian, Kleinian, and relational baby and configures a more complex one. Where the Freudian baby is dominated by (sexual and aggressive) drives, the Kleinian baby, while also driven, carries with her a rich internal world full of objects. The relational baby, yet more complex, is embedded in the social environment from the get-go. Atlas explores the mutual nature of the baby's relational experience. She notes that in our emphasis on the observable (e.g., on infant research), relational theorizing has paid insufficient attention both to sexuality and the enigmatic.

Donna Orange returns to the beginnings of relational theory by examining Mitchell's work and the theories that influenced him (especially Loewald). Orange introduces us to what she believes is missing (or underemphasized) in relational thinking, namely an "ethic of care". Orange locates its absence in the tendency of many (though not all) relationalists to reject the baby metaphor and its attention to patient vulnerability and need. Something gets lost, she argues, when we too-completely embrace Bromberg's notion of multiple self-states. Bringing together the work of Sander, Daniel Stern, Beebe and Lachmann, and Kohut, Orange issues a clarion call for us to appropriate and own a core ethical self that is committed to a position of ethical integrity and personal courage.

Tony Bass' conversation with Adrienne Harris sketches the development of relational thinking within both the psychoanalytic and political contexts. Far from a synthesis, they suggest that contemporary relationalism is a "large tent" more than a single consistent theoretical thread. They give much attention to Jody Davies' suggestion that relational analysts were all originally "immigrants" from other schools of thought, and they are concerned with our building walls or bridges – a metaphor that is unfortunately extremely timely for us all.

Lewis Aron brings these two volumes to a close by arguing for the vital importance of self-critique when informed and stimulated by the critique of the other. Drawing on recent developments in the philosophy of science, Aron calls for a move beyond liberal tolerance in psychoanalytic communities to a genuine appreciation of the other. "Reflexive skepticism" is the assumption that, as much as we may love and treasure our theories, we must also recognize their limitations, flaws, and need for improvement. We search for and expose our vulnerabilities and turn to others for the value of their different perspective, which allows us to remain vital and to thrive.

Taken together, these essays add another dimension to Volume One (*De-Idealizing Relational Theory*) by expanding our theoretical point of entry into the relational canon and linking it to other psychoanalytic contributions. It is our hope that these essays will challenge you to add your own critique and self-critique to the theory with which you identify, so that psychoanalysis begins to bridge differences in a way that enriches the field as a whole.

Chapter 1

Trauma as radical inquiry

Sue Grand

Beginnings

I began studying trauma in the 1980s, prior to the birth of relational psychoanalysis. When I entered my training, there *were* no trauma studies in mainstream psychoanalysis. This was an unfortunate legacy of our forebears. Freud wrote about sexual trauma, the war neuroses, the stimulus barrier, and the repetition compulsions. But in the arena of sexual abuse, Freud would take a problematic path: he repudiated the seduction theory in preference for Oedipal fantasy. Classical psychoanalysis followed him into the realm of Oedipal fantasy and sexual abuse was foreclosed. Throughout the twentieth century, there *were* psychoanalysts studying trauma through the lens of the Vietnam war (Lifton, 1996; Shatan, 1982) and the Holocaust (Bergmann, 1983; Krystal, 1988; Laub, 1992; Laub & Auerhahn, 1989, 1993). But their work almost seemed to confirm mainstream inattention: if war and genocide defined *trauma,* then surely trauma was a condition of *absolute extremis;* it was outside the purview of our daily practice. This only served to distract us. In the U.S. in 1981, psychoanalysis was riddled with these severed links, splits and contradictions, so that trauma was eclipsed by collective amnesia. These amnestic gaps had gathered around Ferenczi, whose work had been disqualified as madness. Thus, in 1992, Judith Herman would begin her classic text with this observation:

> The study of psychological trauma has a curious history – one of episodic amnesia. Periods of active investigation have alternated with

periods of oblivion . . . Although the field has in fact an abundant and
rich tradition, it has been periodically forgotten and must be periodically reclaimed.

(*Trauma and Recovery*, p. 7)

Psychoanalytic training and trauma studies: in that era, these were two
different tracks, non-communicating.

Now, in contemporary relational psychoanalysis, it may be hard to
recall the magnitude of that gap. After psychoanalysis re-awakened to the
reality of childhood sexual abuse (Alpert, 1994; Davies & Frawley, 1994;
Grand, 1995, 1997a, 1997b), 'trauma' and 'dissociation' began to infuse
our lexicon. We wanted to redress our patients' fragmentation and their
secret wounds. To reach into those wounds, to know and speak with the
'un-thought known' (Bollas, 1995): this required us to reach beyond ourselves. In search for a resonant practice, relational psychoanalysis found
Holocaust studies. We accompanied survivors of genocide into their theory
of trauma, PTSD, and survival (Krystal, 1988; Laub, 1992 etc.). I recall
reading about Laub's 'empty circle' (1998), his articulation of knowing
and not-knowing in massive psychic trauma (1993). In the desert of our
ignorance, someone *knew*. Laub saw into the heart of darkness, translating
dead souls back into human discourse. His concepts of absence and the
'empty circle' resonated, for me, with Guntrip's description of the schizoid
problem (1969), facilitating my thesis about the reproduction of evil
(Grand, 2000). I was not alone in awakening to the power of this literature.
Drawing on Laub, (1993); Laub and Auherhahn (1993); and Caruth (1995),
relational trauma praxis would gradually find its home (see Reis, 2009).

This look would be combined with Green's (1986) work on the 'dead
mother', and with Fonagy, Gergely, Junst and Target's (2002) work on
affect regulation and mentalization. We found a new language for intract-
able wounds. We became grounded in the paradox of speech and silence;
in testimony, narrative, and witnessing (Gerson, 2009; Grand, 2000, Reis,
2009). We had already critiqued the unitary self, and clinical enactment
was re-conceived (Davies, 1994). Enactment was the unspeaking per-
formance of the unseen (see Bass, 2003; D. Stern 1997); it was a call for
witnessing. All of this became entwined with attachment theory (see
Howell, 2005). And Salberg (2016) could begin tracing history and trans-
generational transmission through "the influences of disrupted attachment

across multiple generations" (p. 79). As we have made all of these shifts in relational psychoanalysis, our disciplinary boundaries have become more fluid, expansive, and permeable. History, politics, culture, literature, ethics, philosophy, infancy research, neuro-science; the intersectionality of race, gender and class: to apprehend traumatic subjectivity we have needed to breach our insularity, open our borders, and question received knowledge.

All of this began, for me, in the 1980s. It is now 2016. In the intervening decades, trauma study has been a force of radical inquiry. We have gradually retrieved much that had been marginalized and forgotten in our canon (see Aron & Harris, 1993; Aron & Starr, 2013). We returned to Freud's early work on hysteria, to Ferenczi's experiments with mutual analysis, to the social critique that we see in Fromm. We interrogated classical theory, and drew on the interiority of Object Relations theory, and from the mutual social dynamisms originating in inter-personal theory. We cast doubt on analytic authority, invisibility, sterility, and silence. We embraced feminist critiques, re-writing mother as subject, and re-conceiving the mother-infant dyad (Beebe & Lachman, 2014; Benjamin, 1988; Slochower, 1996). We have theorized trans-generational transmission (see Gerson, 2009, Grand, 2000, 2009, 2012, 2016; Gump, 2016; Guralnik, 2014; Salberg, 2016) and trauma's reproduction (see Grand, 2000). In asking what 'cures', we de-centered ourselves from ego, reason, and interpretation. In all of this, we drew on Freudian theory, self-psychology, object relations, and inter-personal psychoanalysis.

Today, trauma is the focal point for relational psychoanalysis. Dissociation, fragmentation, enactment, affect dys-regulation, multiple self-states, somatic communication, disordered attachments, the *gaps* in mentalization: these terms are now our familiars. They are referents to the collective violence imposed on us by the 'out there' *and* to the intimate conundrums of psychic life. The term 'trauma' has truly become a large tent[1] – from genocide and the 'dead third' (Gerson, 2009) to the chronic relational mis-attunements of infancy and early childhood (see Bromberg, 2011; Schore, 2011) – all of it refers to the collapse of mentalization. All of it calls for relational immersion, affect regulation, and relational repair. Once marginalized, trauma study has facilitated larger cultural critique,[2] reawakened us to history and ethics (Goodman, 2012; Goodman and Layton, 2014; Orange, 2011), and reignited our passions for social justice. This convergence happens not a moment too soon. As citizen-therapists, we face dark times: climate change, global violence, rising hatred, fear and inequality, the authoritarian eclipse of democracy.

Listening for the next turn

In psychoanalysis, trauma has tested us; it has been a force for de-stabilization and radical inquiry. Encounters with trauma can seem to destroy our ability to think, vacating whatever we thought that we knew. But in psychoanalysis, this effect has been paradoxical. If trauma study has seemed to destroy links and vacate our minds, it has *also* been human creativity gestating in human bewilderment. At our best, relational psychoanalysis has come a long way *because* we have been listening to that bewilderment. We must recall, however, that traumatic *knowing* is a destination that can never arrive. Trauma is excess, it is the unexpected; it exceeds human experience. Psychoanalytic knowledge will always be partial, unstable, provisional. But this instability is a great teacher: it inspires us to continue our radical inquiry.

And so, in the rest of this chapter, I want to ask: how is trauma testing us, and undoing us, now, in 2018? Where are our limitations and omissions? How might these problematics point us towards our next turn? What do non-analytic trauma therapies know that we do not? In the course of these reflections, trauma will shake the foundations of our discipline. Although my reflections will apply, in many ways, to the underpinnings of all psychoanalytic orientations, I will be following the stated mission of this volume, and focusing on relational literature and thought. As I meditate on these questions I want to be clear: I do not exempt my own work from these problematics. Indeed, this de-stabilizing inquiry emerges directly the limits of my own work. Thinking about destructiveness in culture and psyche (Grand, 2000), I have stood on the solid ground of psychoanalytic theory. But in thinking about what I have called 'small heroes' (Grand, 2009) I felt descriptively fluent but theoretically in-articulate. Since the publication of the latter book, I have slowly been understanding my predicament. In writing about 'small heroes' I was leaning on theoretical fragments; I was confounded by analytic gaps and impossibilities and I felt I kept falling through space. In recent years, I have been trying to formulate what was missing (Grand, 2013). At this writing, I have realized this. In relational psychoanalysis (and perhaps in all of psychoanalysis) there is an absent discourse. In the arena of trauma, we not formulated an expansive field theory, informed by a multiplicity of minds, through which we can theorize mutually influencing forms of *mentalization, resiliency, and enduring love.*

I hope in the course of this essay my meaning will come clear. Even at this writing I am already having difficulty with articulation. I want to say, very simply to my reader, that we don't have a relational field theory of resilience. And that relational psychoanalysts have been rather silent on the topic of resilience in general, with the exception of Richman (2018, vol I in this series). But even as I write the word 'resilience', the term somehow feels banal, and quite inadequate to my search. But the term will have to suffice for now, and what I place under its umbrella will hopefully become clear. Certainly, as clinicians, our primary concern is, and should be, healing our patients' wounds, and we have followed Holocaust studies in our address to these wounds. Relational witnessing literature has emphasized witnessing and testimony; narrative absence; and states of deadness and emptiness, associated with an absent 'thou' (see Gerson, 2009, for example). Powerful, haunting, and often true to traumatic experience, this literature does not address the forms of resourcefulness, strength, and love that are also remarkably present in trauma survival and in the trans-generational heritage of that survival. I have no doubt that our *clinicians* attend to these capacities, but with the exception of Richman (2014; this volume) our *literature* does not. How can we witness survival and promote healing if *resourcefulness and the living human heart* fall through a gap in our theory?

Even during genocide, love is not entirely vanquished by cruelty and the ethos of care is not fully eviscerated (see Bodenstab, 2004; Ornstein, 1985, 1994; 2004). This is evident, for example, in Laub's autobiographical essay about his survival with his mother (2016). Despite terror and brutality, trauma narratives often contain traces of the living 'thou'. And though many trauma survivors do seem scarred by the 'dead mother', they are not hostage to that dead mother. After hundreds of years of severed attachments from their own mothers, African American slaves would risk their lives to find their children (see Williams, 2012):

My father was sold away from us when I was small . . . He missed us and us longed for him . . . He would often slip back to us cottage at night . . . us would gather round him . . . when his master missed him he would beat him all the way home. Us could track him the next day by the blood stains.

(Hannah Chapman qtd. in Williams, 2004, pp. 32–33)

In the shared, struggle of life in near-death, there is a persistence of care. That care is mutually sustained and replenished, even when our minds crack up, even in the midst of starvation in a German concentration camp:

And somehow I found the barrack where she was waiting for me. (Putting her arm around Rosalie) And when I came in, I said, 'Look mother, I have a bowl of soup.' And she said, 'I don't want any. You eat it.' I said, 'I had already a bowl'. She says, 'No. I want you to survive. You are young. I had my life already'. And I said, 'Please, no, you have to survive. Father will be waiting, my brother will be waiting. We both have to survive.' So we decided to share it. My mother took a spoon, but the spoon was empty. She hardly took anything. And when I took a spoon, it was also empty, because I didn't want to take much that she would have. So we realized that we're not getting anywhere, and we decided to feed each other. So she was feeding me, and I was feeding her. And that bowl of soup most likely saved us, because in a day or two we were liberated.

(as cited in Grand, 2015. From Bodenstab, 2004, p. 735,
testimony of Jolly Z HVT-34)

These memories cannot fail to move us to tears. So why doesn't this compel us in relational psychoanalysis? Without this focus, we will have little to inspire us in the meeting with destruction, in the world, and inside the office. Trauma narratives are fraught with the unspeakable, but, often, they are also infused with the remarkable acts of small heroes (see Grand, 2009, 2012, 2013, 2014). Resourcefulness, miraculous acts of human kindness, enduring love and the endurance of the I-Thou; the capacity to say *NO* to bestiality when it would be so much easier to say *Yes*, the re-creation of life after everything is lost: resilience exists and it takes many forms. During and after trauma, these forms are not that rare. We see them in our patients, every hour of the day. If we cannot be awed and sustained by human goodness, resourcefulness, endurance and strength in adversity, we will burn out quickly in our encounters with human darkness.

As clinicians, I think we are all possessed of that awe; but as an *explicit* focus it is vanishingly absent in our literature.

In this chapter, I want to illuminate the roots of that absence. And I want to make a plea for a relational field theory of resilience, even though I can't quite see what it would look like. Currently, in psychoanalysis, trauma survival is largely rendered as terror, fragmentation, and deadness; we largely fail to render the living human heart. Particularly since 9/11 in the U.S., and in the context of unrelenting war, migration, and climate calamity across the globe, resilience has become a central preoccupation in trauma research, and in non-analytic trauma therapies. Our relational work on this topic is very sparse, uncertain in its terms and referents, and fraught with some passionate miscommunications (See Gerson & Richman, this volume). And Gerson, in his study of Holocaust survival, wisely cautions us: if we valorize the 'resilience' of some survivors, we risk colluding in the genocidal narrative: that the strong survive while the 'weak' die. As Gerson reminds us, Holocaust survival was luck, a random fate in a monstrous machine.

Lest we hold an idealized fantasy of the human spirit, Gerson is offering us a corrective. And yet, we cannot fail to honor real human resilience, as it exists, during and after trauma, in the living and in the dead. But all too often we have an either/or vision of the human spirit. Either it is dead or alive. Either it is evacuated or it is heroic. We tend to oppose and essentialize these portraits of the survivor. In my view, neither alone is an adequate rendering of traumatic experience. Neither alone honors the nuances of survival. Both polarities can represent a failure of recognition, de-individuating those who have already been objectified. In seeking a place for resilience in our trauma theory, I hope to avoid this splitting and enhance our theory of witnessing. And I hope to make space in our trauma theory for that which awes us as human beings in a difficult world: the enduring capacity for human goodness.

Certainly, our clinical presentations *do* reveal these enduring capacities. But psychoanalytic literature has always been preoccupied with 'surface' and 'depth', in what Orange, referring back to the work of Ricoeur, describes as the 'hermeneutics of suspicion' (Orange, 2011). As Lachmann (2008) notes, in this posture of suspicion, the analyst:

> looks underneath or behind a person's actions to find the 'real' motivations. Behaviors that appear kind, generous, or perhaps even an

expression of gratitude and appreciation actually conceal baser, unconscious motivations that are aggressive and narcissistic.

(qtd. in Orange, 2011, p. 28)

In psychoanalysis, to go 'deep' is to investigate the wound, the roiling
darkness. When it comes to our trauma patients' endurance of the heart,
I think we need what Orange is proposing in her engagement with
Gadamer, that is: "for a humanistic therapeutics, suspicion must always
remain nested within a hermeneutics of trust" (Orange, 2011, p. 31).

The analytic family: provision and foreclosure

All psychoanalytic theories hold a place for I-Thou love, for ideals and
care and ego strengths and ethical integrity. If we want to formulate a
relational theory of resilience within a 'hermeneutics of trust', we could
reasonably stitch it together from these threads. This is what I tried to do
in my work on 'small heroes', but it was a stretch. For me, stitching these
threads together fails to reach into the core of our problem. I think we
need a more radical inquiry, one that implicates all of us in psychoanalysis.
So here is my radical proposition: I think that our absent theory of resilience
is rooted in the deep structure of the analytic family.

Throughout psychoanalysis, the analytic family is written in dyads and
triangles: mommy, daddy, baby (regardless of sex and gender). In trauma
theory, this family structure has underwritten witnessing and mentalization;
the reparative analytic provisions of attunement, containment, attachment.
But. I will argue that this same family structure *forecloses* our capacity
to theorize the *full range of psychic and relational resources that can be
present during, and after, trauma.* Mommy, daddy, baby: as I suggested
elsewhere (Grand, 2013), this familial formulation proffers, and recognizes,
certain human resources while it *vacates* others. Certain forms of human
sustenance have been written *into* psychoanalysis, while others have been
written *out.* As a result of what has been written out, I think that there are
problematic undertows inscribed in the foundation of psychoanalysis:
unformulated registers of scarcity and sacrifice, depletion and depression,
dependency and hierarchical deference. In our trauma theory, I think that
this problematic undertow haunts our conceptualization of witnessing,

mentalization, and the 'maternal function'. Our analytic family *excludes* too many psychic and relational resources, and leans too heavily on the singular maternal mind. To enhance our capacity for witnessing, we need to construct a relational field theory of resilience. But, in my view, this field theory *cannot* emerge within a practice that simultaneously *idealizes* the *exclusive* mentalizing powers of the maternal function even as it *depletes* the maternal function that it idealizes.

Lonely and over-burdened by her psychic work, called by the pain and excess of trauma, this mentalizing 'Mother' (regardless of sex or gender) would have to be the source: a formidable Good Breast, proffering 'limitless maternal bounty' (Grand, 2009). In the analytic situation, this imago inspires us towards a heroic of care. But this imago also places us at risk for a theoretical regression into maternal splitting. As an idealized 'Mother' confronts trauma and the limits of her witnessing capacity, this Good Mother would keep collapsing into a 'dead Mother' (see also Bassin, 1994; Layton, 2014). For analysts who treat trauma within this model, we might see an uptick in the analyst's fatigue and depletion. And if shame causes us to disown the iatrogenic source of our own condition, we may read this emptiness as the *sine qua non* of traumatic experience. We will be able to work with the 'dead Mothers' and 'deadened babies' whom we have theorized. But a theoretical discourse of resilience is not likely to find its voice, even as it is speaking to non-analytic trauma therapists around the world. To open up a theoretical space for a relational field theory of resilience: I think this requires a re-framing of the analytic family. It requires an expansive concept of human sustenance. We need to cherish the maternal function, and stop leaning so heavily on that maternal function. Our theory needs to recognize all the human resources that exist beyond mommy, daddy, baby.

The limits of dyads and triangles

Despite enormous changes in the relational version of the psychoanalytic family, this family is still fixed in dyads and Oedipal triangles: mommy, daddy, baby. The sexed and gendered arrangements of this family have morphed through time and relational critique. 'Mommy' and 'Daddy' are no longer defined by their genitalia or their gender. Layton (2004) has radically deconstructed gender polarities and the way they are situated in (and reinforce) the normative unconscious, including our own. Given the work on sex and gender by Harris (2005), Dimen and Harris (2001), and Benjamin (1988), 'mentalization' is no longer grounded in a vaginal body. Benjamin's groundbreaking work has reconceived the 'maternal' dyad as a system of 'asymmetrical mutual influence' (Aron, 1996) between an agentic baby and a subjective mother (see Beebe and Lachman, 2014; Benjamin; 1988).

But across diverse psychoanalytic schools, our traditional family structure remains very much as it began (see Layton, 2014). As such, our family is still imbued with significant cultural and inter-subjective constraints, even though we, as Relationalists, would probably not endorse these constraints. We have kept faith with a very small nuclear family; in that nuclear family, mentalization is figured as nested, exclusively, within dyads and triangles. This primary maternal function is exceptionally isolated from its human surround (see also Chodorow, 1999); and it is *overburdened with that psychic work which remains the province of feminization.*

In this construction, the dyad continues to be seen as pivotal, isolated, and responsible; set apart from a much larger mentalizing relational matrix. The dyad's largest relational matrix is an Oedipal triangle. Regardless of whether we acknowledge, and value, maternal subjectivity; regardless of whether that subjectivity has a vagina or a penis or some other sexed embodiment, this dyad is still bearing too much solitary weight. When it comes to witnessing, then, where is everybody else in the human family?

For us, mentalization is linked to 'mother' and *implicitly unlinked* to extended family, the generations, and the collective. We have lost those extended familial forms that reflect diverse class and cultural backgrounds. We still seem to have one parent who has an intimate, micro-relational primary care-giving function (albeit with much more autonomous subjectivity) and another parent of 'the outside world' who comes in and out of this dyadic function (with hopefully more caregiving functions). As a result, there is no one really there to 'mentalize' the psychoanalytic 'baby' except whoever is functioning as our postmodern 'mommy' in relation to our postmodern, Oedipal 'daddy'. I think there is no getting away from it: in psychoanalysis there is still too much weight placed on the mentalizing dyad, and that dyad is still too isolated from its larger human context, despite all of the excellent relational work critiquing the white, middle class underpinnings of our discipline. As Grand and Salberg note (2016, p. 2):

even in the area of trans-generational transmission, the genealogy of trauma is still being mapped onto pre-Oedipal dyads and Oedipal triads. In our view, this mapping is a retreat from radical change in psychoanalysis. In this retreat, the psychoanalytic family remains mommy, daddy, baby, and psychoanalytic theory remains intact, unaltered at its core. Not cracked open by genealogies of trauma, or by the violence of collective wounds.

I would argue, then, that despite the radical changes that trauma study has wrought in psychoanalysis, the maternal function remains intrinsically lonely, readily depleted, and shadowed by sacrifice and depression. Insofar as our theory perpetuates this excessive and exclusive weight on the 'maternal' figuration, we may recycle the very problem we seek to redress: we are wearing out the 'maternal' mind that we hold responsible for traumatic repair. It is no surprise, then, that our trauma theory circulates, exclusively, around deficits, deadness, emptiness, wounds.

The problematics of this family structure have been brilliantly illustrated in Juliet Mitchell's work on siblings (2003). Here, she draws our attention to a peculiar phenomenon: the psychoanalytic family has no brothers and sisters. This exclusion of siblings depletes us of familial, inter-subjective, and cultural resources. Mommy, daddy, baby: this is an exclusively hierarchical structure of resources and authority. As she suggests, sibling relations are horizontal relations; they are the template for peer relations. In the psychoanalytic family there *are* no horizontal forums for conflict, solidarity, love *or* sustenance, no cohort that can provide some autonomous counterweight to authority.

As I discovered in a case of trauma and twinship (Grand, 2013), these horizontal relations are also essential resources of care, attunement, attachment, and mentalization. These resources exist outside of 'mother' and the parental couple. And Mitchell makes a powerful argument that *horizontal relations* are the bedrock of social justice. And in conditions of massive trauma (war, genocide, climatic catastrophe, poverty, terrorist attack, etc.) our *peer* relations are often a primary locus of mutual care and resistance activity. Peer relations form aspects of our subjectivity; they form our cohort and much of our community. From this perspective, then, the *missing* sibling and the missing *peer* are particularly problematic for constructing a field theory of traumatic resiliency. And yet, whenever the peer or sibling appears in developmental theory, as it did with J. Mitchell and with Sullivan, that horizontal relation is re-marginalized. The analytic family is restored to its hierarchical arrangement. All resources flow from authority, from the parent to the child, even though we now consider that child to be mutually influencing and agentic. As we illuminate these missing aspects of the psychoanalytic family, it becomes clear that this family would incline us to reify authority, even as we have tried to deconstruct that authority. And our hierarchical family structure can undermine our faith in our cohort, and weaken our forces of social justice.

The object mother as witness: reconstituting despair

In relational psychoanalysis, the containing, mentalizing 'mother' seems to infuse what Slochower calls our 'analytic ideal' (2006). Certainly, this figuration is central to healing; it sponsors our tenderness, intimacy, containment, reflectivity, responsiveness, and micro-attunement. It has allowed us to greet the patient's affect and body (Hopenwasser, 1998; Rappaport, 2012) and to speak of analytic love (Hoffman, 2009). But this imago can also evoke compassion fatigue. It can actually *subvert* the reality of maternal need and subjectivity, reify the maternal *object,* configure her as the *source,* resurrect the patient as an empty 'baby', exaggerate the developmental tilt (S. Mitchell, 1988), blind us to our patient's adult capacities, and foster maternal depression and catastrophic loneliness (Grand, 2000) in the analyst/witness. Even though, of course, we have long ago repudiated this model of 'mother' (Benjamin, 1988).

Here's a radical thought: perhaps we are co-creating some of the dead mothers that we are witnessing. I think our psychoanalytic family still imagines this 'Mother' as able to, "move fluidly in and out of intense emotional states with no apparent consequences to her mental health" (Kraemer, 1996, p. 770). I am not suggesting that the 'dead mother' of trauma isn't *there* in our patients' minds, enactments, symptoms, dreams, testimony. I am suggesting that our family structure is creating a partial occlusion in our vision, so that we are less likely to theorize *shared, living, relational fields of resourcefulness and care,* and *more likely to theorize the dead mother of trauma.*

Imagine, calling upon this mentalizing 'Mother' to witness human atrocity. To begin this experiment, imagine. One single day of genocide, endured and survived. I cannot. Nonetheless, imagine: one survivor, trying to convey that single day. How long does this story take to recount? How long would it take for this telling to reach its own fullness? And if it were possible for this single day to speak its fullness, how can this 'Mother' have enough ears? This thought experiment haunts me. One day. One survivor. And then, I multiply this day by thousands, and I multiply this voice by millions, all over the world. Each day comprised of infinite hours in an inhuman series; each hour in that series in need of empathic witness. If 'Mother' proffered her ears, still, atrocity would spill beyond all capacity for containment. That single day was too much, and there is always too much of it.

Empathic knowing is an act of ethical devotion, but it also can seem like a call to despair. 'Mother' only has two ears to listen, and in our psychoanalytic family, *there are no other ears.* How much can she possibly hear and hold? It is hard enough on ordinary mothers, caring, alone at home, day after day, for ordinary babies. But when that 'baby' is traumatic experience, maternal ears will eventually grow deaf. In relational psychoanalysis, this deaf/deadened mother always seems to hover over our trauma work. Patients can, and will, feel seen by interpretations of this deadness. But in some way, our patients' experience may *also* be a reading their analyst's subjectivity (see Aron, 1999), *and* our theoretical predicament.

Unconscious objects and longings die hard. In extremity, it is difficult to purge our craving for an all-providing heroic object mother. Insofar as this imago of 'limitless maternal bounty' (Grand, 2009) infiltrates our 'analytic ideal' (Slochower, 2006), we are inspired towards a heroic of care. But this imago can also create an iatrogenic sense of failure and shame in the analytic dyad. We might well see an uptick in the analyst's emptiness and depletion. If shame causes us to disown the iatrogenic source of our own condition, it becomes natural to attribute ALL of this emptiness to the patient's inner world. We can work with those parts of the patient, and we can theorize them. But the discourse of resilience is not likely to find its rightful place, even as it is speaking to non-analytic trauma therapists around the world.

Scarcity and the developmental tilt

In critiquing trauma theory and the analytic family, I have been tracing the paradoxes and impossibilities confronting the maternal mind. I have been arguing that our construction of the maternal function can actually incline us to deplete this maternal mind, and to tilt us towards witnessing traumatic deadness to the exclusion of traumatic resilience. Within this context, our portrait of the survivor can also get stuck in a developmental tilt (see S. Mitchell, 1988; Richman, 2018). In our trauma literature, traumatic interiority tends to be portrayed as a frozen baby, a fragmented child (see Richman, 2018, this volume).

Certainly, these self-states are often *there* inside our patients. But they are not the *only* aspect of traumatic interiority. I do think most clinicians recognize their patients' complexity, their multiple states and parts, including their mature resiliency and strength. These strengths are evident in clinical presentations. Insofar as there is a regressive cast in this field, I believe it exists in our theory, more than in our clinical practice.

But there certainly seems to be a problematic developmental tilt in our trauma theory, a tilt which is further exacerbated by the limits of our developmental theories. With the exception of Sullivan and Erickson, development seems to end in psychoanalysis, rather oddly, before puberty even begins. The full developmental perspectives of Sullivan and Erickson have never been assimilated into mainstream psychoanalysis. We have absorbed some of the early childhood models of Sullivan and Erikson, while ignoring their contributions about later developmental conflicts, relationships, and achievements. To sustain our hierarchical family structure, we have completely ignored Sullivan's attention to maturing peer intimacy and friendship. We have ignored the evolving strengths and capacities that flow from these relationships.

In our psychoanalytic family, we have subtracted siblings; we have idealized, isolated, and over-burdened the maternal function. In our developmental theory, we seem to have a child who never really grows up, but must leap, somehow, directly into adulthood, without any prior sibling template for their peer relationships. Adult intimacy seems to draw, exclusively, on the template of hierarchical parent-child arrangements. All of this narrows the theoretical conduits through which a trauma survivor would be seen to be forging human bonds, questioning authority, resisting destruction, utilizing adult ego strengths, giving and receiving resources and sustenance, renewing the I-Thou capacity, or joining with peers to mobilize for social justice (J. Mitchell, 2003). If we add all of this up, it's hard to see where, and how, we would have a theory of traumatic resiliency.

Intimacy, collectivity, and mentalization

Must the analytic family be organized by one, two, three (see Grand, 2013)? Must mentalization only bear the marker of *Mother?* Must it *always* bear the marker of Mother? Must we keep recycling Good Breast Mothers and Bad Breast Mothers? Must we idealize Mother and deplete the Mother whom we are calling upon for our regeneration? Hasn't *Mother* already borne enough responsibility for the need of the other? How can we re-think the hierarchical structure of the analytic family? Can we expand our definition of the analytic family, and make space for a relational field theory of human resilience?

I am *not* proposing that we abandon the intimacy of 'maternal function', or its reparative attachment and containment. But I am advocating for a radical re-working of the psychoanalytic family at its core. In making this critique, and calling for new directions, I am *not* diminishing the healing powers of intimate engagement with the 'maternal mind'. Dyads are critical sites of relational resources and relational repair. I am a deep believer in the healing effect of attachment, micro-attunement, tenderness, and containment. And there are healing dynamisms that only seem emergent in the analysis of Oedipal triangles. I don't want to throw out these aspects of our theory. But I am arguing that we need to open up our bedrock family structure and re-imagine it, because it is inadequate to the meeting with trauma. I want psychoanalysis to cherish its I-Thou *and* to formulate an I-WE-Thou. What I am looking for is an expansive model of 'maternal function' that honors, and cherishes, the dyadic embrace, and yet radically changes the deep structure and positioning of 'Mother'. I think there is too much weight and solitude in our dyadic formulation of mentalization. I want mentalization to escape some of that solitude; I want us all to share the weight; I want a dynamic collectivity present in the deep structure of empathy, agency, attachment, and containment. And I want to do this, somehow, without compromising the tender intimacy of healing.

I am imagining a relational field theory that expands on the two-person analytic field so well theorized by Aron (1996). To do this, I think we need to liberate the psychoanalytic family from its origins in *nineteenth-century bourgeois Vienna*. If we can return to the radical humanism of Fromm (see Durkin, 2014), incorporate the sibling of horizontal relations and social justice, and integrate a social/ethical perspective with the political/cultural critiques made by relational psychoanalysts[3], we may be able to make this turn. I can sense this turn coming – it is in the ever-widening lens of Relational theory, in the dissolution of disciplinary boundaries, in the porous border of our office, in our inclusive vision of subjectivity, in our link to human collectivities, and in our passion for social justice. Gender, race, class, intersectionality: social conditions are increasingly recognized in the shaping, and the wounding, of the psyche. We have been disentangling oppressive social edicts from the ethics of Buber and Levinas, and claiming the I-Thou ethic that has always existed in psychoanalysis (Benjamin, 1988; Goodman, 2012; Goodman & Layton, 2014; Grand, 2009; Orange, 2011). Where once we ignored Big History, now we honor it through the study of trans-generational trans-mission (Grand, 2000, 2009; Guralnik, 2014; Salberg, 2016). As Salberg and Grand (2016) indicate, if ever psychoanalysis was poised to re-write the psychoanalytic family, it is now:

> The trans-generational turn can radically test this conception of family. In doing so, this turn potentially de-stabilizes the bedrock of our theories . . . the psyche is constituted by a much larger object world. This world is multi-generational. It is no longer exclusively hierarchical but is horizontal: inclusive of the communal cohort effect of massive trauma. This look . . . expands our psychic world and *our relational resources,* as we integrate the social/political/cultural markers of collective trauma.
>
> (Salberg and Grand, 2016 p. 3)

This complex web of relations would be mutually influencing. They would be situated paradoxically, *within, beyond, and outside of* the 'maternal dyad' and the Oedipal triangle. Incorporating siblings, cohorts, history, politics, culture, and the generations, all engaged in processes of contain-ment. This theory would be situated *within* and *outside of* the nuclear family. It would have intimate *and* collective features; a multiplicity of subjects; moveable states and affects that would not be exclusively defined by *dyadic mentalization.*

In such a system, there would be heightened awareness of what Layton (2015) describes as our mutual responsibility for the other's suffering. And care would be the function of the collective, and of multiple forms of familial/peer relations (see Grand, 2015). With this expansion of human resources and psychic sustenance, I think we would enhance the resilience of witnessing *and* our capacity to witness resilience. If we are imagining the future, why not think big?

Every day, in my office, I hear devoted young analysts assailing themselves for the insufficiency of their 'maternal function' with traumatized patients. Somehow, in this, the most feminist school of psychoanalysis, they still think the good analyst should offer limitless maternal bounty. No one explicitly taught them this at their institutes, but my best supervisees have absorbed it. In their meetings with severely traumatized patients, they imagine that they should be without limits. They are devoted, sacrificial, worried, tired, and silently, slowly, burning out. They choke on the *NO* that is arising in their guts, because that *NO* seems equivalent to analytic failure. Like all dissociative communications, this one can best be thought of as a communiqué from our group unconscious. I think it is a cry for help in the lonely task of witnessing. It is a call for us to witness the witness (see Grand & Salberg, 2015) who has been nurturing us without reciprocal sustenance. Only then will the discourse of resilience come into view.

Notes

1 One might wonder if the term 'trauma' has become too large a tent.
2 See Altman, 2012; Botticelli, 2007; Grand, 2013; Hollander and Gutwill, 2006; Layton, 2004, 2006, 2013, 2015; Peltz, 2006; Rozmarin, 2016; Suchet, 2012.
3 See for example: Altman, 1995; Grand, 2016; Layton, 2004; Suchet, 2012.

References

Alpert, J. (1994). Analytic reconstruction in the treatment of an incest survivor. *Psychoanalytic Review, 2*:217 235.

Altman, N. (2012). Whiteness. In: *Relational Psychoanalysis: Expansions of Theory, Vol 4*. Eds: L. Aron and A. Harris. New York: Routledge, pp. 17–199.

Aron, L. (1996). *The Meeting of Minds: Mutuality in Psychoanalysis*. Hillsdale, NJ: The Analytic Press.

Bass, T. (2003). Enactments in psychoanalysis: Another medium, another message. *Psychoanalytic Dialogues*, 13:657–676.

Bassin, D. (1994). Maternal subjectivity in the culture of nostalgia: Mourning and memory. In: *Representations of Motherhood*. Eds: D. Basin, M. Honey, and M.M. Kaplan. New Haven, CT: Yale University Press, pp. 162–173.

Beebe, B. & Lachman, F. (2014). *The Origins of Attachment: Infant Research and Adult Treatment*. New York: Routledge.

Benjamin, J. (1988). *The Bonds of Love*. New York: Pantheon Books.

Bergmann, M.S. (1983). Therapeutic issues in the treatment of holocaust survivors and their children. *American Journal of Social Psychiatry*, 3:21–28.

Bodenstab, J. (2004). Under siege: A mother-daughter relationship survives the Holocaust. *Psychoanalytic Inquiry*, 24, 5:731–752.

Bollas, C. (1995). *Cracking Up: The Work of Unconscious Experience*. New York: Hill and Wang.

Botticelli, S. (2007). Return of the repressed: Class in psychoanalytic process. In: *Relational Psychoanalysis: New Voices, Vol. 3*. Eds: M. Suchet, A. Harris and L. Aron. Hillsdale, NJ: The Analytic Press, pp. 121–135.

Bromberg, P. (2011). *The Shadow of the Tsunami and the Growth of the Relational Mind*. New York: Routledge.

Bueskins, P. (2014). Is therapy a form of paid mothering? In: *Mothering, psychoanalysis: Clinical, sociological and feminist perspectives*. Ed: P. Bueskens. Bradford, ON: Demeter Press, pp. 85–113.

Caruth, C. (1995). Introduction. In: *Trauma: Explorations in Memory*. Ed: C. Caruth. Baltimore, MD: Johns Hopkins University Press, pp. 3–13.

Chodorow, N. (1978). *The Reproduction of Mothering: Psychoanalysis and the Study of Gender*. Berkeley, CA: University of California Press.

Davies, J. & Frawley, M.G. (1994). *Treating the Adult Survivor of Childhood Sexual Abuse: A Psychoanalytic Perspective*. New York: Basic Books.

Dimen, M. & Harris, A. (2001). *Storms in her Head: Freud and the Construction of Hysteria*. New York: Other Press.

Durkin, K. (2014). *The Radical Humanism of Erich Fromm*. London: Palgrave.

Eigen, M. (1996). *Psychic Deadness*. Northvale, NJ: Aronson.

Felman, S. (1992). Education and crisis, or the vicissitudes of teaching. In: *Testimony: Crises of Witnessing in Literature, Psychoanalysis and History*, Eds: S. Felman and D. Laub. New York: Routledge, pp. 1–57.

Fonagy, P., Gergely, G., Junst, E.L. & Target, M. (2002). *Affect Regulation, Mentalization and the Development of the Self*. New York: Other Press.

Gerson, S. (2009). When the third is dead: Memory, mourning and witnessing in the aftermath of the Holocaust. *International Journal of Psychoanalysis*, 90: 1341–1357.

Goodman, D. (2012). *The Demanded Self: Levinasian Ethics and Identity in Psychology*. Pittsburgh, PA: Duquesne University Press.

Goodman, D. & Layton, L. (2014). The historical-political in psychoanalysis' ethical turn. *Psychoanalysis, Culture, and Society*, 19, 3:225–231.

Grand, S. (1995). Incest and the inter-subjective politics of knowing history. In: *Sexual Abuse Recalled: Treating Trauma in the Era of the Recovered Memory Debate*. Ed: J. Alpert. Northvale, NJ: Aronson, pp. 235–253.

——, (1997a). On the gendering of traumatic dissociation: A case of mother-son incest. *Gender and Psychoanalysis*, 1:55–79.

——, (1997b). The paradox of innocence: Dissociative 'adhesive' states in perpetrators of incest. *Psychoanalytic Dialogues*, 4:465–491.

——, (2000). *The Reproduction of Evil: A Clinical and Cultural Perspective*. Hillsdale, NJ: The Analytic Press.

——, (2009). *The Hero in the Mirror: From Fear to Fortitude*. New York: Routledge.

——, (2012). Keeping faith with the other: A commentary on Mario. *Psychoanalysis, Culture and Society*, 17, 1:64–70.

——, (2014). Skin memories: On race, love and loss. *Psychoanalysis, Culture and Society*, 19, 3:232–249.

——, (2013). God at an impasse: Devotion, social justice and the psycho-analytic subject. *Psychoanalytic Dialogues*, 23:449–463.

——, (2015). Circles of witnessing: On hope and atrocity. *Contemporary Psychoanalysis*, 51, 2:262–275.

Grand, S. & Salberg, J. (2016). Introduction. In *Trans-Generational Trauma and the Other: Dialogues Across History and Difference*. Eds: S. Grand and J. Salberg. New York: Routledge, pp. 1–9.

Green, A. (1986). *The dead mother: The work of Andre Green*. London: Routledge.

Guralnik, O. (2014). The dead baby. *Psychoanalytic Dialogues: The International Journal of Relational Perspectives*, 24, 2:129–145.

Guntrip, H. (1969). *Schizoid Phenomena, Object Relations and the Self*. New York: International Universities Press.

Gump, J. Reality matters: The shadow of trauma on African-American sub-jectivity. *Psychoanalytic Psychology*, 27, 1:42–54.

Harris, A. (2005). *Gender as Soft Assembly*. Hillsdale, NJ: The Analytic Press.

Herman, J. L. (1992). *Trauma and Recovery*. New York: Basic Books.

Hoffman, I. (2009). Therapeutic passion in the countertransference. *Psychoanalytic Dialogues*, 19:617–637.

Hollander, N.C. & Gutwill, S. (2006). Despair and hope in a culture of denial. In: *Psychoanalysis, Class and Politics: Encounters in the Clinical Setting.* Eds: L. Layton, N.C. Hollander and S. Gutwill. New York: Routledge, pp. 92–107.

Hopenwasser, K. (1998). Listening to the body: Somatic representations of dissociated memory. In: *Relational Perspectives on the Body.* Eds: L. Aron and F.S. Anderson. Hillsdale, NJ: The Analytic Press, pp. 215–237.

Howell, E.F. (2005). *The Dissociative Mind.* Hillsdale, NJ: The Analytic Press.

Irigaray, L. (1994*). Thinking the Difference.* Trans. K. Montin, New York: Routledge.

Kraemer, S. (1996). "Betwixt the dark and the daylight" of maternal subjectivity: Meditations on the threshold. *Psychoanalytic Dialogues,* 6, 6:765–791.

Krystal, H. (1988). *Integration and Self-Healing: Affect, Trauma, Alexithymia.* Hillsdale, NJ: The Analytic Press.

Laub, D. (1992). Bearing witness or the vicissitudes of listening. In: *Testimony: Crises of Witnessing in Literature, Psychoanalysis, and History.* Eds: S. Felman and D. Laub. New York: Routledge, pp. 57–75.

Laub D. (1998). The empty circle: Children of survivors and the limits of reconstruction. *Journal of the American Psychoanalytic Association,* 46, 2:507–529.

Laub, D. & Auerhahn, N.C. (1989). Failed empathy – a central theme in the survivor's Holocaust experience. *Psychoanalytic Psychology,* 6, 4:377–400.

——, (1993). Knowing and not knowing massive psychic trauma: Forms of traumatic memory. *International Journal of Psychoanalysis,* 74:287–301.

Layton, L. (2004). *Who's that Girl? Who's that Boy? Clinical Practice Meets Postmodern Gender Theory.* Hillsdale, NJ: The Analytic Press, pp. 57–75.

——, (2006). Attacks on linking: The unconscious pull to dissociate individuals from their social context. In: *Psychoanalysis, Class and Politics: Encounters in the Clinical Setting.* Eds: L. Layton, N.C. Hollander and S. Gutwill. New York: Routledge, pp. 107–117.

——, (2014). Maternally speaking: Mothers, daughters, and the talking cure. In: *Mothering and Psychoanalysis: Clinical Sociological and Feminist Perspectives.* Ed: P. Bueskens. Bradford, ON: Demeter Press, pp. 161–177.

——, (2014). Normative unconscious processes. In: *Encyclopedia of Critical Psychology.* Ed: T. Teo. New York: Springer, pp. 1262–1264.

——, (2015). Beyond sameness and difference: Normative unconscious process and our mutual implication in each other's suffering. In: *Psychology and the Other.* Eds: D. Goodman and M. Freeman. Oxford: Oxford University Press, pp. 168–188.

McWilliams, N. (2017*).* Psychoanalytic reflections on limitations: Aging, dying, generativity and renewal. *Psychoanalytic Psychology,* 34, 1:50–57.

Mitchell, J. (2003). *Siblings*. Cambridge, UK: Polity Press.

Peltz, R. (2006). The manic society. In: *Psychoanalysis, Class and Politics: Encounters in the Clinical Setting*. Eds: L. Layton, N.C. Hollander and S. Gutwill. New York: Routledge, pp. 65–831.

Orange, D. (2011). *The Suffering Stranger: Hermeneutics for Everyday Clinical Practice*. New York: Routledge.

Ornstein, A. (1985). Survival and recovery. *Psychoanalytic Inquiry*, 5, 1:99–130.

——, (1994). Trauma, Memory and Psychic Continuity. In: *A Decade of Progress: Progress in Self Psychology, Vol 10*. Ed: A. Goldberg. Hillsdale, NJ: The Analytic Press, pp. 131–146.

——, (2004). *My Mother's Eyes: Holocaust Memories of a Young Girl*. Cincinnati, OH: Emmis Books.

Rappaport, E. (2012). Creating the umbilical cord: Relational knowing and the somatic third. *Psychoanalytic Dialogues*, 22:375–388.

Reis, B. (2009a). Performative and enactive features of psychoanalytic witnessing: The transference as the scene of address. *The International Journal of Psychology*, 90:1359–1372.

——, (2009b). We: A discussion of papers by Trevarthen, Ammaniti and Trentinit, and Gallese. *Psychoanalytic Dialogues*, 19, 5:565–579.

Richman, S. (2014*). Mended by the Muse: Creative Transformations of Trauma*. London: Routledge.

Rozmarin, E. (2016). War and peace. In: *Trans-Generational Trauma and the Other: Dialogues Across History and Difference*. Eds: S. Grand and J. Salberg. New York: Routledge, pp. 187–204.

Salberg, J. (2016). The texture of traumatic attachment: Presence and ghostly absence in trans-generational transmission. In: *Wounds of History: Repair and Resilience in the Trans-Generational Transmission of Trauma*. Ed: J. Salberg and S. Grand. New York: Routledge.

Salberg, J. & Grand, S. (2016). Editors' introduction. In: *Wounds of History: Repair and Resilience in the Trans-Generational Transmission of Trauma*. Eds: J. Salberg and S. Grand. New York: Routledge, pp. 1–7.

Schore, A. (2011). Foreword. In: *The Shadow of the Tsunami and the growth of the relational mind*. Ed: P. Bromberg. New York: Routledge, pp. ix–1.

Shatan, C. (1982). The tattered ego of survivors. *Psychiatric Annals*, 4: 1031–1038.

Slochower, J. (1996). *Holding and Psychoanalysis*. Northvale, NJ: The Analytic Press.

Slochower, J. (2006). *Psychoanalytic Collisions*. Northvale, NJ: The Analytic Press.

Stern, D.B. (1997). *Unformulated Experience: From Dissociation to Imagination in Psychoanalysis*. Hillsdale, NJ: The Analytic Press.

Suchet, M. (2012). Unraveling whiteness. In: *Relational Psychoanalysis, Expansion of Theory, Vol. 4*. Eds: L. Aron and A. Harris. New York: Routledge, pp. 199–221.

Williams, H.A. (2012). *Help Me Find My People: The African-American Search for Family Lost in Slavery*. Chapel Hill, NC: The University of North Carolina Press.

Chapter 2

Otherness within psychoanalysis

On recognizing the critics of relational psychoanalysis[1]

Donnel B. Stern

Some years ago a book of mine (Stern, 2010) was reviewed by a respected colleague, a North American Freudian with Bionian and French
psychoanalytic sympathies (Levine, 2010). He liked my book in many
ways and I appreciated his interest and the effort he expended in reading
the book and offering his thoughts about it. But he was critical on one
score. He felt that it was "problematic that [Stern's] arguments are narrowly rooted in the idiom and context of contemporary interpersonal/
relational discourse and thinking, to the exclusion of Freud and of so
much else in contemporary psychoanalytic literature" (p. 1169). He was
referring to my thinking about unformulated experience, dissociation,
and enactment. He went on to say that, "while being anchored somewhere in some theory is probably inevitable for all psychoanalytic authors,
I suspect that readers who are not fully committed to an interpersonal/
relational perspective may find this book constricted in scope" (p. 1169).
My work, Levine said, risked being so "narrowly cast as to avoid a deeper
engagement with contemporary authors from other psychoanalytic
schools and traditions (such as Bion, Ferro, Lombardi, Matte Blanco,
Tabak de Bianchedi, Cassorla, Hartke, W. Baranger and M. Baranger,
Green, de M'Uzan, Aisenstein, Widlöcher, C. Botella and S. Botella, and
Faimberg)" (p. 1170).

Even in the context of the otherwise positive emphasis of the review,
that seemed to me to be an indictment. In the days following my reading
of this review, though, as I digested my reaction, a thought occurred
to me. I realized that in my book I actually did cite many of the very
writers who my reviewer had criticized me for not considering. It is

certainly true that comparisons between those views and my own were not my primary consideration in that book but I did mention them, indicating my interest in their work. The other side of this thought was that despite the fact that I had been writing about ideas relevant to that list of writers for thirty years, not even one of these same writers had ever cited me.[2]

And so I called the colleague who had written the review and pointed out that, while it was true that I hadn't compared my ideas in any detail to the ideas of the writers he enumerated, I had at least indicated that their ideas and mine bear a significant relationship to one another. But, I went on, because none of those writers had ever cited me, to criticize me for not integrating my ideas with theirs without making the same argument about the absence of their citation of me, seemed to me to reflect a kind of prejudice. My colleague did not agree. And I have not changed my mind.

Nevertheless, I felt he had a point, even with my reservations; and I resolved to do something about this. In the following years I found myself increasingly interested in the work of the Barangers, Bion, Green, Laplanche, Lombardi, and others. Eventually, I wrote about the relationship of the work of the Barangers and the Bionian field theorists, primarily Ferro, to the work of Sullivan (Stern, 2013a) and then to the thinking of contemporary interpersonal/relational writers (Stern, 2013b).[3]

Here is the twofold lesson I took from my colleague's review, my response to it, and other episodes that took place in my professional life during those years. 1) We interpersonal and relational analysts need to become more familiar with the work of European and Latin American psychoanalytic writers. We need to grasp the nature of the intellectual and clinical commitments held by those analysts, especially the commitments that lead them to their perceptions of us. If we comprehend their points of view from their perspectives—that is, not just from our own—we are in a position both to learn from them, and, when it is necessary (and it often is) to take issue with their criticisms. We have a chance to answer effectively those who criticize us, in other words, only if we understand them. The problem is really no different than one of our primary, common-sense, clinical principles: there is no sense in addressing someone about a sensitive subject unless you communicate in a way that really speaks to that person; and that generally requires that one grasp what the point in question means to them. 2) The second lesson to be taken from all of this is the converse of the first: In the same the way I have just described us learning the perspectives of others, those others should become better acquainted with ours.

What we are really talking about here is a specific instance of the general problem of otherness. In all of life's contexts, we must grasp the experience of the other if we are to diminish the emotional distance, alienation, discomfort, and dislike we can feel about the other, experience that so often breeds suspicion, contempt, and even hatred. That otherness may exist between us and actual other people; but of course, in psychoanalysis we are familiar with otherness as an internal problem, as well— that is, as the problem of the unconscious, or of alien self-states. For relational analysts, otherness has become a central clinical concern, a phenomenon that is neither altogether inner nor completely outer, but suspended between the two.

But for my present purpose I am talking about the experience of otherness that takes place between schools of psychoanalysis: in particular, between relational psychoanalysis and Kleinian and Bionian groups, and the various French schools. Of course, the problem we have within psychoanalysis is paltry when compared to the ethnic, racial, nationalistic, and gendered versions of the problem of otherness. Yet it is a problem we psychoanalysts live with on a daily basis, and it is a problem I believe we must solve if psychoanalysis is to endure.

Not all of us share the view that this is a problem that must be solved. I know that some do not see the value in trying to make common cause with those who object to our perspective. Those analysts feel we should simply chart our own path and leave those who disagree with us to chart their own. Isn't there something the matter with offering a respectful hearing to people who often don't approach us in the same way?

I feel, though, that we have so much more in common with other psychoanalysts, no matter how different their views, than we do with anyone else, that it behooves us to find a way to come together. I am convinced that respecting one another and coming together on the basis of that mutual respect is the only way to ensure a future for our field.

And so, with that aim in mind, I discuss in this chapter what interpersonal and relational analysts can do to become better citizens of the psychoanalytic world. Our recognition of analysts who think differently than we do requires greater familiarity with what they have to say, more sympathy with what is dear to them, and a clearer understanding of their perceptions of us.

I hope that analysts with clinical and theoretical commitments different than ours take up the reciprocal challenge to recognize us, and I believe they should; but that part of the problem I have no choice but to leave to them—and to the expansion of the contact between them and us that has become a welcome part of psychoanalysis today.

With Benjamin (1990, 2004, 2017), I generally think of recognition as an intersubjective process, something that occurs mutually, between people, as it does in the philosophy of Martin Buber (Benjamin, 2017)—which means that recognition cannot simply be adopted unilaterally by one of the affected parties toward the other (as Benjamin [2017] and Orange [2011] tell us Emmanuel Levinas describes our unilateral responsibility to the "suffering stranger"). But perhaps mutual recognition can *begin* unilaterally. In fact, Benjamin (2017) does suggest that there are circumstances in which we can jumpstart or awaken a reciprocal, intersubjective process by beginning with one-way recognition. It would seem that adversarial relationships, or aspects of otherwise congenial relationships that have adversarial qualities, must be one of the circumstances in which one party must begin without knowing if the other will reciprocate. Under such conditions, after all, *someone* has to begin the process of recognition. Whether or not reciprocity or intersubjectivity (in Benjamin's way of understanding this term) is the eventual outcome of unilateral recognition, though, it does seem desirable to me to understand and acknowledge how analysts from other schools see us.

In this chapter I consider those criticisms of relational psychoanalysis held by European and Latin American psychoanalysts, which means that I am not considering the philosophical critiques of relational psychoanalysis that have been mounted in recent years by North Americans (e.g. Mills, 2005, 2012). I also will not consider the literature in which North American analysts take issue with relational ideas on clinical, theoretical, and empirical grounds (e.g., Bachant, Lynch & Richards, 1995; Busch, 2001; Eagle, Wolitzky & Wakefield, 2001; Sugarman, 1995; Wilson, 1995).

I want to sound a cautionary note about the way I'm setting up the problem: there can be heuristic value in referring to "us" and "them" because it allows the problem to be conceived in the terms of otherness. But of course nothing is as simple as a dichotomy can make it appear, and not to recognize the complexity of the situation is to risk hardening group boundaries in a way that does not diminish the experience of otherness, but instead inadvertently encourages it. I want to keep in mind in what follows, in other words, that there are many psychoanalysts, with any and all of the passionate theoretical and clinical commitments that are routine in our field, who accept that serious and responsible colleagues can disagree in profound ways and nevertheless deserve one another's respect. In a recent email exchange, my friend and colleague Riccardo Lombardi, a widely known writer who finds inspiration in the work of Bion and Matte-Blanco, lamented the fact that he would not be available to meet me in Rome, where he lives and I was about to visit. In one of the emails of this exchange (Lombardi, personal communication, June 7, 2016), Lombardi spontaneously expressed exactly the sentiment I am trying to describe. After referring to my most recent book, which he described as "beautiful" despite the difference between my orientation and his own, he wrote: "We are fortunate that in our grey time of political monopole we are able to defend our spontaneous interest in the different ways of writing about clinical psychoanalysis." It is this kind of respectful recognition and acceptance of otherness, and perhaps even appreciation of it, that I admire. Lombardi reminds us that it can be done without giving up one's own commitments.

The criticisms we need to understand

So what criticisms do we need to understand? For heuristic purposes, the criticisms that interest me here fall into two broad categories: 1) scholarship and the sources of psychoanalytic concepts and practices; 2) the nature and role of the unconscious in psychoanalytic thought.[4]

All in all, those who criticize what they believe are relational positions on these matters (I put it this way because I do think that a significant part of the problem is a simplistic, and sometimes just mistaken, understanding of relational positions) are often also convinced that the way we think and practice represents a flattened and diluted version of what psychoanalysis should be. By encouraging acceptance of these views I hardly mean that we need to agree with them. I mean that to understand what these views are and why they are held, we need to start out with an acceptance of the situation we face.

I address separately the two issues I have just described. First, I discuss the issue of scholarship and the sources of psychoanalytic thought, which can also be understood as a controversy over who deserves to embrace psychoanalytic identity; then I turn to the question of the place of the unconscious in relational psychoanalysis, which I will address as the issue of who has proper psychoanalytic values.

I. The sources of psychoanalytic thought: psychoanalytic identity

My early reading in the field left me with the impression that the citations of Freud that appeared in the introductions of so many psychoanalytic articles were often more a formulaic obeisance than a genuine intellectual engagement: the price of saying what you want to say, it seemed, was to subordinate it to something in Freud's corpus. I still think that is the case more often than it should be, although obligatory obeisance of that kind seems to be less frequent today in most of our journals than it was then.

There is a long history, though, of psychoanalytic writers in the United States and Canada ignoring this tradition and trying to revise psycho-analytic thought to reflect empirical observations. As a matter of fact, whole psychoanalytic schools have been constructed on the basis of such observations. Take psychoanalytic ego psychology. Not all ego psychology belongs in this category, but much of it does. Hartmann's (1958) conflict-free sphere of the ego and focus on adaptation were conceptions that brought much of academic psychology (notably perception, language, and cognition) under the umbrella of psychoanalysis, and simultaneously brought unconscious motivation into academic psychology. Good examples of bringing unconscious motivation into academic psychology are areas of empirical, quantitative research in which unconscious motivation was understood to play a new and significant role—the New Look in perception research, for example (e.g., Bruner & Postman, 1949), or the beginnings of the new cognitive psychology that in the late 1960s began to supplant learning theory as the dominant academic psychology paradigm (e.g., Neisser, 1967). As an indication that the influence was just as great in the other direction (that is, the influence of empirical research on psycho-analysis) consider the mother-infant observational studies that have been so influential in American psychoanalysis in recent decades, or the voluminous literature on attachment. Or note that the *Festschrift* for Heinz Hartmann (Loewenstein, Newman, Schur & Solnit, 1966) was entitled *Psychoanalysis: A General Psychology*. Much of the literature of ego psychology during those years in the United States concerned matters of general psychology. It is no accident that these were the same years— the 1930s through the 1970s—during which psychoanalysis had its greatest political influence in American academic psychology, psychiatry, and social work.

But ego psychology also preserved much of the psychoanalysis that academics in mental health fields of that era loved to hate. And the academics were not alone: A group of American psychoanalysts—the interpersonalists, or as they were often known, the cultural-interpersonal school—was also critical of many of the same concepts and practices of the mainstream American psychoanalysis of that day (although, of course, being psychoanalysts themselves, they were less thoroughly rejecting than many empirically-minded academics). On the basis of their empirical observations of the centrality of relationships in psychological development and psychoanalytic treatment, what Harry Stack Sullivan (1940) referred to as "interpersonal relations," and what they understood to be the profound formative properties of social life and culture, the interpersonalists rejected many mainstream verities of the day: The inevitable centrality of the Oedipus conflict; the inevitability of the transference neurosis; the insistence on defining psychoanalysis as the application of a single, standard technique in which the analyst as a particular individual should make no difference, resulting in rigid definitions of psychoanalytic neutrality and anonymity; the belief that experience unfolds more or less exclusively from the intrapsychic world; the death instinct; penis envy; drive theory in general, with its internal, biological emphasis, and its de-emphasis of the "real" experience with "real" people that interpersonalists stressed; and the resulting biologized understanding of psychological development, with its theories of libido and inevitable, rigidly unfolding psychosexual stages.

Of course, it is thoroughly understandable that those for whom these rejected positions lay at the heart of psychoanalysis found it difficult to accept the ideas of apostates such as the interpersonalists. But the rejection of the interpersonalists by the psychoanalytic mainstream went far beyond mere disagreement. For generations, the analysts of the American Psychoanalytic Association, largely made up of the same ego psychologists I have already described, excluded the interpersonalists in any way they could. This exclusion was often poisonous and contemptuous: the interpersonalists were characterized as shallow and too focused on the social and environmental—the kind of claim that is always code for the perception that the in-group analysts believe that the out-group analysts not only hold unacceptable views, but are not really psychoanalysts at all. Code was unnecessary, though. In those days the rejection of the psychoanalytic credentials of interpersonalists could be stated quite publicly, and often was.

Eventually, in the 1980s, relational psychoanalysis came into being. To begin with, relational analysts were subjected to the same treatment. Stephen Mitchell, for instance, was invited to speak at the New York Psychoanalytic Institute and then was disrespectfully excoriated in public by the senior members of that organization. But eventually relational thinking was easier for American ego psychologists to accept as part of their discipline than the work of the earlier interpersonalists. Why relational thinking has met with greater respect in mainstream circles is an interesting question that deserves more scholarly inquiry than has been devoted to it to date (but see Stern, 2015b). Some would no doubt point to what they believe are differences in the theoretical contents and clinical practices of interpersonal and relational psychoanalysis (e.g., Frankel, 1998). My own inclination is to attribute the difference to an increasing willingness among mainstream psychoanalysts, as time passed, to consider alternative views.

Today, it seems to me, while disagreements are still frequent between contemporary American Freudians and relational analysts, these are much more respectful disagreements than they once were; and in fact, I find contemporary American Freudians more and more willing actually to consider what relational psychoanalysis has to say. Today, for instance, in stark contrast to the treatment Mitchell received at the New York Psychoanalytic Institute, I teach a required course on interpersonal and relational psychoanalysis at that same institute; and I have spoken to respectful audiences in the auditorium there a number of times in the last few years. I think that the physical proximity of contemporary Freudian analysts and relational analysts in New York, and the sharing of the

American cultural context, has finally led to the beginning of more or less regular contact between these groups. Add to these changes the fact that the William Alanson White Institute recently accepted an invitation to join the American Psychoanalytic Association. None of this could have happened even twenty years ago.

Don't get me wrong: there is still a good deal to work out; and there are still highly conservative contemporary American Freudians who do not approve of the changes I have just described. But I believe that this battle is on its way to becoming a thing of the past. Today, reading the *Journal of the American Psychoanalytic Association* or *The Psychoanalytic Quarterly*, it is impossible not to see the influence of interpersonal and relational psychoanalysis—not in every article, and not always without ambivalence; but the influence is so clear that a colleague of mine has made the cogent observation that certain aspects of contemporary Freudian theory and practice remain "inscrutable" and "historically incoherent" if one does not relate them to the interpersonal and relational theory that preceded them (Blumberg, 2013). Today it seems to me that the relationship between relational psychoanalysis and contemporary American Freudian psychoanalysis is not really a central dilemma for either group. The identity of the North American psychoanalyst has grown to include both.

Ironically enough, as a matter of fact, a good many analysts from the rest of the psychoanalytic world, mainly analysts from Latin America, Great Britain, France, and Italy, have been, and are, critical not only of American relational analysts, but also—and for many of the same reasons—those American Freudians identified with the remnants of ego psychology. The willingness of relational analysts and ego psychologists to find the origin of some of their views in empirical observation that comes from outside psychoanalysis itself, especially when that observation concerns the so-called external world and not the inner one, has provoked criticism that their work is not rooted either in the Freudian canon or in a sufficient appreciation of the power and influence of the unconscious, reflected (so the attitude goes) in an overemphasis on adaptation to the external world. (I take up the points regarding the unconscious and the problem of adaptation in the section below). Neither relational nor ego psychological thinking, for those who take this view, are really psychoanalytic. It seems to me that, as a result of all this, certain American

Freudians, in other words, and many relational analysts, have become, in their relation to the wider psychoanalytic world, the proverbial strange bedfellows.

But what I have said so far about anchoring psychoanalysis in Freud is only one part of the story. Yes, of course it is true: Some of that anchoring in Freud has been, and continues to be, little more than a rhetorical device, a marker of group membership or belonging; and the criticism of relational thought that grows from such a rhetorical position, while we need to understand it, is not a matter of substance, and therefore not something that we need to recognize (in the sense of giving it a respectful hearing). But there are many other writers whose views are more thoughtfully rooted in Freud, while simultaneously diverging from him. Three analysts who immediately come to mind are Loewald, Lacan, and Laplanche. Loewald had nothing to say about interpersonal psychoanalysis, as far as I know (relational psychoanalysis did not exist in his era); but it is rumored that he did learn from Sullivan during his years in Washington, DC. Laplanche did have critical things to say about what he usually referred to as the "intersubjective" view. According to Wainstrater (2012), Laplanche felt that relational psychoanalysis represented a "'vulgar' pragmatism." Wainstrater comments that, "We can see how clearly his thought contradicts the tenets of the intersubjective movement" (p. 298). Lacan did not specifically address relational psychoanalysis, since it came about after he wrote; but he would no doubt have been highly critical of relational thinking, since he rejected object relations, just as he rejected ego psychology, and in fact tended to think of the former as a form of the latter.

All three of these analysts were, at one and the same time, great innovators and staunch defenders of the necessity for psychoanalysis to grow directly from the work of Freud. A brief examination of how they derived their views seems to me to demonstrate that the criticisms of relational psychoanalysis by analysts outside North America do not arise simply as a result of intellectual and clinical disagreement.

I begin with Hans Loewald (2000), who created an important and innovative view of the development and functioning of mind that he always insisted was true to Freud's vision.[5] He claimed that he was merely developing implications of Freud's thought that Freud himself did not see. In the process he created very beautiful ideas about the processes of differentiation and de-differentiation that resulted in the growth of the internal structures that compose the mind. These ideas were so different from Freud's own that it can be hard sometimes to imagine that Freud was their source. In fact, I have heard what seems to me to be the churlish and cynical claim that Loewald professed fealty to Freud only so he could say what he pleased. For my part, when I read Loewald I find his commitment to Freud utterly convincing, even if I must admit to wondering whether he may have been more original, and less inspired by Freud, than he thought he was.

Lacan, while he was accused by some psychoanalysts of being a "recalcitrant, idiosyncratic charlatan" (Nobus, 2000, p. 2) with views that, for many psychoanalytic readers, did not represent Freud, nevertheless did not hesitate to denounce the Freudian ego psychology of Hartmann, Kris, and Loewenstein—the dominant psychoanalysis of Lacan's day— as anti-Freudian and to characterize his own thinking as "strictly loyal to the Freudian enterprise" (Nobus, 2000, p. 1). Lacan's rallying cry was the "return to Freud," a goal Lacan thought could be accomplished only by seeing that the unconscious was structured like a language—and for him language, and therefore the mind, was in continuous flux and conflict, and outside the ego's control. He believed that the ego was established via identifications, and that it was therefore most closely related to the imaginary, the mode in which experience is (falsely and deceptively) stable and unchanging. Therefore, to base psychoanalysis in the ego was to betray Freud. (Frankly, it is not hard for me to sympathize with this view of the mind as a realm fragmented by unconscious events that we can only accept and try to understand.)

Jean Laplanche is perhaps my favorite example of a writer who differs radically with Freud while finding his inspiration in him. What makes him such a good example is the specificity of his very critical reading *of* Freud, and therefore the specificity of his inspiration *by* Freud. Laplanche began his writing career by translating Freud into French, and then, on the basis of this very close study of Freud's body of work, by creating with Pontalis one of the essential psychoanalytic books, *The Language of Psychoanalysis* (Laplanche & Pontalis, 1973). In that work, organized as a kind of dictionary, Laplanche and Pontalis selected Freud's key conceptions and offered pithy and insightful definitions (more like brief discussions, really) of them. During these years, and continuing until his death in the early years of the new century, we see in Laplanche's brilliantly original theoretical work the fruits of these years of immersion in Freud. Every point Laplanche makes—in fact, his entire theoretical corpus—is based on what he analyzes as Freud's "goings astray" (e.g., Laplanche, 2006), which Laplanche "elevates to the rank of a methodological concept" (Fletcher, 2011, p. 83). Laplanche argues that Freud made crucial mistakes and that we must identify those "goings astray" if we are to create the "new foundations" (Laplanche, 1989) that psychoanalysis needs. Over and over again, Laplanche identifies clearly and precisely where he feels Freud diverged from what should have been the implications of his own thought; and then Laplanche fills in the ideas that he claims Freud himself would have come upon if he had been able think more uncompromisingly than he did. Laplanche's work is one long struggle with Freud, who is like a contentious sibling—or perhaps better, a parent one loves and with whom one tangles one's whole life. As in the case of Lacan, Laplanche's ideas, while meaningfully related to Freud's, are not Freud's ideas at all, but elaborations in new directions.

Given what can be accomplished in a single essay, I cannot actually demonstrate in these pages how significantly Loewald, Lacan, and Laplanche diverge from Freud. I must ask instead that the reader simply accept my contention that they do. I cite these writers not in order to present their thinking, but to make the point that ideas very different than Freud's own—quite possibly, no less different from Freud than relational ideas—have been welcomed in the broader psychoanalytic world when they have been anchored, however imaginatively, in Freud's work. I mean "welcomed" in a particular way, since all of these writers have been controversial (especially Lacan) and so were not welcomed in the most simple sense, as if they were eagerly anticipated guests. But they were welcome in the sense that there was never any question in the mainstream literature, or (so I believe) in the minds of most mainstream analysts, about whether they deserved serious consideration—an attitude that is not always what one encounters among these same analysts in regard to relational thinking.

Examples such as Loewald, Lacan, and Laplanche show that it is not necessarily only the differences between mainstream psychoanalysis and relational psychoanalysis that makes mainstream analysts critical. Yes, of course, differences matter enormously (see the following section of this essay) but the reason for mainstream criticism also lies in the fact that relational writers do not necessarily (and sometimes cannot, because the ideas do not allow it) ground their ideas in mainstream psychoanalytic scholarship, and Freud in particular, in a way that encourages traditionalists to grant us psychoanalytic identities.

I am not advocating that relational analysts respond to rhetorical pressures, or to calls for submission to tribal discipline. On the other hand, I do share a profound respect for scholarship with most other psychoanalysts, and therefore I do think it is desirable, when it is possible without twisting ourselves into pretzels in the process, to ground our ideas in all of the relevant ideas that have come before us. I hasten to add that I recognize the fact that many relational analysts already do anchor their work in psychoanalytic tradition.

What we should do in response to this criticism we face is not really my primary point, though. What I want most to convey is this: We need to understand that our approach grows from our pragmatic American approach to empirical observation; our (also typically American) tendency to say things straight out and thereby sacrifice a focus on the emergence of our work from what has come before; and the valorization of individualism in American culture, which I suspect also plays a role in discouraging our awareness of our dependence on our intellectual and clinical forbears. (Bloom's [1973] classic discussion of "the anxiety of influence," despite the fact that it concerns the influences of "strong poets" on poets who came after, is apposite here.) To the extent that these things are true of North American psychoanalysis, our writing can seem disrespectful and shallow to some of our mainstream colleagues. They can feel that we are violating what they most value, the intellectual substance that actually underpins what a psychoanalyst is. For our colleagues in Europe and South America, Freud is an inexhaustible resource, still the font of new thought in psychoanalysis. We need to understand that interaction with Freud is the necessary generative source for our colleagues. Freud is more a father to them than he is to most of us, and their struggle with him is therefore more crucial to them. We should understand this not only as rigidity, but as a creative impetus that we relational analysts are to some extent deprived of, because our relationship to Freud is less intimate, and therefore less precious to us. We need to understand that when they read the parts of our work that do not grow from our encounter with Freud, or in which Freud is at least not an obvious source, even some of those traditionalists who are willing to grant that we have a point will feel that we are disrespecting the history of our field, reinventing the wheel, practicing irresponsible or inadequate scholarship, and/or doing something other than psychoanalysis.

2. The place of the unconscious in relational psychoanalysis: psychoanalytic values

I have tried to recognize critical views of relational *scholarship*, including my own. Now I turn to an attempt to recognize the critical views of relational *theory* held by the same analysts I have already been discussing. This is a more challenging task, because while there is often at least some truth to the claims made about the paucity of scholarly citation of Freud and other mainstream psychoanalysts in the relational literature, the same cannot necessarily be said about claims made by other analysts about relational theory. Some of those who hold the most critical views of relational theory and practice actually do not seem very familiar with the views they are criticizing. Stephen Mitchell (1995), writing about certain American Freudian views, wrote that: "The most appalling thing about these critiques of relational theories is how little effort these authors appear to have expended in trying to understand what it is they think they are arguing against" (p. 574). It doesn't seem unreasonable to take the same view of the familiarity of French, Italian, and Latin American analysts with the relational literature. The job of offering recognition to such views can therefore be quite difficult.

It is true that conceptual and clinical divergences between us and our critics lie at the heart of the views most critical of us. But I have come to believe that the reasons for the negative attitudes toward relational psychoanalysis held by many European and Latin American analysts are not only a matter of simple disagreement. The problem is more profound than disagreement over psychoanalytic questions, just as questioning the willingness of relational writers to anchor their ideas in the history of psychoanalysis is more than a question of scholarship. In the same way that the scholarship issue can be seen as a matter of psychoanalytic identity, the question of theoretical divergence can be understood as a matter of psychoanalytic values.

It is not that European and Latin American critics argue that relational analysts hold *different* psychoanalytic values; the critics claim, rather, that there exists a single set of psychoanalytic values, and that relational analysts do not hold them. Waintrater (2012), for instance, in a very useful explanation of the French response to relational psychoanalysis (for another useful comparative account, see Kernberg, 2001) writes: "Mitchell's (1988) audacity in replacing the drive theory with the relational theory is perceived as a danger, a Trojan horse that could destroy psychoanalysis from within; therefore all such attempts must be fought" (p. 300).

The French characterization of relational psychoanalysis is not a matter of simple disagreement on empirical or philosophical grounds. That kind of disagreement we could probably discuss profitably. Instead, the claim is that relational psychoanalysis is not properly psychoanalytic. This is the kind of criticism that no psychoanalyst, relational or otherwise, can accept. Yet I think—and it is the burden of this chapter to show—that we must accept that these views exist and try to understand how they came about and why they persevere.

For those of us who live in North America, the extremity of these positions about us can come as a shock. Relational and interpersonal psychoanalysts are used to thinking that the wars are over, or at least on the way to being over. We are used to the idea that there has been a significant "interpersonalization" of American Freudian psychoanalysis. And there has been, of course. But to the extent that we treat North American psychoanalysis as the psychoanalysis of the world, we are being short-sighted and narrow-minded.

If we are taken by surprise by the force of the criticism of us from the rest of the world, in other words, it is because of our arrogance and chauvinism, however unrecognized these attitudes may be. Most of us have conceptualized psychoanalysis as if it were simply what we have always thought it was. Only at this late date are we granting the same significance to the psychoanalysis of Europe and Latin America that we have always assumed for our own, homegrown varieties.

Of course, we are not alone in this: Mitchell's work, Waintrater (2012) tells us, is "virtually unknown" in France, and none of his books have been translated into French. *Psychoanalytic Dialogues* "is never mentioned in bibliographies" (p. 296). In France, says Waintrater, ego psychology (hated by Lacan, whose view on this score remains influential) and object relations (including relational psychoanalysis) are equated; and even though it is understood that relational psychoanalysis and self psychology developed in reaction to ego psychology, all these schools tend to be tarred with the same Lacanian brush.

> French analysts react with perplexity, if not astonishment, to such ideas as the relative nature of interpretation, the primacy of the here-and-now, and the deconstruction of authority, especially the analyst's. In the French view, such ideas reflect an ideological tendency, close to cultural relativism; they mark the end of the specificity of psycho-analysis, reduced to a branch of psychology
>
> (Wainstrater, 2012, p. 296)

For the French, "anything referring to cognitive processes, to notions of will and change, belongs to motivational theories and is incompatible with the very idea of the unconscious" (Wainstrater, 2012, p. 296). And:

> The idea of a subject with a unified sense of self gained through understanding and experience is completely at odds with the French conception of a subject divided by the very nature of what constitutes the psyche, that is, infantile sexuality, fantasy, and repression.
>
> (p. 296)

The French reject a central role for affect, according to Wainstrater, continuing to insist instead on the importance of verbal associations and the analyst's interpretations of them. "If the analyst's interpretations are by essence just as subjective as the patient's own experience and both are considered equivalent, then the only thing that matters is shared meaning and knowledge. Thus, according to many French analysts, the relational and intersubjective schools are tantamount to theories of com-munication" (Wainstrater, 2012, p. 297). And of course there is the question of drive: for Laplanche, for instance, "the idea of resolving conflict, and resulting anxiety, through shared understanding and elucidation [as relational writers are understood to recommend] can only be a defensive stance vis-á-vis the drive impulses and their strange and inexplicable nature" (Wainstrater, 2012, p. 298). Perhaps the most critical difference for the French is the Anglo-Saxon rejection of the death drive, which the French see as the "cornerstone of human conflict" (p. 297).

Put these and other points together and the conclusion looks like this:

A watered-down unconscious, or even no unconscious at all: this is how intersubjective theories are perceived in France. For French psychoanalysts, the indomitable force of transference and of the drives cannot be reduced to a transaction between two persons: intersubjectivity and the entire relational movement are criticized as ignoring psychic conflict and the unconscious.

(Wainstrater, 2012, p. 295–296)

I do not have an equivalent example from South America to quote; but it is clear to me that there is no shortage there of this same kind of critique of relational psychoanalysis. Lest it appear that these criticisms come only from France, though, let me offer an example from Italy that echoes some of the same themes. In the passage that follows, Ferro and Civitarese (2013) refer to "interpersonalists" when they actually mean both interpersonal and relational psychoanalysts. Read the comment, therefore, as if it applies to both groups.

The clinical vignettes of the interpersonalists sometimes convey the impression that, first, interpersonal psychoanalysis is based on an interactionism not guided at all times by a model of the unconscious functioning of the individual and group mind as versatile that of BFT [Bionian field theory], which also takes account of the micrometry of the analytic dialogue; and that, second, [interpersonal/relational psychoanalysis] sees change as underlain principally by rational understanding and conscious agreement (which admittedly often rest on a reading of unconscious dynamics and on the joint experience of analysis).

(p. 647)

This chapter is not the place to offer detail about the views of the European and Latin American critics of relational thinking. What I intend here is just to offer enough detail to indicate the scale of the problem. The scale is huge, as even this brief sampling of views indicates.

Given this situation, what can we do if we wish to make better relationships with those who disagree with us? It is simple to begin to answer this question: We must talk to them with the assumption that their attitude toward us is not simply critical, but that, in fact, they wish to have better relationships with us, just as we wish to have better relationships with them. It's just that they, like us, are unwilling to compromise either their psychoanalytic identities or their psychoanalytic values in order to create this state of affairs.

This is all well and good; but let me make sure I am not misunderstood: I am not advocating Pollyannism, nor am I denying that forceful argumentation and rejection of the other's point of view are sometimes necessary and unavoidable.

Let me tell a story. A number of years ago, a group of about a dozen training analysts from two of New York's APsaA institutes asked me to meet with them all day on a Saturday to talk about clinical material. These analysts had read relational and interpersonal literature, but they felt that they weren't able to feel and know what doing this kind of work was really like. We met for about ten hours around a large table one day in the apartment of one of them. Sandwiches were delivered for lunch, and we kept talking. I presented clinical material and did my best to explain how I thought and felt about each clinical situation as it happened, how I intervened when I did, and why I didn't intervene when I didn't. For the first hours, I could tell from their expressions and their comments that a number of these analysts were quite leery of me. I felt defensive, but I tried to be as open as I could, feeling that the only opportunity to create a bond between all of us—and I didn't see any sense in doing this if I didn't aim for that—lay in making an authentic emotional connection through the work we shared. As the day went on, all of us relaxed; and by the end of the day the feeling among us was respectful and collegial, even excited. We felt we had shared something important. I feel confident in saying that it was a terrific day for all of us. You may remember that, earlier in this chapter, I mentioned that I now teach a required course on interpersonal and relational psychoanalysis at the New York Psychoanalytic Institute. That course grew out of this day.

I have had similar experiences with colleagues from Europe and Latin America—although none that were quite as transformative. Often there is discomfort to begin with. But the mere fact of the contact is important. I think that, like some of our colleagues in our own country, Europeans and Latin Americans often imagine relational analysts to be undisciplined and unthoughtful, and perhaps even irresponsible clinicians. They may think we shoot from the hip and do very little besides chat comfortably with our patients. When they see that we are seriously interested in the same clinical problems they are interested in themselves, and interested in the same way, things tend to relax. It is only then that theoretical differences can begin to be discussed.

We cannot have these discussions without accepting our divergences from each other. We do so with the hope that accepting these differences will result in a mutual respect for them. Imagine being an analyst who thinks that negotiation of difference in the clinical situation is simply a defensive maneuver. Imagine believing that the intention to grasp and understand unconscious processes is a superficial accommodation. Imagine thinking that the goal of comprehending the analytic relationship is ephemeral, that such "comprehension" is nothing more than an enactment, an illusion, and that the patient's mind is most usefully contacted by interacting with the patient's unconscious in ways you learn from theory. Imagine thinking that affect is not necessarily your clinical guide, and that the best way to affect the patient's mind has nothing to do with what feels like intimacy, but is instead a matter of correctly interpreting the patient's verbal associations. Imagine believing that analysts' authority rests on the theoretically mediated grasp they have on the patient's unconscious process, an authority patients need to accept if they are to get better. (And imagine having patients who accept this proposition!)

And then imagine sitting with a fellow clinician who thinks in these ways, someone who sits with people in a consulting room, just as you do, someone who hopes that the time and effort they spend with patients is productive. Imagine trying to absorb these enormous differences in the way you and this other analyst think about psychoanalysis. Imagine thinking that, given the aims you share, what you do and what they do must not be as incommensurable as they seem to believe. And then talk about it.

Notes

1 I thank Phillip Blumberg, Ph.D., for his editorial advice and creative additions to this chapter.
2 I have gotten to know a number of the writers on this list over the last several years, and I imagine that the same is true for many other

interpersonal and relational analysts. I suspect that as a consequence of this greater contact across theoretical boundaries, which used to be so much less permeable, citations of relational psychoanalytic literature by analysts of other schools will increase in the coming years.

3 Longer and more complete versions of these articles appear elsewhere (Stern, 2015a).

4 I would prefer not to use the term "the unconscious," because of the reification inherent in it. I prefer something like "unconsciousness" or "unconscious processes" but those expressions are often awkward, and so I often settle for common usage.

5 Loewald is known as an American, and he was, of course. But his cultural identification was European, which is why I include him here. He was one of Heidegger's most prized students prior to arriving in the United States (although he disavowed Heidegger after the war because of Heidegger's Nazism, and refused all attempts by others to arrange a meeting between the two) and while he was usually classified as an ego psychologist, he was really never part of the psychoanalysis established by Hartmann, Kris and Loewenstein.

References

Bachant, J.L., Lynch, A.A. and Richards, A.D. (1995). Relational models in psychoanalytic theory. *Psychoanalytic Psychology*, 12:71–87.

Benjamin, J. (1990). Recognition and destruction: An outline of inter-subjectivity. In: *Relational Psychoanalysis: The Emergence of a Tradition*, Ed: S.A. Mitchell and L. Aron. Hillsdale, NJ: The Analytic Press, pp. 183–200.

——, (2004). Beyond doer and done to: An intersubjective view of thirdness. *Psychoanalytic Quarterly*, 73:5–46.

——, (2017). *Beyond Doer and Done To: Recognition Theory, Intersubjectivity, and the Third*. New York and London: Routledge.

Bloom, H. (1973). *The Anxiety of Influence: A Theory of Poetry*. New York: Oxford University Press.

Blumberg, P. (2013). Personal communication.

Bruner, J.S. and Postman, L. (1949). On the perception of incongruity: A paradigm. *Journal of Personality*, 18:206–223.

Busch, F. (2001). Are we losing our mind? *Journal of the American Psychoanalytic Association*, 49:739–751.

Eagle, M.N., Wolitzky, D.L. and Wakefield, J.C. (2001). The analyst's knowledge and authority: A critique of the "new view" in psychoanalysis. *Journal of the American Psychoanalytic Association*, 49:457–488.

Ferro, A. and Civitarese, G. (2013). Analysts in search of an author: Voltaire or Artemisia Gentileschi? Commentary on 'Field Theory in Psychoanalysis, Part II: Bionian Field Theory and Contemporary Interpersonal/ Relational Psychoanalysis' by Donnel B. Stern. *Psychoanalytic Dialogues*, 23:646–653.

Fletcher, J. (2011). Editor's note. Countercurrents. In: *J. Laplanche, Freud and the Sexual*, Ed: J. Fletcher. New York: International Psychoanalytic Books, pp. 83–97.

Frankel, J.B. (1998). Are interpersonal and relational psychoanalysis the same? *Contemporary Psychoanalysis*, 34:485–500.

Hartmann, H. (1958). *Ego Psychology and the Problem of Adaptation*, trans. D. Rapaport. New York: International Universities Press.

Kernberg, O. (2001). Recent developments in the technical approaches of English-language psychoanalytic schools. *The Psychoanalytic Quarterly*, 70:519–547.

Laplanche, J. (1989). *New Foundations for Psychoanalysis*. Trans. D. Macey. Oxford: Basil Blackwell.

——, (2006). Exigency and going astray. *Psychoanalysis, Culture and Society*, 11:185–189.

Laplanche, J. and Pontalis, J.-B. (1973). *The Language of Psychoanalysis*. New York: Norton.

Levine, H.B. (2010). *Partners in Thought: Working with Unformulated Experience, Dissociation, and Enactment*. By Donnel B. Stern. New York/London: Routledge, *Psychoanalytic Quarterly*, 79:1166–1177.

Loewald, H. (2000). *The Essential Loewald: Collected Papers and Monographs*. Hagerstown, MD: University Publishing Group.

Loewenstein, R.M., Newman, L.M., Schur, M. and Solnit, A.J. (Eds.) (1966). *Psychoanalysis: A General Psychology. Essays in Honor of Heinz Hartmann*. New York: International Universities Press.

Lombardi, R. (June 6, 2016). Personal communication.

Mills, J. (Ed.) (2005). *Relational and Intersubjective Perspectives in Psychoanalysis: A Critique*. Lanham, MD: Jason Aronson/Rowman and Littlefield.

——, (2012). *Conundrums: A Critique of Contemporary Psychoanalysis*. New York: Routledge.

Mitchell, S.A. (1988). *Relational Concepts in Psychoanalysis: An Integration*. Cambridge, MA: Harvard University Press.

——, (1995). Commentary on "Contemporary Structural Psychoanalysis and Relational Psychoanalysis". *Psychoanalytic Psychology*, 12:575–582.

Neisser, U. (1967). *Cognitive Psychology*. Englewood Cliffs, NJ: Prentice-Hall.

Nobus, D. (2000). *Lacan and the Freudian Practice of Psychoanalysis*. New York: Routledge.

Orange, D.M. (2011). *The Suffering Stranger: Hermeneutics for Everyday Clinical Practice*. New York and London: Routledge.

Stern, D.B. (2010). *Partners in Thought: Working with Unformulated Experience, Dissociation, and Enactment*. New York: Routledge.

——, (2013a). Field theory in psychoanalysis, Part 1: Harry Stack Sullivan and Madeleine and Willy Baranger. *Psychoanalytic Dialogues*, 23:487–501.

——, (2013b). Field theory in psychoanalysis, Part 2: Bionian field theory and contemporary interpersonal/relational psychoanalysis. *Psychoanalytic Dialogues*, 23:630–645.

——, (2015a). *Relational Freedom: Emergent Properties of the Interpersonal Field*. New York: Routledge.

——, (2015b). The interpersonal field: Its place in American psychoanalysis. *Psychoanalytic Dialogues*, 25:388–404.

Sugarman, A. (1995). Psychoanalysis: Treatment of conflict or deficit? *Psychoanalytic Psychology*, 12:55–70.

Sullivan, H.S. (1940). *Conceptions of Modern Psychiatry*. New York: Norton. First published in book form 1953.

Waintrater, R. (2012). Intersubjectivity and French psychoanalysis: A misunderstanding? *Studies in Gender and Sexuality*, 13:295–302.

Wilson, A. (1995). Mapping the mind in relational psychoanalysis. *Psychoanalytic Psychology*, 12:9–29.

Chapter 3

Reflections and directions
An interview of Jessica Benjamin by Sue Grand

Jessica Benjamin and Sue Grand

September 2014

SG: Jessica, I think this is going to be a really interesting conversation. One area of interest of mine is that, we have a legacy of splitting applied psychoanalysis from clinical psychoanalysis. The relational turn at NYU Postdoc was socially conscious and politically progressive. You work allows for a deep interpenetration of applied and clinical psychoanalysis. Social concern and multi-layered cultural critique are at the core of your theory of developmental theory. Do you think we're doing enough to end this sort of split between applied psychoanalysis and clinical psycho-analysis? Are there directions that we could be taking, so that cultural critique and social consciousness would become even more inseparable from clinical thinking and process?

You're also one of the few people that talks explicitly about ethics. You use the term, "moral Third." Are we doing enough to address the problem of ethical living?

JB: This question is very close to my heart, but in some ways I think it's less of a controversial question within the field. It's true that because of my unique opportunities and education and the way that I came into the field – not simply through psychology but through critical social theory – I saw certain conceptual problems within the psychoanalytic canon as it was passed down from Freud. As a critical theorist, which is a kind of neo-Marxist theory, I tended naturally to try to identify (looked for) those contradictions that gave rise to the problems. But in the case of women, motherhood and femininity, you actually didn't have to look for them, they banged you over the head. The question was less how to find them than to understand them in a more nuanced way than early feminists did when they simply rejected psychoanalysis. So how do we preserve an analysis of the unconscious mind, of the idea of internal objects, of the way that human beings actually impact each other outside of awareness? How do we preserve that, while integrating the feminist critique? This, in a sense, was the first goal.

Reading *Civilization and Its Discontents* immediately gave rise to certain questions. Do we really want to attribute what human beings do that is destructive, to a kind of destructive drive? Donnel Stern addressed this in his recent discussion of Field Theory. He pointed out that there are theories of intersubjectivity that are narrowly clinical and others that imply a revision of the whole human social dimension.

My idea of the Third is much broader, more social, and also more like Lacan than, say, the idea of the "analytic third" in Ogden, where it refers primarily to the relationship created by the two partners. Ogden came up with the idea of using the term "the Third," not merely from Green but more from Lacan. I was reading Lacan not for his clinical position but for his social conceptualization of the Third, maybe we should say his meta-psychological conception.

If you're trying to create an alternative way of understanding psycho-analysis to Freud's, you have to have some social presuppositions. For example, Mitchell and Greenberg talk about the idea that human beings are fundamentally social. I believe they said something like: you either believe that human beings live and die alone, or you believe that they live in the community, that they are embedded socially. For me the issue was to think dialectically – to continue to understand why people thought and think that human beings live and die alone, even though *our explanatory model understands us to be essentially social*. So I never throw out that other side of the equation. How do we not throw out the other side of the dialectical opposition, but actually learn from that tension? In other words, we would try to struggle with our sense of not being social, that is to say not really believing in the other's existence as a true human other subject, not being able to dignify the other, and in that sense recognize the other.

We think that we're social beings but we don't really act as though we are. We think that we reject Hobbes and that we reject the idea of individualism and we have all these critiques of individualism, but in many senses we act as though we don't feel that way. Freud's theory of narcissism in a sense was meant to understand that. And the theory of narcissism and the theory of aggression are very closely related, as I try to show in *Bonds of Love*. They both have to do with a certain erasure of the other. So, I tried to *develop* intersubjective *theory to* analyze how the erasure of the other in our minds, or the inability to actually let the other come and live in our minds, is something that is psychodynamically understandable, not simply as primary narcissism. I saw it as an alienation of recognition, that is to say some failure or defect in the developmental process.

From the very beginning, the baby is never alone, that is, without the mother, yet we know that babies can experience primal agonies related to feeling alone. So how is one able to be so alone when one is not alone? One would have died if one were truly alone, yet one feels so alone. From the very beginning, this tension between the fact that ideally and in some material sense we're never asocial, and yet we can feel so alone in our agonies, has to be understood. One wants to integrate the wonderful infancy research that shows how the infant is interacting from the very beginning and one wants to retain next to that Bion's perspective on how alone the infant can feel when containment is lacking—of course based on an intersubjective notion that the mother should be containing the baby. His theory has a much stronger emphasis on the ways in which those failures and containment leave the baby in the state of primal agony and that we have to connect with that primal agony. So it's holding those things in tension, the sunnier-minded American view of the development of recognition (Dinnerstein used that phrase, the more sunny-minded American view of how things could be and should be). We have to hold a tension with the sunnier side of good mother and baby and the dark side, holding those two positions in tension clinically and intellectually. That's really the goal.

SG: So, can I stop you for one second? First of all, one of the things that I'm very excited about is that you try to hold *both sides*, which I think has been a dilemma in relational psychoanalysis in general. Holding *both* the isolated experience that seems to be profoundly human and the understanding of us always in social, relational contexts. The other thing I think you're getting at implicitly is that what we mean by social can have different definitions. We can be growing in a social context in which we're constantly shaped, in relation, and yet there's a different kind of social, which has to do with actually knowing the other person is a human other. They can go together, right? That's what I think a lot of your work is about.

JB: Recognizing that distinction and disparity.

SG: Yes, exactly.

JB: Which really is best thought of, I think, in a Hegelian way, although I am not an expert on Hegel. I simply read and studied enough in Frankfurt to have a sense that the key concept here is the difference between "for itself" and "in itself". Inherently, that is, "in itself" we're all social, but we only come to the consciousness of our social being through certain struggles or experiences, and it's this coming to consciousness of our social nature that is the "for itself". So the social can be either merely "in itself", that is to say only objectively observable from some outside god's-eye point of view, or it can be that which we actually come to realize, at least incipiently, within the mind, within consciousness. So that distinction is something that I've applied to the Third. That's why I've said that Ogden's Third is a different conceptualization than the Third as I discuss it. Ogden's Third refers to the third "in itself", that is an objective observer can see these two people are co-creating the dynamic *as an independent entity*, but when you are in the dynamic and it is not going well, you feel very much like it's either something that's all your fault or all the other person's fault (**SG**: right) and you can't actually experience the co-creation. So the "for itself," the co-created quality, is not seen itself as "for itself" in that situation, but the "for itself" is really the salient point here. *This distinction shows* why we both feel that we are alone or, shall we say, we are in a world of objects rather than a world of others, and we are capable of coming to consciousness being in another self-state where we feel we are in a world of living others.

Given that, you then can return to the question of whether it would be helpful for people to have certain social perspectives, to have this perspective on social theory or some other relevant perspective on social theory that gives you the same ability to think. (**SG**: yes) So that is separate from the question of our social practices, but at the very least to have that level of sophistication and education would be useful. And since psychology programs do not emphasize social theory it certainly would be good if we (psychoanalytic educators) could provide that.

SG: So I'm going to keep focusing us on where there's a critique of relational at this point, or where we might go. How you see relational theory, clinical process, and also our culture – the way we've constructed relational culture or training – is there anything that you would critique about these two forms of being social that you're talking about, the "in itself" and the "for itself"? I'm going to keep asking you that question as we go along.

JB: I can just say that if people had more of these basic conceptual tools, then I think some of the misunderstandings that we're talking about, regarding recognition, or regarding aggression, would not be as likely to happen. Their understanding of what it means *in theory* to recognize the other would be mediated by a sense of something much richer. Much of this is spelled out in my article "On Recognition and Destruction," which is frequently read but *has some implications that weren't spelled out, that I hope will be clear in my new book.*

SG: Well it, it really gives a wonderful, essential, portrait of the way you think. And that's why people are always rereading it.

JB: Right, but what I'm saying is that it must embody something of this elusive distinction, between a simplistic idea of recognition and a more sophisticated idea of recognition where we understand via Winnicott that it is something that comes into being as a knowledge of the other's independence that is tolerable to the self, not threatening to the self, even joyful for the self, but *sadly* not in fact, a requisite for people getting through life. I mean they're getting through life somewhat badly, but in fact they are getting through life without having much of a strong sense of others as being real and alive to them, and this problem of the other's unreality, the fundamental schizoid dilemma that others don't feel real to you and thus you do not feel real to yourself is, perhaps, another way to see what I was trying to say about recognition. The real point about recognizing the analyst's subjectivity is that once we have that experience of the other as another center of being, as a responsive, living, breathing other, it not only means that they are another equivalent mind who knows me, it means they know me because of something inside them. And *this means* they must be somehow like me. *They have their own* unique experience but one that has to be similar enough to mine that they can understand me. Without experiencing this similarity someone would be liable to imagine, in a kind of schizoid way, that you're applying rules and theories, and that's how you understand other people, as if you're a kind of automaton.

SG: Can I underline this point? (**JB**: Sure) One question is whether relational thinking has tended to overemphasize the introduction of the analyst's subjectivity, that growth requires encounters with the analyst's separate subjectivity.

A related critique is that the analyst's subjectivity is either too in the room, too foreclosing, given too much space, or doesn't allow enough for private space or interiority. And I think that what you just said has a lot of bearing on what is perhaps a misunderstanding or a simplification, that the analyst is a living, breathing human being who is responding with their own unique experience.

JB: Exactly. Patients can of course be initially unable to recognize that this is from whence this empathy is coming and they can be unable to recognize the empathy for what it is. We can recognize that as dissociation or we can call that schizoid, we can think of it as fear of intrusion, we have to analyze what that is. But if you go back to your original question, does there have to be growth in terms of that recognition? Yes, there absolutely has to be growth in terms of recognition of the analyst's empathy for what it is.

SG: As coming from the analyst's human interior, so to speak.

JB: *Yes.* First of all, it has to be recognized as empathy, that is to say felt as something positive, because *initially* it may not be. Until it's recognized as something positive with at least a part of the self, it will not be usable. Now it could be recognized by *one* part of the self while another part of the self is attacking it. So these are the kinds of things we want to be aware of.

SG: And what I hear you now saying is that even therapeutic approaches that primarily involve empathy and empathic immersion would in a very subtle way involve the analyst's subjectivity. After all, we can only empathize through our own human interior.

JB: *Yes*. We have to be aware of the way in which nothing like empathy can be taken for granted as something that the other can receive. When the patient rejects our empathy, we do feel unrecognized and we should be aware of that fact so we can process how it comes to affect us. And to return or to loop in here the question of aggression: what is taken to be aggression, let's say in a Kleinian theory, might be taken to be in a Guntrippian way as a patient's inability to receive because of the withdrawal of the self into this frightened place of interiority, or, as the patient's inability to use the object, if you're thinking like Winnicott

This may appear as an attack on you and your subjectivity and all the good things you want to give the baby, like in "Hate in the Countertransference," but to interpret it therefore as aggression to me seems actually simple-minded. I've seen analysts who feel attacked and become very aggressive with patients who cannot receive. This is of course a failure of analysis. So to use the idea that the patient is attacking the analysis or attacking the analyst or attacking the analyst's mind as certain Kleinians do, can become iatrogenically very perverse.

SG: And to read it as destructive motivations inside the patient instead of reading it as much more complicated.

JB: *Yes,* to read it as helplessness, or shame, or fear of injury, and so forth. I had to supervise a presentation publicly in England by an analyst who kept interpreting the patient as being destructive when the patient was being, in my opinion, very frightened and submissive toward the analyst. I thought that this idea of aggression was a very blunt instrument. Now I think the same thing when I read certain interpretations of Betty Joseph's. There's a paper in particular where Betty Joseph sees the patient as expressing manic excitement about the death of someone he knew in conjunction with expressing anxiety related to his son's upcoming surgery, whereas I hear the patient as expressing terror, but being dissociated. So, from my perspective, it is not "deeper" to grasp aggression than to grasp terror,

(SG: Right, or shame) or a kind of primal agony that's combined of the two. I believe that there's a sort of idealization in the notion that if you see people as being more destructive, you are somehow more profound, more capable (SG: Working deeper), of grasping the dark side of human beings. And I think that one of the great contributions of object relations, relational thought and self-psychology, is to understand the degree to which human beings are disorganized and terrified not only by their own hatred, but by the injuries and persecution and fear that have caused that hatred to arise. So I have a sense that any general critiques of one school by another as e.g. inattentive to aggression are far too global and unspecific to ever be clinically useful, except insofar as it is sometimes helpful to me personally to say to myself: Am I missing something negative or hateful here that would frighten me? Do I, am I paying enough attention to the way this patient may be compliant, rather than truly connected?

SG: You know one of the things that I think is problematic for clinicians is that the perception of certain communications from a patient as destructive occurs because the analyst cannot allow themselves the fullness of their own subjectivity inside. I'm not even talking about what they're telling the patient.

JB: No, inside their own internal experience, right.

SG: Because people can do a lot of things that have a destructive impact on the other but that's not necessarily at all what the subjectivity inside is about. It's about shame, it's about terror, it's about disintegration, it's about loneliness, it's about all kinds of things.

JB: Right, someone's shame may make you feel very rejected.

SG: Exactly. Because we're not processing what we're experiencing in the room, we can readily read it as the patient's hate or destructiveness.

JB: Ok, so, to put that in slightly different language, a language of affect regulation theory, we become disregulated by the patient's shame, for instance, and then because of our own disregulation we feel ashamed, inadequate. If we belong to a certain way of thinking, we could be saying the patient is trying to put this shame into me or this patient is attacking me and trying to bring down my analytic function. Or we could say, the patient is attacking my mind and making me unable to think. But, what you're saying, and I fully agree, is it's useful to have certain categories to be able to understand that I am now unable to think, what this patient does causes me to be unable to think. It doesn't mean that they're *trying* to make me unable to think but it is true that I am now having an experience of being unable to think. And it's even possible to say to a patient: You know, when you're like this, it makes me unable to think (laughs). And that can be a really useful intervention because the patient could say: Yes when my father yelled at me, I always felt unable to think.

SG: Right, but you're not starting with an assumption that your counter-transference is a veridical reading of what the patient's internal subjectivity is about. And one of the things that I think has been a critique of relational psychoanalysis is that we can sound like we're slipping in the direction of reading our countertransference as veridical, a kind of direct knowledge of what the patient's subjective motives are, or history is.

JB: But see, that's exactly what I experienced reading Betty Joseph, that because she's having a manic dissociative reaction to the patient's anxiety, that the patient must be having a manic reaction, while the patient might actually be feeling ashamed, anxious, worried about what the analyst is thinking, and his dissociation is actually affecting the analyst but that effect can't be owned and reflected upon by her.

SG: Exactly, I mean that's, to me, the major problem with a Kleinian approach, that kind of slippage is really clear in a Kleinian approach. In your language, the analyst has trouble allowing the patient to be a separate subject. Instead it's as if because I'm having a feeling the patient must be either doing that to me, or motivated to do it to me.

JB: Or feeling that same thing and putting that into me in some way. Now all of those things are useful things to know about (**SG**: Or to question, to raise as questions). Yes and it's useful to know about the possibility that this can happen. But, at the same time what I would underscore is that this type of conflation of self and other happens to everyone across the board

and it is not actually an attribute of a particular theory. It is not the failing of a particular theory, it is in fact something that we have to address with our theory and any school can show evidence of this kind of behavior.
SG: Because it's part of the human struggle.

JB: And it's part of the analytic situation to create this.

SG: So, can I . . .? I'm interrupting but I'm getting very excited.

JB: Ok, but first I want to go back to just this one thing. When we talk about the problem of recognizing subjectivity, we're talking about recognizing subjectivity along different axes and dimensions. The first one was the axis of realizing that this empathic other actually is a person. There are gradations of that realization; perhaps that realization can be had by one part of the patient's self, but still strenuously rejected by another part that is mistrustful, that wants to stay closed off, that does not want to open up. One part of the patient becomes healthier and begins to do better in their life, shows external progress, but another part is still holding onto original trauma, is mistrustful. This is where we need the most help, all of us, all the time. The question is how you're going to overcome the dissociation or splitting between those parts of self, so that the person doesn't come back to you ten years later with this part of the self still manifesting in one aspect of their life with their children, or their sexuality, or their work life, and they're saying: You know you really helped me Doctor, but there's this thing that I just haven't been able to get over. It seems as though it's very easy for the self to split into the healthier part and the more damaged part. And the healthier part keeps getting better and better, and I don't have a solution for this. This is what I want us to work on and I feel there are many different directions through which we can work on this.

SG: Let's try to link that to where you feel relational psychoanalysis is now, either theoretically or clinically as a culture, and how we need to work on that in the future. Is there anything you'd like to say about that?

JB: There's something I want to insert sort of back earlier relating to the question of the more nuanced approach to recognizing the analyst's subjectivity. Let's just go back and then we'll return to this point. I remember discussing this point with Lew Aron in the nineties when he was writing his first articles about working relationally. The problem with the higher level of engagement by the analyst is it is likely to foreclose certain kinds of transitional space in which the patient just rummages around in her or his aloneness and has certain experiences that would not be had otherwise. And I still feel that's a problem. My dilemma with that is that I think some people really do well with that and prefer having a lot more of that space.

SG: That quiet space.

JB: And they need that. I think that in the nineties, really in the eighties and nineties when I was much more under the influence of Winnicott and object relations, before relational theory developed, I certainly worked more in that way. Gradually, I found myself becoming more interactive, through the relational approach, and making more use of enactments. When I present some of my work to students who are having very successful, positive experiences in a kind of Winnicottian mode, they really don't like what I'm saying because it conflicts with what they're experiencing. I don't know yet how those two things could or if they ever could go together. Which is really a misfortune because then we would have to say the best possible outcomes for people would be achieved if we could send them to the right sort of analyst, but so often people aren't.

SG: I know, I know, well match is a hugely important thing.

JB: Yes, because there really are different ways of working. And I respect that way of working and I have used that way of working to good effect with certain people, but I've also found that while that way of working goes on well for a certain amount of time, when you hit the area of greatest trauma, it may not be the way that you can work. I therefore am agnostic about this but I feel that people should work on it and try to explore what the difference is between what it really means internally for people to experience a certain kind of quiet and space in the treatment, and what it means to work more through play and active involvement. Because the alternative to that kind of analytic – not exactly withholding –

that analytic restraint, is a certain kind of play. And what happens if you develop from the very beginning a much more playful relationship with the patient?

SG: And what do you mean by playful? Are you talking about Winnicott's squiggle game where you both squiggle?

JB: Well, but how does that come about in an actual talking cure relation? It comes about because you throw certain emotive responses into the hopper. You associate along with the patient, you share the metaphors that come to mind for you, and let the patient either reject those or work with them. But you put more material into the play space. It's like the squiggle is just one line, but what happens if you give the kid some clay, some finger paint.

SG: Right, but you're also playing along. You're not just sitting there while they –

JB: You might be offering them a tea party set to make a little tea party with, for example, or put other stuff into the playroom. And some people, of course, quite obviously signal that they will get very flooded, and you really want to put very little in, and other people are signaling that they want more in. So that's one dimension, the dimension of play and how there are some people with whom you can get into tremendously active play relations and they will flourish, come alive and they will feel very resentful if you don't give them more of that. Then again, there's a whole other dimension that has to do with affect regulation. What Schore and Beebe write about. I went to a conference on affect regulation a couple of years ago, organized by Schore and, Siegel. I was really impressed at the possibilities that open up, including in the work of Russell Meares, who has such a creative way of using affect regulation in the analytic process. That is another way to go forward, an incredibly nuanced and careful and very un-intrusive way in relation to the patient, but at the same time deeply aware of trauma. I don't think there's so much a lack of possibility here, as there is the problem of a plethora. When the relational school or method is characterized in such a narrow way and branded as being just this one thing, analysts acting and putting their subjectivity into the room, this is such an oversimplification of what is happening in the actual field, and the breadth of it.

SG: This is extremely important and I'm really loving the way you're talking about this clinical process in such a nuanced way, and also, the very subtle, gentle ways that the analyst's subjectivity is in the room, which is so different than this brand that relational has, right? Which is a portrait of us putting our subjectivity in the room in a much more flagrant, much more noisy, possibly intrusive way. I'm wondering what you think about why the impression of the analyst's subjectivity in the room has been distorted. Because the way you're actually describing the analyst's subjectivity in the room, it can be extremely gentle, virtually invisible, for long periods of time, very much about attunement, listening to the patient's reactivity. At conferences and case presentations, we can create the impression that we focus on Big enactments, which require Big moments of the analyst's subjectivity in the room.

JB: Well, I don't necessarily agree that that's all we show, actually. But I think that the reason that the emphasis has been on enactments and on these kinds of crises is that these are the ruptures that have classically undone analyses, they are the things that people suffer with. Ruptures and impasses are what students are constantly bringing into consultation – when you give a seminar and someone raises their hand and says: I'd like to discuss a case that I'm having trouble with – very often it's not an overt rupture, it's an impasse because they're, if they're young and inexperienced, then they're being very careful, but they're feeling completely tied in knots by the patient, they don't know how they're going to move through that. I do sometimes feel not that the problem is that it's explosive, but that there's a lack of analytic tools and that some of these impasses could be resolved if therapists had more tools in their tool chest relating to analyzing the patient's indirect communications, really a way to symbolize what the patient is doing in the moment. They don't have enough working metaphors, enough symbolic interpretive capacities to start working with these things in a way that, even if it's not utterly correct, will make them feel less helpless. I think you need a toolkit to be an analyst and that the psychodynamic, intrapsychic toolkit is insufficient among some of our students. I said this to Steve Mitchell before he died.

I said I don't think our students are getting enough intrapsychic theory. He asked me why was I writing about penis envy, for instance, and I said, because people still present with material that needs to be symbolically understood as feeling that they need a phallus and don't have one and I think it helps them to put it in that way. Because, as I've written, both little girls and boys are usually covetous of what the other has and want to have both, all.

I don't think that people are merely over-emphasizing enactments. I think enactments are crucial moments when the most dissociated, traumatic material comes forward and we needed to learn how to work on that. I don't think it's a bad thing that we spend a lot of time on that because nobody did that for virtually one hundred years in which so many analyses failed and all those people either quit or just sucked it up and went through their analysis and when you ask them, they say they had an analysis, it helped me in certain ways, but there's still something in me that feels unhealed.

SG: The gift here is that we have created space to deal with clinicians' most difficult experience – all clinicians struggle with 'Big' impasses and enactments; previously there was little room for us to discuss this openly. Now we have ameliorated analytic shame, decreased the analyst's sense of defectiveness, and increased our capacity to move through these moments.

Previously, analysts reckoned with impasse in private spaces, in dread of exposure and failure. The relational lens is an important corrective; it is no surprise that analysts may over-focus on this aspect of relational work. As a result, however, our more subtle daily work can be eclipsed, or even seem non-existent. Do you know what I mean?

JB: Yes, absolutely, I think that, right. Because we added a whole big, new, you know, layer to the box. And not just one tool.

SG: And since everybody's desperate for help with that, including us, then it begins to look as if this is all we do, all we talk about. And in that context, it can appear that the insistent presence of the analyst's subjectivity is looming very large as if we don't do the other kind of work that you're talking about, and I think it's very much because we've been deprived of help with this.

JB: But I also don't think that all enactments get resolved through expressions of the analyst's subjectivity. I think some enactments involve the analyst's subjectivity, but what resolves them is much more the analysis of what the patient experiences because the patient is not *always* that interested in what you experience and so what you experience has to be reframed for them in terms of what they experience.

SG: Ok that's terrific. And I think that what you just said is a big gift to re-orient the way people's impressions of relational can be formulated, right? Your subjectivity guides you and it's going to be used, but that there may be times, plenty of times, when you get through an enactment by working within the patient's experience.

JB: The critique that I made of Steiner in the paper that you discussed a long time ago. In that enactment, which seemed to be an ongoing enactment, he said, the patient always seemed to feel that he wasn't taking enough responsibility for his contribution to things but he also said I think just a few seconds earlier, that he had been having that feeling that he often had that she was always making *me* responsible for everything.

But he doesn't stop then and say, huh, that's interesting, I feel like she's making me responsible, she feels like I'm making her responsible, we're both blaming each other, let's talk about that. The point isn't necessarily that you have to disclose or "confess," as Steiner put it, you don't have to say, "Yes it's true, I was making you responsible." It would be sufficient to say, "It seems like you're always telling me that I'm making you responsible for everything, and it also seems like, at times, I'm putting blame back on you." And it seems as if there's a kind of dynamic here between us, in which each person is trying to offload the blame and perhaps you feel that as the analyst, I ought to be the bigger person. (laughs)

SG: That's nice, I like that.

JB: I haven't fully figured out how I want Steiner to speak to this patient, because I don't know enough of the rest of it. But to say, it seems like there's a contest here about who's to blame and that you feel to blame all the time, and that you think you know, if I were really a bigger person, I'd be taking on the blame. How much disclosure is involved in that? Very little, because the part where I'm feeling blamed by you is obvious.

SG: And it's a very important distinction that you're making. That to describe the dynamic in the room is not a disclosure, it's not saying and imposing on the patient. 'You're making me feel blamed' (which is a self-disclosure) is a very different statement than our more frequent descriptor: 'blame seems to be bouncing around in this room'.

JB: Right, because "You're making me feel blamed" is an accusation, a reproach, a complementary interaction. It situates us inside the doer-done to dynamic. And there are different ways to speak to someone in which you take account of how much they want your subjectivity to be involved. So certain patients would say: Well, are you blaming me? And you would have to be able to have enough internal processing to say: Oh, I guess I must be doing that. Right, you'd have to be able to own that in some way, for such a patient. For another patient, it would be a little horrifying if you owned something (**SG**: Exactly) too specifically and personally because they would feel that was so shaming of you, and there-fore you would be so shaming of them, and they're really so careful about shame (**SG**: Or they're so worried about being destructive towards you). Exactly. I think what you're describing as the standard relational view is almost a template, *a simplified model of enactment.*

Fitting in with this idea of recognizing the subjectivity of the analyst, there *was* an ongoing struggle that was really territorial more than anything else, between the relational and the self psychological point of view. Not to say there weren't real disagreements between the position that Mitchell articulated in '88 and self psychology, but the self psychology focus on rupture and repair has been at the core of our work on enactments.

I thought that Bromberg's work came over toward the self psychological view. The more he got into affect regulation, the more he was moving closer to infancy theory. On the other hand, the dissociation aspect is something that came more from the Interpersonal side, so obviously there are these different conglomerations that people were working with. Reifying the theory in terms of where it was at any one moment involves a mistake that goes back to how psychoanalysis was structured around

Freud, as though there had to be some kind of a uniform theory for psychoanalysis to be scientifically legitimate. And there simply could not be such a unified theory for the relational movement. There was necessarily an ongoing process that involved many quite diverse thinkers and practitioners. Many different people were in dialogue with one another and constantly changing their positions – as, for instance, Steve Mitchell did when he started to write about attachment and intersubjectivity.

One of the most crucial misconceptions about my work, and you can see it in Steve Mitchell's book on intersubjectivity, as well as in people who are more critical of me such as Reis and Orange, was that I saw the main developmental moment as simply being the so-called Hegelian clash of wills in the rapprochement period, in this moment of the struggle for recognition. That's simply a misreading of my work, which proposed an outline of development that we can trace, *beginning* with the earliest forms of recognition, which are much more asymmetrically based on the parent recognizing the baby's signals, needs, gestures, affect states. But the earliest moments of recognition still have an element of feedback from the baby and the baby's differentiated responses, i.e. she can differentiate between mother and other. My idea of recognition as a developing capacity began with the initial importance of attunement, and face-to-face play which allows for an early version of mutual recognition. The dimension of matching versus non-matching that Beebe describes was a crucial element of my original theory of recognition. The idea that I saw recognition simply as something that occurs when the baby finally recognizes the mother's subjectivity is a distortion of my idea that children ultimately are able *to* do that. But they do that because the mother is recognizing their subjectivity, and no baby is going to recognize the mother's subjectivity who hasn't been well and truly recognized by the mother.

There is a constant proclivity among people to try to differentiate themselves by denying the complexity of other people's thoughts so that they can juxtapose what they have to say to that other person – and I think it's unavoidable – we all do it. At the risk of being self-serving, I would say that the difficulty in truly immersing yourself in the other's thought *as the other intended* it is the form of recognizing another person's thought that demands real discipline, it is an effort of differentiation that I miss in the misreadings of those who harp on the supposed lack of emphasis on attunement, harmony, oneness what-have-you in my theory of recognition. To be honest, I think such differentiation requires enormous effort and while I like harmony just as much as anybody, I think attunement and empathy often requires us to stretch ourselves to accept that others don't want what we want or feel as we do.

SG: Well, this goes back to what I wanted to say before, that in the room the analyst's subjectivity is always present in some kind of implicit, environmental way. And that the analyst is always attuning to what level of awareness of the analyst's subjectivity the patient needs, will welcome, that will facilitate their growth. So your fundamental position is one of attunement and mutual regulation around how the patient needs, wants, or grows from a direct encounter with the analyst's subjectivity, and that you're very much attuning to the signaling of the patient. (**JB**: Right.) All the time.

JB: But the problem is, if we go back to Ogden, he talks about there being a thinking subject, an independent subjectivity, and then there's the third that's the interaction of the two subjectivities. The analyst is a thinking subjectivity, thinking in the broadest sense of thinking, feeling, processing. The analyst is often very preoccupied with just keeping her or his own mind.

SG: With self-regulation really.

JB: Exactly, with self-regulation. And with trying to think in the face of what might be overwhelming stimuli. And at certain moments the analyst has to recognize: I can't do this, I can't actually regulate, I may have to just sit through this. At other moments, the analyst is inclined, perhaps correctly and perhaps not, to imagine that they can think or communicate their way out of this dilemma by offering themselves to the patient in some way.

SG: Like describing their dilemma.

JB: The analyst is in effect inviting the patient to help him or her get out of this (**SG**: Collaboratively) place because the analyst is thinking: I'm not getting out of this by my figuring it out by myself.

SG: The analyst's attitude would be: 'I could use some input from you'. In my inter-personal training, we talked about this as getting good supervision from the patient!

JB: Bromberg stresses that things really changed for him clinically when he realized he didn't have to figure things out by himself, that he could invite the patient. What happens when we stop thinking we have to figure everything out for ourselves and conversely, in what moments do we find ourselves thinking, we had better figure it out for ourselves because we are too ashamed and too dysregulated, or the patient is. You can now query to what degree would that be intrusive, to what degree will that be helpful and even if it's intrusive, perhaps it's pretty helpful (**SG**: Unavoidable). Unavoidable, right. Exactly, and it can have both an up and a downside. All of those questions are intersubjective questions.

There's this arena of query and discipline where we can now become familiar with a whole other range of activities that used to occur *sub rosa* and now we're going to actually expose them to the light and see that they're not simply damaging. We're going to stop being so afraid of them.

SG: Right, and stop feeling like such failures if we have to (**JB**: Right) consult the patient. Even if it can feel temporarily intrusive, or destabilizing –

JB: The de-idealizing process.

SG: Certainly de-idealizing – with the exception of Searles and some interpersonalists, it was rare to express such faith in the patient's mind and perceptions. In the old model, we were the 'doctor' – how could we ask our patient for assistance? Often, my patient can give me some very good supervision in a moment where I feel lost or confused or stuck. This can happen explicitly, upon my request, or through implicit communications. My faith in their collaboration potentiates their faith in themselves. And that, yes, it can be very de-idealizing and anxiety-provoking for the patient to realize that the analyst is feeling somewhat lost. But it is often a very empowering moment of discovering their own capacities, and the analyst's flawed humanity.

JB: Or doesn't know everything.

SG: Or doesn't know or, whatever that is. But also, at the same time, it invites the patient to have more faith in their own mind, their own capacity, even to discover their own capacity for love and provision to the other–

JB: And in my theoretical perspective, it's also about faith in the Third as a process of rupture and repair. The basic expression of the Third in analysis is rupture, repair, and recognition and that repair/recognition is a kind of a unity. It is part of a superordinate process by which recognition becomes strengthened; what becomes idealized is not merely the analyst now, but our ability to create a relationship with each other. So the idealization flows more and more into the process.

I wrote this back in '94, in "What Angel Could Hear Me." I was working in a more, shall we say, Winnicottian mode, but I can now expand the idea to see how that which is idealized is not just the transitional space but the rupture and repair process.

SG: So if you link to self psychology, it's the process that becomes the self-object, in a certain sense, the actual excavation, exploration, mutuality, collaborative working through of a rupture.

JB: Perhaps you could say that the self-object now becomes part of a larger process that is governed by the Third and that your implicit understanding of what makes for a safe and positive self-object for you in life is somebody who is willing to become governed by the Third.

SG: I feel in this whole conversation, that you are making a critique if not of relational, then something about when relational gets distilled, or understood, or branded. We always tend to oversimplify ideas, to mimic it, to identify with it. So I would say that this notion of what it means to have the analyst's subjectivity in the room – my feeling, and this may not be yours, is that, there's some way that our culture, the way students are starved for a certain understanding to help themselves out of bad moments, that there's some kind of distilled received wisdom that's not exactly what you mean. Listening to some case presentations, I hear a crude understanding of the way the analyst puts their subjectivity into the room – without grasping the subtleties of caution, attunement, and regulation.

JB: I think a lot of that representation is coming from the outside, that is to say, it's not so much the self-understanding and self-representation. It could be of students, but students always simplify things.

SG: The issue of branding always collapses complexity. Is there anything you want to say about relational branding?

JB: I just think I'm the kind of person that doesn't pay enough attention to that sort of thing. . . . If I can introduce another piece. You raised the issue of aggression and of therapists' inability to deal with aggression and getting into a submissive relationship to the patient. That has to do with the therapist's inability to sufficiently embrace their own hatred, aggression, and destructive feelings, and their fear of being harming and destructive.

I remember saying to a therapist in supervision: You know, you really just want to kill the patient. You know what, you need to accept that you are a killer. Accept it. If you would just accept that you're a killer, this would all change. And so she said afterwards, she left the group, and she went skipping down the street, thinking, more like singing to herself: 'I'm a killer, I'm a killer, I'm a killer.' And then things did change with the patient of course. I want people to have the experience in supervision of learning that they can play with these emotions without becoming so dysregulated, and that has to be done through play and at the same time we have to recognize how terrifying these things can also be. So we need to hold a tension between a kind of non-dissociative recognition of terror and a creatively dissociative use of play in order to accept painful emotions of shame, horror, and destructiveness. What I think was lacking in self psychology was this playful relationship to aggression. But, I don't think the relationship to aggression in the interpersonal tradition was playful either, I think it was punitive. And I don't think it was particularly playful in the Kleinian tradition.

SG: Interesting – I found my interpersonal training to be refreshingly frank about human aggression on both sides of the couch; and I especially appreciated that interpersonal theorists, such as Fromm, embedded aggression in its cultural conditions.

JB: We're doing better today because we have people who really are paying attention to dissociation. What I think we have trouble with is having a sufficiently intellectually saturated theory of unconscious meanings, which people who grew up in the Freudian tradition had, because that gives you so much more to play with.

SG: You mentioned before that we need more intrapsychic tools. And so that might be something that you would like to see us focus on more, integrate more.

JB: Yes, you see, I think that all of these people who use unconscious communication and reverie, I think people like Ferro and Ogden have a great toolkit of working with metaphor and working with unconscious content. That is different from what I see as the basic New York position, which is working with affect.

SG: It's an interesting question.

JB: I tend to think that my students come very equipped to track affect but not so equipped to track things that aren't presenting affectively but rather are presenting through metaphor and symbol, such as through dreams, fantasies, and also through odd moments of interaction that have symbolic meanings.

SG: That's interesting because I think that most of my students have no experience working with dreams at all. They are not communicating to the patient that dreams are interesting and tell us a lot about what's going on unconsciously. So their patients don't tend to bring in dreams. I think that there is a deficit in exploring unconsciousness in that way.

JB: But, the problem is for me that I don't want that exploration to be opposed to our ability to track the affective and the procedural and the implicit levels, which I think our students are much better at than people who are trained in the Freudian tradition. I think the whole idea of ranking and saying that one modality is better or saying that one approach is the correct approach is not useful.

SG: So you're also saying that affect and inter-subjectivity should not sideline or foreclose the intrapsychic/ symbolic work with the unconscious.

JB: Right, but because historically psychoanalysis developed up until the 1970s with this exclusive focus on the intrapsychic and the unconscious, not to mention very pernicious forms of defense analysis and abstinence on the part of the analyst, there was so much correction to do. The 80s and 90s were a period of intense correction and the last decade has been a period in which we've really been trying to evolve beyond, you know, swinging over into correction. But we had to introduce so many important concepts –

SG: Yes, corrective concepts.

JB: In terms of how we worked with our subjectivity, in terms of affect, in terms of dissociation, in terms of affect regulation. This was a period of immense correction and addition, and now we can have a period of integration and synthesis. So, from my perspective, it's not so much that we did something wrong but this was how our learning process went. I see it just like analysis, we had to do these things first, but now we are able to go back and move towards other pieces that we may have left behind in development.

I'd like to see our students become more synthetically trained so that they're able to do work with serious trauma, so that they have at least some familiarity with therapeutic modalities that are primarily oriented to trauma, but at the same time I would like them to be able to work with people who are appearing in a very different way, who are more schizoid, who work more symbolically. I like people to have that range but clearly everyone is going to locate themselves somewhere . . .

Evolution of theory always . . . theory develops somewhat reactively. There was this question that was raised by Steve Mitchell about whether we were engaged in a revolution. I think that it was revolution but I think that a good revolution does not eat its children or its grandparents.

So I think that intersubjectivity is a revolution in thought, as compared to the subject-object position. It's a hugely important moment in twentieth-century thought that we move into an intersubjective perspective. The news of this revolution, unfortunately, has still not gotten out in academia, you know, they still are working basically with Freudian theory.

SG: You know it's remarkable, isn't it?

JB: Yes, they just have no knowledge of intersubjective psychoanalysis and so even their own experience in psychotherapy is disconnected with their ideas about what psychoanalysis is. What concerns me more at the moment is the complete absence of reflection in the public sphere of what we've achieved, we are unknown in the public intellectual sphere and the academic world. That's a truly disturbing fact that I don't know what to do about.

SG: So we're going to stop in a few minutes but I think this is very enlightening, both in terms of a much subtler, nuanced, broad-ranging representation of the way you see things, and also the kind of synthetic turn that you would like us to be making, the ways that you would like us to balance our emphasis on affect and interaction with more intrapsychic work, more symbolic work about the unconscious.

JB: And I should add that symbolic work about the unconscious includes a real understanding of how we are constantly enacting internal object relations, which I think is something that Jody Davies' work exemplifies. And so, when we talk about the so-called unconscious, I think we really want to talk more about the inner object world and I think relational psychoanalysts have been concerned with the inner object world all along. I think that everyone who has been central to this movement believed in the inner world of object relations. It was in our formulated statement about why we were splitting with the interpersonal as well as the Freudian track. I don't think we ever intended to leave those behind.

SG: That's wonderful.

Chapter 4

Toward a more fully integrative and contextual relational paradigm

Paul L. Wachtel

It is broadly understood that the relational point of view emerged as an integrative effort, bringing together the insights and perspectives of inter-personal theory, object relations theory, and self psychology (Aron, 1996). Prior to the relational synthesis, these different points of view were largely seen as separate and competing psychoanalytic paradigms. Proponents of one were often dismissive of the others and understood their own perspective as in opposition, failing to appreciate the common shift from a primarily drive model to a concern with how *relationships* were at the center of the development and dynamics of personality. After the pioneer-ing efforts of Greenberg and Mitchell (Greenberg & Mitchell, 1983; Mitchell, 1988), the landscape changed. Although the identifications of groups of analysts with only one (or at least primarily one) of these perspectives certainly continues to be robustly evident, the consensus increasingly emphasizes their convergence, and there is by now a vast relational literature in which their differing contributions are brought together in a fruitful and evolving synthesis.

Up till now, however, the integrative impulse that led to the explosive growth of the relational movement and the identification of large numbers of analysts throughout the world as relational has not been widely carried forth beyond the confines of the viewpoints first integrated by Greenberg and Mitchell. The open-minded spirit that created the capacity to look across boundaries and find both commonalities and synergies seems to have lost its momentum.

By this I do not mean to suggest that creativity per se has declined. The relational literature continues to manifest significant creative energy and to yield new insights, and I continue to be an avid reader of that literature. Rather, what I am pointing to is the persistence of the boundary between ideas that derive from the world of psychoanalysis and ideas deriving from elsewhere. This boundary, to be sure, is by no means impermeable. In recent years, there has been substantial interest among some relational writers in the ways that relational formulations intersect, for example, with attachment research, cognitive and affective neuroscience, trauma theory, and a range of other research domains, and some relational analysts have explored issues of race and class as well. Moreover, from the very beginning, the relational paradigm incorporated in significant ways elements of feminist thought, postmodernist and constructivist perspectives, and other points of view from outside of psychoanalysis (Aron, 1996).

But when it comes to serious attention to the contributions of other *therapeutic* orientations, the receptiveness has been much more limited. To be sure, even here there has been increasing attention in recent years, at least among a subset of relational analysts, to incorporating ideas and methods from non-psychoanalytic therapeutic orientations (see especially the important volume by Bresler & Starr, 2015). In a sense, one of my key aims in this chapter is to contribute to the furtherance of this tendency. In that sense, my argument is less a critique than a friendly prod, an effort to contribute to the further acceleration of a trend that has already begun. But a clear-eyed look at the overall literature of the relational movement makes it clear that attention to the ideas of therapeutic orientations outside of psychoanalysis is still not close to mainstream in the relational world. And although there are some creative relational thinkers who continue to venture outside the usual boundaries of relational discourse, the courageous spirit of challenge to long-revered and unquestioned psychoanalytic assumptions that characterized the relational movement in its early years has given way, it seems to me, to a period of consolidation. Put differently, the questioning of what could be called the received version of psychoanalytic thought and practice, which was so central to the evolution of the relational paradigm, has not been matched, in recent years, by an equivalent questioning of whether the (by now) received version of *relational* thought and practice is sufficient.

One of the most powerful obstacles to continuing innovation and questioning of basic assumptions is consensus. When everyone one interacts with shares the same basic assumptions, it is much less likely those assumptions will be re-examined or looked at afresh; indeed, it can seem dangerous. Thus, conversely, one of the experiences most likely to promote innovation and critical inquiry is to encounter people who think differently. In addition to the psychoanalytic meetings I attend, such as IARPP and Division 39, I regularly attend the annual meetings of the Society for the Exploration of Psychotherapy Integration (SEPI). And while I derive much from attending the former, it is at SEPI that I find my thinking especially challenged and most likely to evolve or change.[1] There I regularly attend sessions by therapists of other orientations, and panels in which analysts exchange ideas and clinical experiences with behavior therapists, family therapists, Gestalt therapists, and others. In these meetings I encounter experienced clinicians who work from very different premises than I do and use very different approaches to patients, and I almost always come home from them not just with new ideas and clinical strategies but with new *questions* about my own ideas.

Of course, to be stimulated and challenged by ideas, one must have at least a modicum of respect for those who hold them. The ideas I might encounter at a rally of the Tea Party would almost certainly depart sharply from my own, but they would be unlikely to contribute in any way to changing my mind because I have so little sympathy or respect for what the Tea Party stands for. The aversion toward cognitive and behavioral therapies on the part of most relational analysts may not approach in intensity that of mine toward the Tea Party, but it is certainly significant, and there is little inclination to look in this direction for stimulation, new ideas, or potential questions about long-held assumptions. But given how influential these approaches currently are in the world of psychotherapy in the United States and in many other parts of the world, it seems to me that it behooves relational analysts to at least look more closely than has been common thus far at just what this 800-pound gorilla in our field is actually like and whether it is as thoroughly alien (and as thoroughly worthy of dismissal) as many relationalists are used to thinking.

The aversion is probably less intense with regard to the other two broadly influential non-psychoanalytic paradigms in our field, family systems and humanistic-experiential. As a consequence, the barriers in this regard are not as rigid; various forms of systems thinking, for example, have been of substantial interest to a significant subset of relational analysts. In concentrating in this chapter particularly on the potential interface with cognitive-behavioral modes of thought and practice, I do not mean to downplay the contributions of these other points of view, whose intersection with psychoanalytic ideas has been a matter of interest to me for some time (see, for example, Wachtel, 1997; Wachtel & Wachtel, 1986). Rather, I concentrate here on the more difficult, less "natural" feeling question of whether there are potential points of intersection or mutual enrichment to be found between relational thought and practice and that of cognitive-behavioral therapists precisely because it has been less explored. I do so as well because the increasingly dominant influence of cognitive-behavioral thinking in the therapeutic world more broadly makes the question one of some urgency to examine.

It is not that I think the fit between the two paradigms is an easy one. There are aspects of the way that cognitive-behavioral therapy is frequently practiced that truly do not sit well with the values or sensibilities of relational analysts or therapists. But as I shall discuss below, there are *many different versions* of cognitive-behavioral therapy, and some are more readily compatible with a relational approach than others.[2] Moreover, it is important to note that although some degree of *compatibility* is required for an integration or synthesis between relational and cognitive-behavioral practice, there would be little reason to even attempt such an effort if there were not also significant *differences* between the two paradigms. Nothing, after all, would really be added if they were found to be essentially bringing to bear the same therapeutic processes, simply with different packaging, vocabulary, or ideological overlay.

To be sure, there has been much evidence that common factors (especially the quality of the therapeutic relationship) underlie much of the effectiveness of the nominally different and competing schools of therapy that characterize the landscape of contemporary practice (e.g., Duncan, Miller, Wampold, & Hubble, 2010; Norcross, 2011; Wampold & Imel, 2015). These findings, combined with related data demonstrating that the overall therapeutic impact of therapies approached from the vantage point of different schools of thought in our field is remarkably similar, offer a powerful argument against the self-serving assumption that one's own approach (whatever tribal group in our field one identifies with) is uniquely capable of being helpful to people in psychological distress. It is the combination of compatibility/underlying similarity *and* difference or distinct contribution that makes a synthesis of two approaches of value (Wachtel, 1997).

My own history of engagement with the world of cognitive-behavioral therapy has been far from simple or unconflicted. On the one hand, I was an early advocate of the integration of psychoanalytic ideas and methods with those of behavior therapy, at a time when the behavioral point of view had not yet achieved its current prominence (Wachtel, 1977), and the version of relational thought that characterizes my own thinking, cyclical psychodynamics (Wachtel, 2014), has been shaped in significant ways by this long-standing interest. On the other hand, I have been a particularly strong critic of certain trends in cognitive-behavioral practice (Wachtel, 1997, 2011) and of the claims by many cognitive-behavioral advocates that their approach is uniquely "evidence-based" or "empirically supported" (Wachtel, 2010). Indeed, for the very reason that I have explored and engaged the cognitive-behavioral paradigm more seriously and extensively than most relational analysts, I have also articulated my *objections* to certain of its features more fully than have most relational writers, who rarely examine in any detail the premises or practices of a paradigm they rather thoroughly dismiss. Thus, in elaborating in this chapter why I think that relational psychoanalysis can benefit from more serious engagement with this other major paradigm in the world of mental health and psychological therapy, I will also elaborate on why certain directions in cognitive and cognitive-behavioral therapy are problematic and largely *in*hospitable territory for therapists with a relational sensibility. In its overall intent, however, it is certainly the case that my aim in this chapter is to reinvigorate the original integrative thrust of the relational turn and to point toward ways in which exploration of the seemingly alien territory of the cognitive-behavioral world can contribute to expanding the horizons of relational practice and to promoting the kind of rethinking and reexamination essential to keep any point of view fresh and vital.

I am aware that the agenda to which I am pointing here may seem to some readers like it strays too far from what they understand as the essence of the relational outlook and frame of mind. But in part, the re-examination of just what it does mean to be relational is one of my aims. The relational movement is in fact a loose coalition or broad umbrella (Wachtel, 2008). Consequently, understanding both the commonalities that unite the diverse set of thinkers under that umbrella and the ways that the various elements of the relational framework overlap only partially, and sometimes even clash, can yield a more sophisticated understanding of the nature of relational thinking and the meaning of the relational turn. The relational movement is almost defined by its diversity (see the May 2014 online IARPP colloquium on the work of Stephen Mitchell for a good example of the range of views and substantial differences in viewpoint).

There are, to be sure, sufficient ideas and assumptions that are shared by significant numbers of relationalists – though rarely by all – that the term relational clearly has meaning, at least as a configurational term denoting overlapping and interweaving commonalities (Aron, 1996; Wachtel, 2008). But whereas the earlier Freudian consensus pointed to a set of ideas and practices which – even if often departed from in actual practice – was "officially" adhered to, to a very significant degree, the landscape of relational practice is much more variegated; one can be "relational" in one's practice in a rather wide range of ways. It is in part for this reason that I wish to suggest that venturing beyond the confines of psychoanalytic practice altogether – even beyond the more flexible boundaries of *relational* practice as they are currently understood – is (perhaps paradoxically) truer to the values and the spirit of exploration that drew relationalists to psychoanalysis in the first place than is retaining relational psychoanalysis as a gated community, screening out ideas from the riff-raff. Gated communities are rarely vibrant ones.

Why CBT (of all things)?

The possibilities for incorporating insights and ways of working from other orientations cover a wide range of therapeutic approaches (see Bresler & Starr, 2015; Wachtel, 1997, 2002; Wachtel & Wachtel, 1986 for examples). But since space is limited, I want to focus in this chapter on one source of ideas and methods in particular – the realm of cognitive-behavioral therapy. I choose this realm in particular for several reasons. First of all, as I alluded to above, it is scarcely a secret that CBT is currently the most influential paradigm in the overall world of psychological treatment, exercising a hegemony in the field comparable to that held by psychoanalysis several decades earlier. Second, and perhaps equally important to my choice, CBT is the "other" orientation that is likely to feel most alien to relational analysts and therapists. Indeed, to many readers, the idea that any aspects of cognitive-behavioral thought and practice can really be integrated into a therapy informed by a relational sensibility may seem close to outlandish. Thus, I am at the very least pointing to an area *worth talking about* rather than one that will elicit a bland "yes, of course."

Third (and related), I choose CBT in particular because it is the therapeutic realm about which many relational analysts are most likely to be largely *ignorant* or (what often amounts to the same thing) to view with a degree of stereotyping or caricature that is useful to reexamine. Thus, although the incorporation of ideas and methods from family systems or humanistic-experiential approaches may be easier for most readers of this chapter to imagine, discussion of the role of CBT seems a more challenging – and hence more interesting – focus to pursue.

When worlds collide: serious incompatibilities between CBT and relational psychoanalysis

To be sure, there are features of much cognitive-behavioral theory and practice that do not fit well at all with the values or concerns of relational analysts.[3] In particular, for many years CBT was dominated by an overly rationalistic point of view that clashed in important ways with a number of central features of relational thought and practice. The patient was viewed as holding "irrational" assumptions about the world which were the source of his difficulties, and the therapist was understood as in a position to *correct* this erroneous view. Moreover, cognitive-behavioral therapists operating from this rationalistic perspective were uninterested in, and at times even hostile to, affect. Often they would attempt to "talk patients out of their feelings" (see Wachtel, 1997, 2011), arguing that if the patient would only think more "rationally," he *wouldn't have to* feel depressed or angry.

It is little wonder that relational analysts, looking at such ways of thinking and working, did not feel drawn to incorporate them into their work. Indeed, in my own efforts to combat stereotypic visions of behavior therapists as clinically inept and lacking respect for the complexity and meaningful subjectivity of their patients, and to interest analysts in the possibility that behavioral methods could valuably complement what we do, the emergence of this rationalistic mode of thought and practice in the increasingly dominant "cognitive" versions of behavior therapy was nothing short of an embarrassment (see for example, Wachtel, 2011, pp. 23–27).

By now, however, there have emerged a wide range of other ways of thinking and working that are important parts of the cognitive-behavioral world and that fit much better with relational assumptions and sensibilities. One particularly important element is the evolution of a *constructivist* form of cognitive therapy that differs quite considerably from the rationalist approach I just described (Arnkoff & Glass, 1992; Guidano, 1991; Mahoney, 1995, 2003; Neimeyer, 2009; Neimeyer & Mahoney, 1995). Cognitive therapists operating from a constructivist rather than a positivist-rationalist perspective actually have much in common with relationalist thinking, which is, of course, strongly constructivist in viewpoint. Yet there is remarkably little knowledge on *either* side of the divide of their constructivist twin.

In a separate, but certainly related, trend, an influential and growing cohort of cognitive-behavioral therapists has been highlighting the ways in which earlier proponents of the cognitive-behavioral paradigm had paid insufficient attention to affect (e.g., Samoilov & Goldfried, 2000) and to the therapeutic relationship (e.g., Gilbert & Leahy, 2007; Leahy, 2008). Attention to these critical dimensions of human experience and the clinical process brings cognitive-behavioral work into considerably closer alignment to the sensibilities and ways of working more common to relationalists.

Alongside these developments, and further interweaving with them in the ongoing evolution of cognitive-behavioral thought and practice, has been still another development that contributes to bridging the gap[4] between cognitive-behavioral and relational ways of working – the evolution of what has come to be called "third wave" behavioral and cognitive-behavioral therapies (Hayes, Follette, & Linehan, 2004). These include acceptance and commitment therapy (Hayes, Strosahl, & Wilson, 2012), dialectical behavior therapy (Linehan, 1993, 1994; Robins, Schmidt & Linehan, 2004); mindfulness-based cognitive therapy (Segal, Williams, & Teasdale, 2002) and functional analytic psychotherapy (Kohlenberg & Tsai, 1991). These therapeutic approaches, while rooted in the cognitive-behavioral tradition, also have a strong emphasis on mindfulness and acceptance, including acceptance of *affect*. In contrast to the dismissal or downgrading of affect (or the outright critique of affect as "irrational") that can be evident in the rationalist versions of cognitive therapy, these perspectives actually *highlight* and address very focally the role of affect.

Their clinical strategy shares much in common with Bromberg's (1993) point that:

> The ability of an individual to allow his self-truth to be altered by the impact of an 'other' ... depends on the existence of a relationship in which the other can be experienced as someone who, paradoxically, both accepts the validity of the patient's inner reality and participates in the here-and-now act of constructing a negotiated reality discrepant with it.
>
> (p. 160)

Moreover, in contrast to the problematic assumption by rationalist cognitive therapists that they know what is rational and their patients do not – akin to the stance of the "knowing" analyst and the benighted patient that was a key focus of the relational critique of more traditional psychoanalytic thinking (e.g., Hoffman, 1998; Renik, 1993) – the approaches I am referring to here share the humility of the relational perspective that neither therapist nor patient have a monopoly on what is true or realistic.

Relatedly, in contrast to what is sometimes seen as a manipulative tendency in other behavioral therapies, these "third-wave" cognitive-behavioral therapies, in common with the constructivist cognitive therapies noted earlier, emphasize a *collaborative* therapeutic stance. And, just as mindfulness has begun to be an interest of increasing numbers of relational analysts (see especially Wallin, 2007), so too is it increasingly of importance in these versions of cognitive-behavioral therapy. In general, the evolution of these newer cognitive-behavioral approaches – differing from their predecessors without dismissing everything about the foundations or tradition from which they arose – resembles the parallel evolution of relational psychoanalysis, which in similar fashion remained firmly rooted in the psychoanalytic point of view even while engaging in radical revision of certain aspects of its underlying epistemology and stance toward the therapeutic relationship. Future intellectual historians, I suspect, will be fascinated with these parallel evolutions, occurring in different corners of the therapeutic world with little awareness on the other side of the divide of rather similar revisions going on across the river.

My point, it is important to be clear, is not that these newer cognitive-behavioral approaches are simply *the same* as relational psychoanalysis, differing only in their terminology, in superficial matters of form, or in which authors they cite. Far from it. In fact, if they really *were* the same, there would be little value in attempting to integrate them; from either direction, there would be nothing new to add. It is the very complementarity of the different strengths and different perspectives of these two broad approaches that offer nutriment for the creative therapist to address more effectively the many points in the course of the work in which the patient (or the therapist) feels "stuck". The differences between the approaches are a generative resource.

But for this borrowing and complementing to be coherent, it is essential that the two different ways of thinking or working not be utterly incompatible. In the case of rationalist CBT and relational psychoanalysis, they very largely *are*. And because it is the rationalist version that is more likely to be familiar to most relational analysts, interest in the prospect of learning or incorporating anything useful from the cognitive-behavioral realm is understandably low.[5] It is only with sufficient understanding of the *wide range* of ways in which cognitive-behavioral thought and practice has evolved that at least the potential for such enrichment can be seen.

In this brief chapter, there is insufficient space to spell out in any detail the various ways in which attention to the more compatible versions of cognitive-behavioral therapy might enhance work undertaken from a relational vantage point (see Wachtel, 1997, 2008, 2011 for a more comprehensive account of how such integrative work can be pursued). Among the potential contributions that might be briefly noted are different (and often more systematic) ways of monitoring the patient's experience and his progress (or, at times and importantly, his lack of progress); useful means of attending to and addressing the patient's behavior and experience *outside* the consulting room to complement the strengths of the relational paradigm in exploring the intersubjective experiences within the room; a range of interventions designed to directly promote change in the daily interactions in the patient's life space; and, perhaps most important of all, attention to the dimension of *exposure* and its powerful contributions to the reduction of anxiety (Wachtel, 1997, 2008, 2011).

The especially important contribution of the concept of exposure and the procedures that derive from it follows from the understanding offered by Freud, in *Inhibitions, Symptoms, and Anxiety* (1926) that anxiety (often signal anxiety that is not consciously experienced) lies behind almost all of the patient's complaints. For this reason, the massive body of evidence deriving from cognitive-behavioral work pointing to the effectiveness of exposure procedures in overcoming anxiety is directly relevant to the aims of psychoanalytic work as well. Psychoanalytic thought greatly expands and clarifies our understanding of just what it is that the patient needs to be exposed to – most often the crucial sources of anxiety do not just lie in external stimuli such as dogs, airplanes, or open spaces, but include very centrally one's own thoughts, feelings, and perceptions. But serious attention to the concept of exposure increases our ability to go beyond simply generating verbalizable insights and to effectively promote direct *experience* of the warded off wishes, feelings, and experiences of self and other from which the patient has retreated. Adapting behavioral methods of exposure to the context of relational psychoanalytic work requires a sophisticated understanding of both paradigms. What emerges from such combining of the strengths of both is likely to look somewhat different from standard conceptions of *either* exposure *or* interpretation. But the result is likely to be a therapeutic approach that is both more deeply experiential and more successful in enabling the patient not just to *know* the parts of himself he has tried to cast aside but to *reintegrate* and *reassimilate* those parts of himself into a more vital, full, and genuine experience of self (Wachtel, 2008, 2011).

Beyond theoretical tunnel vision: integrating the developmental and the contextual

The original charge for the authors in this book was to examine the relational paradigm and consider what features of relational thought or practice have been insufficiently developed or require reworking. I have focused in this chapter on one element in particular, calling for a revival of the boldly integrative mindset that launched the relational movement, and for extending the sights of our integrative efforts beyond the boundaries of the psychoanalytic model and into the larger world of therapeutic practice more generally.[6] The value of this kind of exploration of convergences and integrative possibilities includes important ways in which, in many specific clinical situations, the incorporation of additional perspectives or methods can help resolve impasses that threaten to derail the work or can enable the patient to move more rapidly toward living in a more fulfilling and less painful way. But it includes as well simply the way that serious confrontation with ideas that are unfamiliar or have been prematurely rejected as alien or unworthy of interest can shed new light on one's own assumptions and one's own paradigm.

As I noted earlier in this chapter, when one interacts too predominantly with others who share one's assumptions and biases, the very consensus among the members of the choir is likely to impede the kind of probingly reflective thought so essential to keeping an intellectual tradition alive and vibrant. In my own work, I have found that the encounter first with behavioral modes of thought and practice and then, successively, with a range of other alternative paradigms and modalities has been a valuable and stimulating challenge from which emerged a form of psychoanalytic and relational theorizing I could not have anticipated. The cyclical psychodynamic model that was the result of these explorations (Wachtel, 2014) remains strongly rooted in the psychoanalytic and relational point of view, but it has modified and reworked a number of key assumptions and formulations in response to new observations that I would have been unlikely to encounter had I remained completely bounded by the psychoanalytic world in which I was originally trained.

Our field as a whole has evolved in such a way that different groupings of theorists have each developed their own particular brand of tunnel vision, and, as a consequence of the social dynamics common to all circumscribed social reference groups, have essentially persuaded themselves that the observations afforded them by their method and their theoretical prism are all that really matter. It is the aim of an integrative mindset to go beyond that tunnel vision by continually challenging and examining one's comfortable assumptions and attempting to become familiar with how thinkers of other persuasions root their thinking in a differing set of observations and a different way of making sense of what they do observe. This effort is always of only limited success – we can never completely transcend our present point of view, which inevitably filters what we are able to notice and put together; but the integrative endeavor at the very least calls these tendencies to our attention and directs us toward ideas and observations that we otherwise would be likely to screen out.

It was precisely this kind of thinking that lay at the foundations of the relational turn. By attempting to consider how interpersonal theory, object relations theory, and self psychology each had something to add that was missed by the others, and yet had enough in common that they could be reconciled and fruitfully brought to bear to create a coherent and more comprehensive understanding, the early relationalists created a sounder and more generative foundation for psychoanalytic thought. And in that very process, still further questions arose and still deeper probing of assumptions was pursued – leading, for example, to the further articulation of what came to be called the two-person point of view; to the development of a thoroughgoing constructivist perspective; to challenges to the standard assumptions of drive theory; to questions about authoritarian versus collaborative structures for the therapeutic relationship; to new challenges to the ideas of abstinence, anonymity, and neutrality; and to a host of other, related but different probings of formulations and assumptions that had long been psychoanalytic givens. This questioning proceeded in tandem with the integrative effort – both a product of that effort and an impetus for it. The lines of influence were reciprocal and bidirectional rather than linear, but clearly the new, integrative mode of thought that was relational psychoanalysis was a hothouse for generating questions about assumptions long held dear by analysts without sufficient examination.

In some ways, the potentially revolutionary implications of this rethinking have yet to be fully realized in the mainstream of relational thought. In particular, the emphasis on understanding personality dynamics and development in the context of the matrix of relationships that frames the person's life points to ways in which the influence of the past can be understood not in terms of a sealed off internal world (whether that internal world be understood in terms of drives and their derivatives or in terms of internalized objects and representations) but rather in a more transactional and contextual fashion. The "internal" and the "external" are not separate realms but aspects of psychological life that mutually evolve and mutually maintain each other via a complex web of reciprocal influences and feedback loops (Wachtel, 2014, 2017a, 2017b).

Central to Mitchell's seminal fusion of interpersonal theory and object relations theory (e.g., Mitchell, 1988) is that the contributions of object relations theory to understanding the complexities of intrapsychic structure and the contextual, field-theory formulations of personality dynamics offered by interpersonal theory can be brought to bear on each other in synergistic ways that overcome deficiencies in each and create a stronger, more comprehensive and more clinically adequate theory. Interpersonal theory, Mitchell felt, had an insufficiently developed conceptualization of internal psychological structure (for which object relations theory provided a useful and ultimately compatible depiction), and object relations theory had a problematic account of how these early internalized experiences manifest and perpetuate themselves over the course of a lifetime – an account insufficiently distinguishable from the older Freudian portrayal of "the patient as an infantile self in an adult body, fixed in developmental time" (Mitchell, 1988, p. 170). Putting together the complementary strengths of each perspective, Mitchell argued that:

> disturbances in early relationships with caretakers seriously distort subsequent relatedness, not by freezing or fixing infantile needs [as object relations theorists depicted it], but by setting in motion a complex process through which the child creates an interpersonal world (or world of object relations) out of what is available.
>
> (p. 170)[7]

The critiques by Mitchell of the "developmental tilt" and the "metaphor of the baby" have been seen by some commentators as an early way-station (perhaps even a wrong turn) on his path toward a fuller embrace of the insights of object relations theory. In contrast, I view these critiques as instances of Mitchell at his most incisive. Indeed – apropos the theme of this book as a whole – I view some of the problematic features in the subsequent history of relational psychoanalysis as a failure to take seriously enough just how incisive Mitchell's critique was *and*, importantly, how brilliantly it created a foundation for incorporating what was valuable in the object relations tradition into a broader and more theoretically coherent framework that was able to address a fuller range of observations. If infantile needs and experiences are not "frozen in time," but are instead, as Mitchell argues, the initiator of a complex lifelong set of feedback processes, in which the successive relational contexts that the person encounters both shape and are shaped by the dynamic mixture of wishes, fears, perceptions, and expectations that characterize the inner world, then we have a theoretical means to take into account *both* continuity *and* change in the same terms. We have as well a way of understanding both why the person continues to think and act in ways that can seem "primitive," "infantile," or "archaic," *and,* at the same time, the many ways in which even very troubled individuals are nonetheless responsive to the immediate context in which they are participating (Wachtel, 1973, 2011, 2014).

Attention to people's variability in behavior and experience in response to the continually varying contexts that frame our lives is closely related to one of the key developments in contemporary relational theorizing, the focus on multiple self-states (e.g., Bromberg, 1998, 2008; Davies, 1996, 1998; Harris, 1996, 2011; Mitchell, 1993; Slavin, 1996, 2013; Stern, 2003). Putting these two perspectives together, we may note that the variability in self-state is not just a "spontaneous" event, like a random quantum leap, but is better understood as reflecting that the structures of personality are, by their very nature, *contextual structures* (Wachtel, 2008, 2014). Our responsiveness to variations in the contexts we encounter does not reflect the slavish stimulus-response link posited by a crude behaviorism; we always shape, filter, interpret, and alter the situation according to our proclivities. But neither do we slavishly persist in experiencing the world in terms of a single underlying "developmental level" or "personality organization." Rather, as is implicit in a contextualized version of multiple self-state theory, we bring to bear our multiple potential ways of being and experiencing as different relational and emotional contexts bring forth different facets of our complex psychological organization.

Concluding comments

The conceptualization of the relational synthesis offered by Mitchell created fertile ground for incorporating into psychoanalytic thought the still broader set of observations and methods potentially available to us from outside the psychoanalytic world.[8] For this reason, as one of the founders of SEPI, I invited Steve to participate in a panel when the group met in New York and I subsequently invited him to serve on SEPI's advisory board. Steve did so for several years, and then he resigned, telling me he needed to conserve his energies for his integrative efforts *within* psychoanalysis and therefore couldn't participate in the broader effort to also integrate ideas from outside of psychoanalysis. I understood and respected Steve's choice – we are all stretched and must acknowledge our finiteness. But still, I felt it was one of the few times when Steve made an unfortunately – and uncharacteristically – narrow choice and that not only was SEPI made poorer by the absence of his participation but so too was Steve. A brilliantly integrative mind like Steve's would have found much to enrich his thinking in the exchanges at SEPI between analysts and therapists of other orientations and between clinicians and researchers. I would like to think that if Steve were alive today, he would be revisiting his earlier decision and seeing this further expansion of perspective as the next important challenge for psychoanalysis in general and relational theory in particular – and as the logical extension of his own pioneering efforts. In any event, it has been my aim in this chapter to suggest to the reader that such an expansion of perspective and attention to a broader set of ideas and clinical observations represents a return to, and vitalizing extension of, the integrative spirit that lay at the heart of the relational turn.

Notes

1   In the spirit of full disclosure I should note here that I was one of the founders and a past president of SEPI, so I clearly have a certain stake in acknowledging its strengths.
2   There are, of course, multiple versions of the relational paradigm as well, and these differences also bear on how readily other points of view may be usefully integrated or incorporated.
3   These tend, unfortunately, to be the versions of CBT with which analysts are most familiar.
4   It is important to be clear that bridging the gap does not mean that the two approaches are the same; they in fact remain quite different in a great many ways. I discuss shortly how building on those very differences is of the essence of the integrative agenda.
5   It is not that most relationalists know this trend by the term "rationalist" or as a subset of cognitive-behavioral modes of thought and practice. Indeed, for the very reason that they are unfamiliar with developments in that realm, many relationalists are likely to implicitly equate rationalist cognitive-behavior therapy with cognitive-behavioral therapy per se.
6   It may be noted that implicit in my entire argument is a strong agreement with Aron and Starr (2013) that one of the unfortunate and unnecessary obstacles to progress in the evolution of psychoanalytic thought and practice was a problematic value-laden binary between "psychoanalysis" and "psychotherapy." I do not draw the traditional sharp distinction between the two in my own thinking or in the arguments offered here.

7 This conceptualization closely parallels that offered by cyclical psychodynamic theory (e.g., Wachtel, 1977, 2011, 2014) a perspective that emerged slightly earlier from a different kind of integrative effort and whose structural similarities eventually pointed to its being a variant form of relational theorizing (Wachtel, 2008).
8 A strong case has been made (Bresler & Starr, 2015) that, more than other versions of psychoanalytic thought, relational theory is particularly fertile ground for the integration of other modalities and perspectives into a psychoanalytically informed way of working.

References

Arnkoff, D. B. & Glass, C. R. (1992). Cognitive therapy and psychotherapy integration. In: D. Freedheim, H. Freudenberger, J. Kessler, S. Messer, D. Peterson, H. Strupp, H., and P. Wachtel (Eds.), *History of Psychotherapy*. Washington, DC: American Psychological Association, pp. 657–694.

Aron, L. (1996). *A meeting of minds: Mutuality in psychoanalysis*. Hillsdale, NJ: Analytic Press.

Aron, L. & Starr, K. (2013). *A psychotherapy for the people: Toward a progressive psychoanalysis*. New York: Routledge.

Bresler, J. & Starr, K. (2015). *Relational psychoanalysis and psychotherapy integration*. New York: Routledge.

Duncan, B. L., Miller, S. D., Wampold, B. E., & Hubble, M. A. (2010). *The heart and soul of change*. Washington, DC: American Psychological Association.

Freud, S. (1926). Inhibitions, symptoms, and anxiety. *Standard Edition*, 20 (pp. 87–172). London: Hogarth Press, 1961.

Gilbert, P. & Leahy, R. L. (Eds.). (2007). *The therapeutic relationship in the cognitive behavioral-psychotherapies*. New York: Routledge.

Greenberg, J. & Mitchell, S. A. (1983). *Object relations in psychoanalytic theory*. Cambridge, MA: Harvard University Press.

Guidano, V. E. (1991). *The self in process: Toward a post-rationalist cognitive therapy*. New York: Guilford Press.

Hayes, S. C., Follette, V. M., & Linehan, M. M. (Eds.). (2004). *Mindfulness and acceptance: Expanding the cognitive-behavioral tradition*. New York: Guilford Press.

Hayes, S. C., Strosahl, K. D., & Wilson, K. G. (2012). *Acceptance and commitment therapy: The process and practice of mindful change* (Second Edition). New York: Guilford Press.

Kohlenberg, B. S. & Tsai, M. (1991). *Functional analytic psychotherapy: Creating intense and curative therapeutic relationships*. New York· Plenum.

Leahy, R. L. (2008). The therapeutic relationship in cognitive-behavioral therapy. *Behavioural and Cognitive Psychotherapy*, 36(6), 769–777.

Linehan, M. M. (1993). *Cognitive-behavioral treatment of borderline personality disorder*. New York: Guilford Press.

——, (1994). Acceptance and change: The central dialectic in psychotherapy. In: N. Jacobson, V. Follette, and M. Dougher (Eds.), *Acceptance and change in psychotherapy*. Reno, NV: Context Press, pp. 73–86.

Mahoney, M. J. (Ed.). (1995). *Cognitive and constructive psychotherapies: Theory, research, and practice*. New York: Springer.

Mahoney, M. J. (2003). *Constructive psychotherapy: A practical guide*. New York, NY: Guilford Press.

Mitchell, S. A. (1988). *Relational concepts in psychoanalysis*. Cambridge, MA: Harvard University Press.

Neimeyer, R. (2009). *Constructivist psychotherapy: Distinctive features*. New York: Routledge.

Neimeyer, R. A. & Mahoney, M. J. (Eds.). (1995). *Constructivism in psychotherapy*. Washington, DC: American Psychological Association.

Norcross, J. C. (2011). *Psychotherapy relationships that work:Evidence-based responsiveness*. New York: Oxford University Press.

Renik, O. (1993). Analytic interaction: Conceptualizing technique in light of the analyst's irreducible subjectivity. *The Psychoanalytic Quarterly*, 62(4), 553–571.

Robins, C. J., Schmidt, H. & Linehan, M. M. (2004). Dialectical behavior therapy: Synthesizing radical acceptance with skillful means. In: Hayes, S. C., Follette, V. M., and Linehan, M. M. (Eds.), *Mindfulness and acceptance: Expanding the cognitive-behavioral tradition*. NewYork: Guilford Press, pp. 30–44.

Samoilov, A. & Goldfried, M. R. (2000). Role of emotion in cognitive-behavior therapy. *Clinical Psychology: Science and Practice*, 7, 373–385.

Segal, Z., Williams, J. M. G., & Teasdale, J. D. (2002). *Mindfulness-based cognitive therapy for depression: A new approach to preventing relapse*. New York: Guilford Press.

Slavin, M. O. (1996). Is one self enough? Multiplicity in self-organization and the capacity to negotiate relational conflict. *Contemporary Psychoanalysis*, 32, 615–625.

——, (2013). Why one self is not enough: Clinical, existential, and adaptive perspectives on Bromberg's model of multiplicity and dissociation. *Contemporary Psychoanalysis*, 49, 380–409.

Stern, D. B. (2003). The fusion of horizons: Dissociation, enactment, and understanding. *Psychoanalytic Dialogues*, 13, 843–873.

Wachtel, E. F. & Wachtel, P. L. (1986). *Family dynamics in individual psychotherapy*. New York: Guilford Press.

Wachtel, P. L. (1973). Psychodynamics, behavior therapy, and the implacable experimenter: An inquiry into the consistency of personality. *Journal of Abnormal Psychology*, 82, 324–334.

——, (1977). *Psychoanalysis and behavior therapy: Toward an integration.* New York: Basic Books.

——, (1997). *Psychoanalysis, behavior therapy, and the relational world.* Washington, DC: American Psychological Association.

——, (2002). EMDR and psychoanalysis. In: F. Shapiro (Ed.), *EMDR as an integrative psychotherapy approach: Experts of diverse orientations explore the paradigm prism.* Washington, DC: American Psychological Association, pp. 123–150.

——, (2008). *Relational theory and the practice of psychotherapy.* New York: Guilford Press.

——, (2010). Beyond "ESTs": Problematic assumptions in the pursuit of evidence-based practice. *Psychoanalytic Psychology*, 27, 251–272.

——, (2011). *Therapeutic communication: Knowing what to say when* (Second Edition). New York: Guilford Press.

——, (2014). *Cyclical psychodynamics and the contextual self: The inner world, the intimate world, and the world of culture and society.* New York: Routledge.

——, (2017a). Psychoanalysis and the Moebius strip: Reexamining the relation between the internal world and the world of daily experience. *Psychoanalytic Psychology*, 34, 58–68.

——, (2017b). The relationality of everyday life: The unfinished journey of relational psychoanalysis. *Psychoanalytic Dialogues*, 27, 1–19.

Wallin, D. (2007). *Attachment in psychotherapy.* New York: Guilford.

Wampold, B. E. & Imel, Z. E. (2015). *The great psychotherapy debate: The evidence for what makes psychotherapy work.* New York: Routledge.

Chapter 5

The pathologizing tilt
Undertones of the death instinct in relational trauma theory

Sophia Richman

Twenty-eight years ago I was invited to give my testimony to the Fortunoff Video Archive for Holocaust Testimonies at Yale. It was a very positive experience until the last moments of the interview. I had been told ahead of time that the plan was to first talk about my prewar experience, then my wartime memories, and then to talk about my life after the war. Since I was born into the Holocaust, there was no personal prewar experience to talk about. With regard to the second task, I didn't have much to say either, since I was a very young child during the war years and my memories of life in hiding were few. It was the last part of the interview, which I had looked forward to, where I would have a chance to talk about the reverberations of the trauma and how I had coped. I had thought a great deal about the impact of those years in hiding, and I was quite proud of the life I had created. So when, after about an hour, before I had a chance to talk about my current life, the interview suddenly came to an end – I felt abruptly cut off.

Several days later, I received a phone call from one of the interviewers, my friend and colleague, who asked me how I was doing and I took the opportunity to let her know about my disappointment at having been cut off in the middle of my narrative. She invited me to return and complete my testimony, which I did. While I appreciated the sensitivity with which my reaction was subsequently handled, and I ultimately felt heard and truly witnessed by the two interviewers, nevertheless, I have sometimes wondered why the testimony was prematurely terminated in the first place. Was the focus of the interview meant to highlight traumatic events at the expense of coping mechanisms? Was the resilience it took to create a new meaningful life, of less interest to the interviewers than the details of traumatization? In this chapter I address these questions and deconstruct what I believe to be misguided relational theorizing as linked to trauma theory.

With the evolution of the relational perspective in psychoanalysis, we have come to increasingly value the uniqueness of the self and self-other configurations, but when it comes to the trauma of genocide this principle is often abandoned. Many of the conceptual formulations put forth by psychoanalysts who are considered experts on Holocaust trauma are based on highly abstract theoretical ideas and presented in the form of sweeping generalizations that gloss over vast individual differences in the capacity of human beings to cope with traumatic circumstances. These theories, which are widely quoted in the literature, and find their way into Holocaust study curriculums, have totalized the psychoanalytic field of trauma studies. Survivors seen through the prism of psychopathology are viewed as "other." They are painted as one-dimensional, devoid of complexity, and often characterized in dichotomous, extreme terms, such as either "irreparably damaged" or "amazingly resilient." Relational psychoanalysts who subscribe to a view of the mind as composed of multiple shifting self-states seem to forget about multiplicity when discussing trauma survivors.

The notion that psychoanalytic theories are derived from the subjective world of the theorist (Stolorow & Atwood, 1979) is not a new idea, but it is one which is often forgotten. We fail to remember that theory is a construction which reveals the analyst's theoretical biases, shapes what he/she understands, and influences what is discovered. When elegant theoretical constructions are presented with conviction and authority, they tend to take on the status of facts and it is sometimes difficult to remember that these are actually hypotheses in need of validation. To be clear, I am not anti-theory, but I am against the unexamined deployment of theory. Ultimately what concerns me is the leakage of questionable theoretical speculations into relational practice.

Entrenched assumptions and clashing paradigms

Contemporary trauma theory has been greatly influenced by Dori Laub, a child survivor psychoanalyst and co-founder of the Fortunoff Video

Archive for Holocaust Testimonies at Yale, the organization that interviewed me in 1990. This worthy project was one of the first to videotape testimonies of Holocaust survivors. With his vast experience, Laub has a great deal of credibility in the area of trauma and is well respected in the relational psychoanalytic community. He has mentored countless psychoanalysts who are interested in trauma and his theory of the effects of catastrophic trauma is widely and uncritically accepted and repeatedly quoted in the literature. His basic theory about the nature of Holocaust trauma has been unchanged since the early 1980s when the Archive was first established. As he summarizes it in a recent publication devoted to Holocaust witnessing:

> The Holocaust was an event and an experience that annihilated the *good object* (humanity, God, the intimate other) in the internal world, and in individual and collective representation. In its wake, experiencing, remembering, and imagining were severely compromised, if not abolished. In the absence of a protective parental shield, the processes of symbolization, mental representation, and narrativization came to a halt.
>
> (Laub, 2015, p. 216)

Laub's object relations theory can be located within a drive model of the mind, and the death instinct is the centerpiece of his trauma theory: "The concept of the death instinct is indispensable to the understanding and treatment of trauma. . . . It is a clinical and theoretical necessity" (Laub & Lee, 2003, p. 433).

Although I expect that most relationalists would have difficulty accepting that premise, nevertheless they seem to embrace assumptions which originate in a drive paradigm. For instance, paraphrasing Laub's basic theory of trauma, Donnel Stern (2010) writes: "massive psychic trauma, because it damages the processes of association, symbolization, and narrative formation, also leads to an absence of inner dialogue, curiosity, reflection, and self-reflection" (p. 126). Stern accepts Laub's idea of a shutdown in these essential cognitive processes due to the annihilation of the good internal object, without acknowledging Laub's underlying rationale for this idea, namely the role that the death instinct plays in this presumed shut-down. Laub's explanation is: "Such death instinct derivatives come unleashed once the binding libidinal forces of object cathexis are abolished and identification with the aggressor (the only object left in the internal world representation) takes place" (Laub, 2005, p. 307).

Similarly, Ghislaine Boulanger (2007), another relational analyst who has been deeply influenced by Laub's theory of trauma, accepts the idea that a failure in symbolic functioning is at the heart of trauma's legacy. "Survivors of massive psychic trauma frequently experience deficits in symbolic functioning affecting the capacity to dream, to entertain fantasies, and to think productively" (p. 15). Unlike Laub, who claims that all survivors experience this, Boulanger qualifies her statement with "frequently" while still accepting his basic drive theory. Ignoring the fact that Laub subscribes to a one-person model of the mind, and that traumatic shutdown of symbolization and narrative is a death instinct derivative as he conceptualizes it, Boulanger presents his ideas as if he were a relationalist. For instance, in her book, she introduces a chapter titled "The Relational self in crisis," with the following epigraph taken from Laub & Auerhahn's 1989 paper: "*It is the context of our thesis that psychic structure is relational and trauma is deconstructive*" (Boulanger, 2007, p. 95). The use of terminology which sounds relational but derives from a drive theory paradigm is confusing at best.

More evidence of how Laub's work has infused the relational perspective is to be found in the work of Philip Bromberg, a well-respected relational pioneer. He writes: "As Laub and Auerhahn (1989) succinctly expressed it, 'because *the traumatic state cannot be represented*, [emphasis added] it is unmodifiable by interpretation . . .'" (Bromberg, 1998, p. 400). In this quote, Bromberg takes for granted the rather strange assumption that trauma cannot be represented, despite the fact that there seems to be no evidence for this assertion (Alford, 2009b; Leys, 2000; Richman, 2014; Trezise, 2013). Chana Ullman, another relational psychoanalyst who generally avoids common stereotypes about survivors, uncharacteristically accepts the party line when she writes: "Turning *the dead third* into a witness is an attempt to recover a history of genocide when the events are beyond words, beyond narrative, and beyond representation" (IARPP Colloquium, 2012). In these instances, both Bromberg and Ullman are verbalizing unwarranted, entrenched assumptions originating in postmodern deconstructive theory.

Literary theory has infiltrated the field of trauma studies and resulted in a trauma paradigm based on the deconstructive ideas of philosophers such as Jacques Derrida and trauma scholars such as Shoshana Felman and Cathy Caruth. This theory leads to mystifying statements such as: "Massive trauma precludes its registration" (Laub, 1992, p. 57); "Massive trauma precludes all representation" (Caruth, 1995; qtd. in Leys, 2000, p. 266.). These puzzling assertions, often quoted, are presented as though they are irrefutable facts rather than the philosophical and literary speculations that they actually are.

Theoretical acrobatics and their critics

Those who take issue with the idea that Holocaust trauma cannot be represented, tend to come from disciplines other than psychoanalysis. For example, C. Fred Alford (2009b), a psychoanalytically informed political scientist, has criticized the genesis of this idea in the work of Caruth – the literary critic, Bessel van der Kolk – the neurobiologist, and Dori Laub – the psychoanalyst. These three theoreticians all share the belief that trauma creates a wound, a structural deficit, which renders the survivor incapable of narrating his experience or expressing it symbolically. Ruth Leys (2000), an intellectual historian who is another critic of contemporary trauma theory, states that the entire theory of trauma proposed by these theoreticians is immune to refutation as it is designed to preserve the truth of the trauma as a failure of representation.

If trauma cannot be represented, then testimony about the past is inevitably a misrepresentation, with the result that there are no witnesses to the Holocaust. Supposedly, the inherently incomprehensible nature of the event precluded its own witnessing, even by its very victims. "What precisely made a Holocaust out of the event is the unique way in which, during its historical occurrence, *the event produced no witnesses*" (Laub, 1992, p. 80). If this dramatic statement was to be taken literally, then how could we justify or reconcile the vast enterprise of testimony gathering which Laub himself has spearheaded?

Ultimately Alford offers a psychodynamic understanding of the exaggerated assertion that the Holocaust cannot be imagined or represented. He conceptualizes this belief as an attempt to protect ourselves from a terrible knowledge that we already know, namely that under certain circumstances human beings are indeed capable of such horrors.

Thomas Trezise (2013), a scholar in psychology, history and philosophy, challenges widely accepted theoretical views about the representation of trauma as set forth in Caruth and Laub among others, and takes issue with their tendency to use hyperbolic generalizations and to universalize. According to Trezise, their theorizing obscures the very history they are trying to record and impairs their ability to listen to survivors.

Lewis Aron is one of the lone voices in relational psychoanalysis who speaks to the complexities and variability among survivors. He is concerned about the tendency to pathologize and reminds us that survivors of genocidal trauma represent a wide spectrum of adaptations and therefore it is not appropriate to consider them as a group entity. Aron identifies circular thinking in trauma studies: "The logic is so simple – they suffered trauma, so they are dissociated, hence there are gaps and deadness" (IARPP Colloquium, 2012). When it comes to this subject, we note a preponderance of unwarranted assumptions and illogical pronouncements, such as – because trauma survivors have lost the capacity to symbolize, narrate, or represent their trauma, they cannot bear witness to their own experience. Presumably, only through the giving of testimony to a specially trained listener, can these processes be restored.

In my writing on trauma (Richman, 2014), I conclude that the notion that Holocaust trauma defies representation or narrativization stands in direct contradiction to the countless acts of narration, such as memoirs and testimony, that have emerged from the Shoah. The assertion that in catastrophic trauma there is a shutdown of psychological processes of reflection, association, symbolization, and integration, is a sweeping and highly questionable generalization. While this may be true for some survivors, it is patently not the case for all. In fact, if one examines the creative outpouring of survivor art in poetry, memoirs, and other art forms, it is evident that on the contrary, many survivors have a heightened need and capacity for self-expression, reflection, cognitive and emotional integration, narrative formation, inner dialogue, and meaning making. Moreover, artistic creations can be seen as important forms of testimony which provide a window into the experience of the survivor and have the potential to heal the creator.

Bearing witness and being witnessed

It is in the area of Holocaust witnessing and testimony that this issue of recognition and healing becomes especially significant. Witnessing is a relational process which goes on in an interpersonal field between two subjectivities (Stern, 2012), and as such, it holds particular interest for relational psychoanalysis. A number of relationalists have written about the importance of witnessing in psychoanalysis, with special attention to its significance in the case of trauma survivors (Boulanger, 2007; Gerson, 2009; Reis, 2009; Richman, 2014; Stern, 2010, 2012; Ullman, 2006, among others). As the co-founder of the Holocaust Video Archives in the 1980s, Laub is seen as the expert on Holocaust witnessing. An entire special issue of *Contemporary Psychoanalysis* (2015) is devoted to relational witnessing of the Holocaust, and Dori Laub has a prominent presence in it. He has inspired a number of relationalists such as Gerson (2009) and Stern (2010, 2012) who have built their own theories of witnessing on the foundation which he created. Stern (2012) acknowledges Laub's expertise in the following passage:

> Laub's seminal work on the significance of witnessing, and about the "restoration" that can occur when one is witnessed, grew from Laub's experience of directing the Archive, experience from which he (Laub, 1991) concluded that the Holocaust destroyed the very possibility of witnessing.
>
> (p. 74)

Stern borrows an example from Laub's work on testimony to illustrate the significance of the creation of an internal witness to substitute for the absence of a real life significant other. Five-year old Menachem, separated from his parents during the Holocaust, clung to a photograph of his mother, praying to it, having conversations with it, and thereby maintaining his relationship with her. This photo functioned as his witness and helped him to survive on the streets of Krakow (Stern, 2012). I agree with Stern that this is a wonderful example of the creation of an internal witness, but I also see this as evidence that under traumatic conditions, symbolization does not come to a halt as the theory predicts, in fact this capacity to symbolize is enlisted in the service of coping. The photo of mother became a symbol of her presence, her love, her goodness, and protection. It facilitated and solidified Menachem's connection with her; by looking at her photograph, the child was able to engage in dialogue with her, and develop a narrative about her return. Rather than a loss of these capacities, Menachem relied on them more than ever. As is suggested in this story of Menachem, the child had found a creative way to *bear witness to himself.*

Eventually, the adult Menachem is invited by Laub to contribute his testimony to the Archive. Until that time, the only person who had heard the story of his childhood was his wife, but her role as his first witness is virtually ignored in both Laub and Stern's accounts of the restorative effects of Holocaust witnessing. The implication is that only a trained mental health professional can gather testimony in a dialogic context and be an authentic listener who communicates the sense . . .

> That you are not alone any longer – that someone can be there as your companion – knowing you, living with you through the unfulfilled hope, someone saying, 'I'll be with you in the very process of your losing me. I am your witness.'
>
> (Laub, pp. 91–92, qtd in Stern 2012, p. 75)

This description seems more fitting when the witness is a significant other – like one's close friend, or one's partner in life. When the interviewer is a virtual stranger, whose main purpose is to record the horrors of genocide, he/she seems better described as a researcher gathering data than a genuine witness to the suffering of the individual sitting before him.

The notion that in order for the survivor to become a witness to his/her own trauma and give authentic testimony requires a formal setting and interview by a specially trained professional seems somewhat self-serving and pretentious. As Alford points out, those who listen to the testimony of the survivor consider themselves co-witnesses who presumably transform into narrative what the survivor can only act out. "This is the task of those who would listen to testimony, and only a tough and giving few are capable of doing this." Picking up on the arrogance of this position, Alford wryly adds "Do not overlook the self-congratulation at work here" (2009b, p. 9).

Giving and recording testimony is a complicated process – it is not just about the memories and narrative of the survivor, rather it is a mutual process between the giver of testimony – the survivor, and the receiver of testimony – the witness. Recent psychoanalytically inspired research features a new and creative approach to the understanding of the testimonial process (Hamburger, 2014). It applies a relational micro-analysis to recorded narratives gathered by the Fortunoff Video Archive for Holocaust Testimonies at Yale. In a detailed account of an interview conducted by Dori Laub (the main interviewer) and an associate, the testimony is analyzed and rated by a team of observers.

The results show how the multilayered process of mutual reenactment takes place during the testimony. The dialogue is hampered not just by the survivor forgetting and fragmenting, but also in the emotional reactions of the witness (p. 253). Transference and countertransference entanglements and ruptures are evident throughout this five-minute segment. It becomes clear that numerous defensive shifts take place in both the survivor and his interviewers; there are paramnesias (false memories), parapraxes (slips of the tongue), hearing errors, as well as an occasional loss of boundaries, distortions, and denial. Sometimes Laub insists on going in a direction that the survivor resists, he asks him distracting questions, and shows moments of temporary loss of reality and merging, confusing his own story with that of the survivor (Hamburger, 2015).

The fact is that subjectivity is always involved in perception and the creation of meaning. It is inevitable that each partner in a dyad has an effect on shaping the dialogue. While this can be valuable and productive in clinical work, in testimony gathering, where the objective is presumably to provide data about the persecution experience, it can be problematic. When the witness/interviewer also has a clear conscious agenda based on theoretical biases, the problem is compounded.

Most troubling however, is the use of data obtained from testimonies to develop theoretical constructs about survivors of massive psychic trauma and present them as if they are objective facts rather than speculative theoretical constructions deeply influenced by the intentions and perceptions of the interviewer. When documenting persecution is the exclusive goal of Holocaust witnessing, and the death instinct is conceptually linked with trauma, then it is no wonder that there is a pathologizing tilt to the conclusions that follow.

The dead mother complex, the dead third, and the death instinct

A striking example of the tendency to pathologize survivors, is the metaphor of the *Dead Mother*, a favorite among some psychoanalytic thinkers. The *Dead Mother Complex*, is a concept taken from Andre Green's writings on the absence of maternal care and stretched to apply to the survivor's plight. Green's (1983) definition of the Dead Mother Concept is:

> an image which has been constituted in the child's mind, following maternal depression, brutally transforming a living object, which was a source of vitality for the child, into a distant figure, toneless, practically inanimate, deeply impregnating the cathexes of certain patients . . . and weighing on the destiny of their object-libidinal and narcissistic future . . . [The] dead mother . . . is a mother who remains alive but who is, so to speak, psychically dead in the eyes of the young child in her care.
>
> (p. 142)

It was never Green's intention to apply this concept to Holocaust survivors, but Laub (2005) has appropriated it to make his point about the damages of catastrophic trauma. He writes: "The contribution of Green's concept of 'The Dead Mother Complex' to the understanding of the connection between death instinct derivatives and massive psychic trauma is of greatest value" (p. 325).

Andre Green is a drive theorist who retained Freud's concepts and metapsychological framework while synthesizing the contributions of other psychoanalysts such as Bion, Winnicott and Lacan. His theoretical position has been identified as a compromise between the Freudian and object relations traditions by Fonagy and Target (2003). Drives are the centerpiece of Green's theory of psychoanalysis and Laub has been greatly influenced by his ideas. Green's emphasis on *absence* and *nothingness* is particularly compelling for Laub (2005). "Nothingness is characterized by blocking of thought processes, the inhibition of the function of representation . . . The final result is paralysis of thought . . . a hole in mental activity and an inability to concentrate, to remember . . ." (Green, pp. 40–41, qtd. in Laub, 2005, p. 317).

Green's preoccupation with the negative and with the dialectics of presence and absence have been incorporated into the thinking of a number of relationalists including Gerson (2009), Harris (2012), Salberg (2015), and Stern (2012). It is quite puzzling to me that relationalists who do not subscribe to the idea of a death instinct in particular, or drive theory in general, seem nevertheless to be quite enthralled with this concept of the Dead Mother and have joined Laub in extending it to all instances of massive psychic trauma where the good internal object is lost – presumably the case with all survivors of genocide according to Laub and those who have been influenced by him.

Samuel Gerson (2009), like Laub, has heavily relied on Andre Green's concept of the Dead Mother to explain the experience of victims of genocide and has developed his own version of it in the concept of the *dead third*. From the drive theory of Green and of Laub, to the relational model which Gerson is identified with, seems a huge theoretical leap across paradigms, but the unifying themes of deadness and nothingness bring them together – "This tendency towards nothingness is the real significance of the death instinct" (Green, 55, qtd. in Laub, 2005, p. 317).

In a frequently cited article on Holocaust trauma, Gerson develops his ideas about the long-term effects of genocide on the psyche of generations of survivors. His ideas, as expressed in this paper, have been very well received by many relational psychoanalysts – Adrienne Harris has described this paper as "One of the most generative essays of this decade" (IARPP Colloquium, 2012). Donnel Stern (2012) finds Gerson's work on the *dead third,* as it applies to genocide, convincing and moving.

Gerson has written a poetic and dramatic treatise on the tragedy of the Holocaust. His primary focus in this piece is on the *survival* of genocide not on *survivors* of genocide. He is less interested in the narratives of survivors – how they coped with the assaults on their bodies and mind, or how they created new lives in the aftermath – and more concerned with the horrors of genocide and the general effects it has on a population of its victims.

There is no question that genocide is the ultimate evil, an ever-present menace with far reaching reverberations on generations of survivors. My concern is that Gerson's ideas, which are expressed in dramatic, mystifying metaphors and hyperboles, paint all survivors as hopelessly damaged human beings, thereby robbing them of their subjectivity and of the complex meanings of their experience. Gerson extends the Dead Mother concept to survivor's experiences of the world at large as unconcerned about their fate and indifferent to their suffering. I find his pivotal concept of "Mankind as a Dead Mother" (p. 1347) to be a highly abstract generalization which does not add to our understanding. It suggests an unrealistic and idealized expectation that the world should care, while at the same time it ignores the reality of countless caring individuals who risked their lives to rescue others.

Gerson tells his readers that the Dead Mother is an absent presence whose effect on the child is like that of a black hole that relentlessly sucks the child's vitality. According to him, this is the lot of many children of survivors whose mothers, traumatized by their own losses, leave them with a legacy of deadliness at their core. This disturbing image of the Holocaust survivor as parent is another example of pathologizing. It is presented not as an aberration, but as a compelling portrait of the psychology of many children of survivors. Although Gerson qualifies his statements with words such as "many" or "often" the implication is that this is the norm rather than the exception. He may not intend to lump all survivors into this pathological group, but it is certainly implied in his writing.

A further example of this premise is Gerson's position that the inevitable consequence of catastrophic trauma is deadness, or an enduring presence of absence within the psyche of the survivor. Individual differences among survivors, as well as different states of mind within the same individual, are overlooked in this conceptualization. Gerson's focus is on deadness to the exclusion of life-affirming strivings on the part of the survivor; he cautions the analyst against aligning himself with the patient's hopes and vitality because "the states of mind that herald the presence of absence, or gaps, or phantoms, are often experienced as more enduring and real than are the moments of creative engagement" (p. 1354). Similarly, in an online colloquium based on his paper, he warns the participants that:

> valorizing the traits that might be associated with resilience and the creation of a new life is a grievous error as it obscures our contact with the deadliness that enveloped and destroyed their pre-genocide lives, shadows our present, and threatens the future.
>
> (IARPP Colloquium Series, 2012)

These assertions are made in the context of Gerson's emphasis on the importance of attuned affective responsiveness of the witnessing analyst. I agree with Gerson that attuned witnessing is an essential function for the analyst to engage in, but I expect that we differ with regard to what we consider *attuned* witnessing. For me, authentic or attuned witnessing means approaching the individual with curiosity and a willingness to be surprised in the encounter with his/her subjectivity. When Gerson valorizes certain traits over others, or aligns himself with one or another aspect of the personality, he is engaging in what I call *selective witnessing*; that is, witnessing informed by certain theoretical presuppositions. Behind *selective witnessing* is the belief that the analyst is in possession of certain truths and that the survivor's story is understood in the context of these truths. Given the intersubjective nature of the witnessing process and the inevitable co-construction of narrative, my concern is that the story which emerges is unduly influenced by the expectations of the theoretician/psychoanalyst.

Anna Ornstein, a psychoanalyst survivor, shares my disappointment with widespread Holocaust-related theoretical speculations. Her very life challenges survivor stereotypes. From the moment of her liberation she has lived a rich and meaningful existence. Now in her late 80s she continues to be creative and engaged in life and makes important contributions to the literature of psychoanalysis. For many years, Ornstein has been taking issue with the narrow view of survivors perpetuated in the trauma literature. In a recent paper she commented on the fact that psychoanalysts have missed an important opportunity to understand what allowed for psychological survival by their exclusive focus on the pathological consequences of the survivor's experience (Ornstein, 2014). In the same article, she expressed surprise that even with the relational turn in psychoanalysis, when the co-construction of meaning in psychoanalysis is generally accepted, "Holocaust survivors' emotional lives are still conceptualized in idiosyncratic, theoretical terms . . . the more extreme the language, the more likely it will be quoted by others" (p. 89). Referring to Gerson's (2009) paper, she continues: "I consider these metapsychological speculations to be not only poor substitutes to an attempt to *understand* what the survivors have been actually experiencing, but also ideas that could have prevented a meaningful therapeutic engagement" (p. 90).

Intergenerational transmission of trauma stereotypes

Unfortunately, such metapsychological speculations which pathologize survivors have serious implications for clinical work for generations. When we approach our survivor/patients as if vulnerability is their exclusive state, and we do not acknowledge the strengths which enabled them to survive and thrive, we are failing to recognize them fully. As new generations of psychoanalysts enter our field, flawed theoretical assumptions about survivors are passed down by their supervisors, psychoanalysts, and teachers.

In a recently published work on individual and collective trauma, Clara Mucci (2013), a former English literature professor newly trained in psychoanalysis, looks to a previous generation of psychoanalysts for understanding Holocaust trauma. She acknowledges a profound debt to Dori Laub and seems to have entirely adopted his trauma theory. It is noteworthy that in a reference section totaling 44 pages, there is not a single mention of Anna Ornstein's work. Mucci makes numerous references to contemporary relational psychoanalysis, but her use of the term *relational* does not connote a two-person model. The analyst is presented as the expert who is guided by theory and proceeds accordingly to "cure" the patient. Implied in this formulation is that the expert analyst knows exactly what it is like for the patient to have experienced massive psychic trauma, and she knows just how the treatment should proceed, even before the patient has entered her office (Richman, 2015). Mucci's stance on intergenerational transmission of trauma similarly replicates the predominant current view, which stresses severe psychopathology passed on from one generation to the next. Thus she writes:

> Since symbolization was impossible in the first generation, this burdensome task must be acted out by the second generation in other forms of illness. While the first generation, as we have seen, mostly suffered from anxiety, depression, anhedonia, and inability to describe their own conditions, psychosomatic illnesses (incapacity to symbolize and to mourn, incapacity to express their suffering in words) with a predominant incapacity to 'recount the trauma,' it is this task that is left to the second generation.
>
> (p. 178)

With regard to the third generation, she states: "the third may actually develop more severe symptoms because the working-through of the resolution of the trauma inherited is somehow 'foreclosed' to the third generation" (p. 189). At the same time that Mucci makes these dire pronouncements about generations of survivors, she acknowledges that research studies actually find no evidence of psychopathology in the children of survivors. However, determined to view survivors as damaged, she goes on to contradict the empirical finding.

It is evident in reading Mucci's work that her intentions are well-meaning; that she is dedicated to understanding the intricacies of the issues that she is writing about, and has worked hard to master the trauma literature. Regrettably, that literature is replete with unfortunate and erroneous generalizations. I do not take issue with the idea of intergenerational transmission of trauma, nor do I dispute the disastrous effects of genocide on generations. My intention is to provide a corrective to the current tendency to pathologize. My plea is for a more balanced and nuanced understanding of trauma transmission.

The dialectics of resilience

Jill Salberg (2015) is another relational psychoanalyst who has been influenced by the work of Laub, Kestenberg, Bergmann and Jucovy and others who have labeled generations of survivors as damaged and disturbed. Like Laub and Gerson and Mucci, Salberg uses the metaphor of the Dead Mother to describe the emotional lives of Holocaust survivors and their children. She writes: "Absence, deadness, and dysregulated attachment are seen as common features of survival ... the dilemma of second and third generation who, from birth, have been cared for by parents with dysregulated affects and possibly dissociative self-states" (p. 34). There seems to be no room for the "good enough mother" in this formulation. What about the parent who is attentive and empathic much of the time, but is subject to occasional moments of dissociation? If we accept that the human mind consists of multiple self-states, well, don't we all have occasional moments of dissociation or dysregulation? As Bromberg points out, there can be a cohesive core personality which tolerates moments of dissociation and shifts in self-state (Bromberg, 1998, p. 131). Why should one assume that trauma survivors can't have a cohesive core sense of self that transcends such shifts in emotional states?

It is reassuring to read that Salberg does recognize that not all children have to manage fragmentation resulting from parental traumatization; she acknowledges that survival resilience can also be transmitted. Thus she writes: "When the traumatized parent remains resilient and alive, this state-shifting or fragmentation may be tolerable and fleeting for the child" (p. 36).

The problem with this type of reasoning is that it presents resilience in a dichotomous way: Those who don't fit the stereotype of the damaged survivor must be amazingly resilient. The implication is that while most survivor parents are suffering from "absence, deadness and dys-regulated attachment" some parents are able to remain "resilient and alive." Such a dichotomous view misses the complexity of human beings as well as the universal potential for existing in multiple self-states (Richman, 2006). In my view, survivors are not *either* damaged *or* resilient – they are *both* damaged in some ways *and* resilient in others. Survivors, like other people, are multifaceted and have the capacity to be vibrant and engaged at one moment, depressed and despairing at another, or numb and dissociated on occasion. Such states are not mutually exclusive; they co-exist.

The notion of resilience is a complicated phenomenon. In my experience resilience is not limited to those fortunate individuals who possess this "rare" quality, rather it is a potential which exists in all survivors and emerges under certain circumstances and in certain self-states; more frequently in some individuals than in others. According to Valent (1998), there is an internal dialectic in the term *resilience*. We can focus on the side that expresses the triumph of having overcome a tragedy, or we can look at the devastation caused by it. Survivors can be both resilient and vulnerable at different times, and in different situations. Their lives can be seen as testimonials to the indomitable human spirit, but also as examples of trauma's debilitating long-term effects.

It is interesting that when Laub and Auerhahn (1989) observed some higher-level functioning among Holocaust survivors, they were surprised by it. "The character structures of many survivors show a *surprising* [emphasis added] mosaic of areas of high level psychological functioning coexisting with the potential for severe regression" (p. 391). I personally do not find it surprising that areas of high-level functioning coexist with moments of confusion or dissociation in the lives of most survivors. It is only surprising to the theoretician, when he/she does not recognize the multiplicity of mind and when the survivor is viewed exclusively through a psychopathological lens.

While many psychoanalysts tend to conceptualize survivors in such one-dimensional terms, Alford (2008, 2009a, 2009b) recognizes that survivors, like the rest of humanity, are capable of living a rich life in the aftermath of catastrophic trauma. Based on his listening to hours of testimony from the Fortunoff Video Archives, he concludes that it is the capacity for *doubling* which allows survivors to live with the self that endured trauma, and to function well in present time in spite of it. The term doubling refers to a process of altered consciousness, which results in the creation of a dual self. This type of dissociation alters an unbearable reality by compartmentalizing experience, thoughts, or feelings and thus allows the traumatized individual to mourn the profound losses of the past, even as she is able to celebrate her survival and look forward to the future with gratitude (Richman, 2006). I believe that when we speak of resilience in the face of trauma, we address this duality and multiplicity.

Laub, too, has recognized that in their testimony . . .

> Survivors emphasize that they indeed live in two separate worlds, that of their traumatic memories (which is self-contained, ongoing, and ever-present) and that of the present. Very often they do not wish, or are completely unable, to reconcile these two different worlds. The memory is thus timeless; the experience is frozen. It is automatic and purposeless, bereft of meaning.
>
> (Laub, 2005, p. 311)

It is noteworthy that for Alford living in two separate worlds is adaptive, while for Laub this is more evidence of the hopelessness of the survivor's lot. The idea that survivors may not wish to reconcile these two different worlds, makes sense if seen as a way to continue the essential mourning process. Once we depart from the classical view of the mind as a private closed system that regulates an inner world of energies and defenses, and move into a relational perspective on mourning, a continued tie to lost objects can be seen as a desirable outcome (Richman, 2014).

The concept of resilience has been given short shrift in most of the trauma literature until recently (Prot, 2010; Valent, 1998). There has been a shift in the research focus concerning Holocaust survivors from investigating psychological problems to discovering the sources of strength enabling survival and good social adjustment (Prot, 2010).

We can learn from psychoanalyst survivors such as Anna Ornstein and her husband the late Paul Ornstein what helps people live through trauma, and not just to survive it, but to thrive and lead a creative meaningful life in its aftermath. The Ornsteins lost countless relatives and friends; all of their siblings perished, and each of them lost a parent. Paul Ornstein survived the war as a forced laborer in a battalion in Hungary. He eventually escaped and found Anna, his childhood sweetheart, who had survived Auschwitz with her mother. They married shortly after the war and began their new life in Germany where both enrolled in medical school. In a recent memoir, which Paul Ornstein co-wrote with Helen Epstein (2015), he described life shortly after liberation when he and Anna were settled in a DP camp in the U.S. occupied zone of Bavaria, Germany (Richman, 2017).

> I can't say that, at the time, we mastered our rage and grief. We postponed dealing with them. In retrospect, I can see that we were numb in a certain way, more than we realized then. The fact that Anna and I met again brought us back to life together. I have often thought that the so-called "survival guilt" is in many ways a figment of the imagination of psychoanalysts who escaped from Europe on time. We did not suffer from "survival guilt." In spite of everything, we were able to enjoy life.
>
> (2015, p. 54)

The capacity to enjoy life, a sense of optimism, and the ability to develop deep friendships and intimate relationships are personal characteristics that I have observed in survivors such as Paul and Anna Ornstein who have been able to successfully cope with devastating trauma. Valent (1998), who studied attributes of resilience in child survivors of the Holocaust, concluded that ubiquitous resilience factors included "positive attachment figures, accessing supportive networks, competence, and positive self-esteem" (p. 531). Characteristics of resilience which mitigated the long-term effects of traumatic experience included emotional attachment to good objects, hopes of being reunited with them, as well as the ability to cut out thoughts and emotions inconsistent with survival, which I would call a capacity for healthy dissociation (Richman, 2014).

The ability to bounce back after adversity seems to be a relatively stable character trait that is manifested during and after the devastation. But this does not mean that one's life is trouble free. I believe that residual scars of traumatic experience remain forever, despite the healing effects of time, or of good relationships that provide mutual care, or of psychotherapy and psychoanalysis. Wounds may heal, but scars remain. Resilience does not exclude vulnerabilities; both co-exist in the same individual and take center stage at different times and under different circumstances. Mourning lost relatives or a lost childhood has no end; with the monumental losses of genocide there cannot be completion in the work of mourning. Mourning goes on throughout life, but that doesn't mean that only deadness prevails. Yes, living with memories of profound loss and grief which can never be "worked through," is always a challenge, but most of the survivors I have known are able, at least most of the time, to rise to this challenge and to experience life fully with vitality and hope, even as they mourn their profound losses.

Throughout one's life, certain situations can trigger strong emotional reactions even sometimes retraumatize the survivor. But this does not constitute psychopathology or what has been labeled as a pervasive sense of deadness. Many are coming to believe that "the process of the survivors' recovery should be construed not as a lack of symptoms, but rather an ability to cope despite their symptoms, or an ability to invest their life with meaning" (Prot, 2010, p. 62).

Another anecdote taken from Paul Ornstein's memoir illustrates the power of relationships, both internal and in real life, to sustain us.

Two hundred yards from the trenches, I suddenly realized that I left my jacket behind. Gyuri told me to leave it behind, afraid that the rockets would hit me. But I had photographs of Anna and my family in the pocket of that jacket and they were my talisman. Gyuri returned with me to retrieve my jacket. We then crawled back on our bellies.

(2015, p. 40)

This anecdote is reminiscent of Laub's case cited by Stern (2012) of Menachem, the child who clung to the photo of his mother when he was separated from her. These photo images, which represented home, love, and security, were the stand-ins for the people left behind. Through their ability to use symbols and their imagination, Paul, Menachem, and so many others separated from their loved ones, could keep their good objects safe in the place where imaginary witnesses reside.

Listening to survivors

As is apparent by now, it is my contention here that many of the assumptions about survivor experience derive from metapsychological speculations rather than from the actual lived experience of survivors. For example, one of Laub's often repeated assumptions is that in the wake of massive psychic trauma, the processes of exploratory curiosity come to a halt and there is a shutdown of reflection and self-reflection. Reading and listening to the words of survivors about their actual experience does not corroborate such an idea.

For instance, we note that Primo Levi wrote about his intense need to understand and the powerful curiosity he observed among inmates when he was imprisoned in Auschwitz. Addressing the reader, he writes: "It might be surprising that in the Camps one of the most frequent states of mind was curiosity. Besides being frightened, humiliated, and desperate, we were curious: hungry for bread and also to understand" (Levi, 1987, p. 99). Levi was acutely aware of his environment and determined to record the world and people around him. When interviewed years later, he reported that he considered his capacity for reflection, thinking, and observation to have been survival factors. He also described his state of mind in Auschwitz as one of "exceptional spiritedness," and "exalted receptivity" – terms suggestive of vitality and aliveness.

Much of what we read in memoirs and what appears in recorded testimonies that I have been privileged to watch, is a direct contradiction of Laub's basic assumptions about trauma that have been adopted by so many relationalists – that catastrophic trauma destroys the good object in the internal world of the victim. On the contrary, survivors report that it is relationships that kept them alive. In his writing Levi highlights the importance of relationships in providing hope for the inmates and allowing deeply held values to be maintained despite relentless attacks on their humanity.

Throughout his memoirs, Primo Levi refers to the friendships that sustained him; those from the past which he encountered in the camp, and men he met in Auschwitz. These relationships, old and new, helped him to maintain a sense of humanity amidst the brutality around him, and in some cases literally saved his life. For example, his relationship with Lorenzo, an Italian civilian worker who provided him with extra food regularly during the last six months of his imprisonment, at great risk to himself, was a constant reminder of the existence of a just world outside for which it was worth surviving (1995).

In his last book, written 40 years after Auschwitz, Levi (1989) reflected on, and attempted to integrate, his personal trauma experience in the light of how the world had dealt with the Holocaust in the intervening years. With some bitterness, Levi noted that those who were not there in Auschwitz tend to stereotype and oversimplify complex human responses to catastrophic trauma. He also pointed out that there is a tendency to think in binary terms such as good and evil, or right and wrong, and to overlook important characteristics of human behavior.

It has been my plea throughout this essay that, instead of imposing our trauma theories on survivors of genocide, we listen to what they have to say to us about their experience. At the same time, I am well aware that in our intersubjective universe, we usually only hear what we want to hear, and often dismiss the rest which doesn't fit in with our expectations. Nowhere is this more evident than with the life and death of Primo Levi. Everyone seems to find something in Levi that confirms his/her own ideas about human nature and the tragedy of genocide. The way that one believes he died, after only 67 years on this earth, depends on who is telling his story; the most popular version is suicide, but this is controversial. Diego Gambetta (1999), the eminent Italian sociologist, did extensive research into Primo Levi's untimely death. He gathered the evidence and the testimonies of people on both sides of the issue, and concluded that there is no proof of suicide – no witnesses, no suicide note, and no direct physical evidence. If Levi, who was a lifelong chemist, wanted to kill himself, he would have known, or had access to, better ways than jumping into a narrow stairwell with the risk of becoming paralyzed. On the basis of his research, Gambetta concluded that there is overwhelming evidence that Levi's supposed suicide was actually an accident. Gambetta pointed out that despite the evidence, the suicide theory of his death continues, thus reflecting a general bias that if one survives Auschwitz, everything that happens subsequently tends to be interpreted in the light of that experience. The readiness with which people assume that Levi's death was suicide driven by bad memories reflects the stereotype – that survivors are forever and irreparably damaged by their trauma experience.

Artist/survivors such as Levi take charge of their own mending. They create witnesses and find ingenious ways of giving testimony on their own terms. Many feel safer that way. Trauma creates a great divide. I fear that our attempts at understanding survivors often backfire – the experience-distant theoretical formulations, the dramatic metaphors, the insulting analogies, all meant to capture the experience of survivors, actually widen the chasm. The ways that we distance ourselves from others are often out of our awareness. I find myself agreeing with Trezise (2013) when he says: "the routinely repeated claim that the traumatic experience of Holocaust survivors is unrepresentable or unspeakable appears to stand in for a refusal to listen" (p. 211).

In conclusion, some of our best and brightest relational psychoanalysts have uncritically accepted antiquated ideas which originated in death instinct theory. These theoretical assumptions are repeatedly quoted in the trauma literature by seasoned and respected contemporary relationalists who neither accept death instinct theory or subscribe to a one-person perspective, psychoanalysts who view the analytic process as co-constructed and think in terms of multiple states of self, yet when it comes to massive psychic trauma seem to forget these relational ideas and instead embrace metapsychological speculations based on drive theory. We know that these models have fundamentally different premises and are basically incompatible (Greenberg & Mitchell, 1983). Surprisingly, when it comes to the subject of catastrophic trauma, relationalists have not addressed the inconsistencies and contradictions inherent in mixing these two different models of the mind.

One wonders if there is something sacrosanct about Holocaust trauma that intimidates psychoanalysts and makes it less likely that they will challenge those who are perceived as experts. Laub has been seen as the authority on the subject of the Holocaust since the inception of the Fortunoff

Video Archive for Holocaust Testimonies. Citing his work gives those who want to write about the Holocaust the legitimacy they seem to need to venture into this difficult and dangerous territory. If the Holocaust lies in a quasi-sacred realm beyond history, and traumatic experience is believed to be intrinsically unspeakable, then the effect may be the silencing of the voices of victims as well as of those of critics (Trezise, 2013). But it is the implications for clinical practice which are most disturbing. The *one size fits all* premise applied to Holocaust survivors and their children and grandchildren unwittingly reenacts the persecution; survivors who were once objectified by their enemies are now indistinguishable to the professionals who are dedicated to helping them.

References

Alford, F. (2008). Why Holocaust testimony is important, and how psychoanalytic interpretation can help … but only to a point. *Psychoanalysis, Culture & Society*, 13, 221–239.

——, (2009a). *After the Holocaust: The Book of Job, Primo Levi, and the Path to Affliction*. New York: Cambridge University Press.

——, (2009b). *The Holocaust Is Not Traumatic; The Holocaust Can Be Represented*. Paper prepared for presentation at the 2009 Annual Meeting of the American Political Science Association, Toronto, Canada.

Aron, L. (2012). IARPP Colloquium Series, No. 20.

Boulanger, G. (2007). *Wounded by Reality: Understanding and Treating Adult Onset Trauma*. Mahwah, NJ: The Analytic Press.

Bromberg, P. (1998). *Standing in the Spaces: Essays on Clinical Process, Trauma and Dissociation*. Hillsdale, NJ: The Analytic Press.

Caruth, C., Ed. (1995). *"Introduction," to Trauma: Exploration in Memory*. Baltimore, MD: Johns Hopkins University Press.

Fonagy, P. & Target, M. (2003). *Psychoanalytic Theories: Perspectives from Developmental Psychopathology*. New York: Brunner-Routledge.

Gambetta, D. (1999). Primo Levi's last moments. *Boston Review*. http://bostonreview.net/diego-gambetta-primo-levi-last-moments.

Gerson, S. (2009). When the third is dead: Memory, mourning and witnessing in the aftermath of the Holocaust. *The International Journal of Psychoanalysis*, 90, 1341–1357.

Gerson, S. (2012). IARPP Colloquium Series, No. 20.

Green, A. (1983*)*. The dead mother. Reprinted in: A. Green, (Ed.), *On Private Madness*, pp. 142–173. London: The Hogarth Press and the Institute of Psychoanalysis, 1986.

Greenberg, J. & Mitchell, S. (1983). *Object Relations in Psychoanalytic Theory*. Cambridge, MA: Harvard University Press.

Hamburger, A. (2015). Refracted attunement, affective resonance: Scenic-narrative microanalysis of entangled presence in a Holocaust survivor's testimony. *Contemporary Psychoanalysis*, 51, 239–257.

Harris, A. (2012). IARPP Colloquium Series, No. 20.

Laub, D. (1992). An event without a witness: Truth, testimony, and survival. In: S. Felman & D. Laub, (Eds.), *Testimony: Crises of Witnessing in Literature, Psychoanalysis, and History*, (pp. 75–92). New York & London: Routledge.

——, (2005). Traumatic shutdown of narrative and symbolization: A death instinct derivative? *Contemporary Psychoanalysis*, 41, 307–326.

——, (2015). Introduction. *Contemporary Psychoanalysis*, 51, 216–218.

Laub, D. & Auerhahn, N. (1989). Failed empathy: A central theme in the survivor's Holocaust experience. *Psychoanalytic Psychology*, 6, 377–400.

Laub, D. & Lee, S. (2003). Thanatos and massive psychic trauma: The impact of the death instinct on knowing, remembering and forgetting. *Journal of the American Psychoanalytic Association*, 51, 433–464.

Levi, P. (1987). *Moments of Reprieve*. New York: Simon & Schuster. (Original work published in Italian in 1981).

——, (1989). *The Drowned and the Saved*. New York: Vintage International. (Original work published in Italian in 1986). Translated by Raymond Rosenthal.

——, (1995). *Survival in Auschwitz*. New York: Simon & Schuster. (Original work published in Italian in 1947). Translated by Giulio Einaudi.

Leys, R. (2000). *Trauma: A Genealogy*. Chicago, IL: The University of Chicago Press.

Mucci, C. (2013). *Beyond Individual and Collective Trauma: Inter-generational Transmission, Psychoanalytic Treatment, and the Dynamics of Forgiveness*. London: Karnac Books.

Ornstein, A. (2014). Reflections on the development of my analytic subjectivity. In: S. Kuchuck, (Ed.), *Clinical Implications of the Psychoanalyst's Life Experience: When the Personal Becomes Professional*, (pp. 81–97). New York and London: Routledge.

Ornstein, P. with H. Epstein (2015). *Looking Back: Memoir of a Psychoanalyst*. Lexington, MA: Plunkett Lake Press.

Prot, K. (2010). Research on consequences of the Holocaust. *Archives of Psychiatry and Psychotherapy*, 2, 61–69.

Reis, B. (2009). Performative and enactive features of psychoanalytic witnessing. *The International Journal of Psychoanalysis*, 90, 1359–1372.

Richman, S. (2006). Remembering to forget to remember: Response to Anna Ornstein. *Contemporary Psychoanalysis*, 42, 673–680.

———, (2014). *Mended by the Muse: Creative Transformations of Trauma.* New York: Routledge.

———, (2015). Review of beyond individual and collective trauma: Intergenerational transmission, psychoanalytic treatment, and the dynamics of forgiveness by Clara Mucci. *The Psychoanalytic Quarterly,* 84, 502–510.

———, (2017). Review of looking back: Memoir of a psychoanalyst by Paul Ornstein with Helen Epstein. *The Psychoanalytic Quarterly,* 86, 198–211.

Salberg, J. (2015). The texture of traumatic attachment: Presence and ghostly absence in transgenerational transmission. *The Psychoanalytic Quarterly,* 84, 21–45.

Stern, D.B. (2010). *Partners in Thought: Working with Unformulated Experience, Dissociation, and Enactment.* New York: Routledge.

———, (2012). Witnessing across time: Accessing the present from the past and the past from the present. *The Psychoanalytic Quarterly,* 81, 53–81.

Stolorow, R. & Atwood, G. (1979). *Faces in a Cloud: Subjectivity in Personality Theory.* New York: Jason Aronson.

Trezise, T. (2013). *Witnessing Witnessing: On the Reception of Holocaust Survivor Testimony.* New York: Fordham University Press.

Ullman, C. (2006). Bearing witness. Across the barriers in society and in the clinic. *Psychoanalytic Dialogues,* 16, 181–198.

———, (2012). IARPP Colloquium Series, No. 20.

Valent, P. (1998). Resilience in child survivors of the holocaust: Toward the concept of resilience. *The Psychoanalytic Review,* 85, 517–535.

van der Kolk, B. (1987). *Psychological Trauma.* Washington, DC: American Psychiatric Press.

Chapter 6

The injurious impact of failed witnessing

Reflections on Richman's "pathologizing tilt"

Sam Gerson

Sofia Richman begins her critique of the great majority of contemporary work on the psychological impact of genocidal trauma on Holocaust survivors and their offspring by describing a trauma of her own, one that occurred "twenty-five years ago". She recalls being surprised that that the interviewers at the Fortunoff Video Archives for Holocaust Testimonies at Yale University did not ask her to describe her post-war adaptations. Richman asks: ". . . was the focus of the interview meant to highlight traumatic events at the expense of coping mechanisms? Was the resilience it took to create a new meaningful life, of less interest to the interviewers than the details of traumatization"?

To these questions, clearly asked in pain and protest, we must probably say "yes" – that the primary focus and purpose of Holocaust testimonies is to record the horrors of genocide and not post-war forms of resilience and creativity. Clearly, Richman is arguing for a change.

This notwithstanding, the failure of the testimonial project to garner Richman's experience of survivorhood appears to have evoked her dispute with the focus on the sequela of trauma that marks most scholarly and clinical work about the Holocaust, and leads to her corrective call for us to consider post-war resilience and creativity. Her experience at the testimonial interview also, I believe, strikingly reveals the power of engaged witnessing to serve reparative functions, and the power of its absence to solidify the trauma of non-recognition. Her story of the failed testimonial highlights, albeit in an inadvertent way, how engaged witnessing is an essential relational mode of therapeutic action.

Richman's experience lends itself to her questioning what she believes are a set of 'highly abstract theoretical ideas' that have narrowed the view of coping with trauma into a perspective wherein survivors are pathologized, and resilience is not recognized or integrated into relational trauma theory. She writes that "Survivors seen through the prism of psychopathology are viewed as "other", they are painted as one-dimensional, devoid of complexity, and often characterized in dichotomous terms such as either "severely damaged" or "amazingly resilient." Richman goes on to argue that this approach indicates that relational theorists neglect the idea of multiplicity in discussing self-states, and she traces this position to relationalists' uncritical absorption of Laub's one-person trauma theory.

I wish first to take up two points here – one is that the "pathologizing" of survivors did in fact occur through the creation of the concept of "survivor's syndrome". Certainly one must account for selection bias, as the psychiatrists who first created this term were referring to individuals who were seen as patients rather than the general population of survivors. Yet there was another, and perhaps more determinative, selection bias – one created in an act of unacknowledged collusion between survivors and the mental health field. The creation of the term "survivor syndrome" (Niederland, 1968) owes at least some part to the wish of survivors, and the mental health provider community (a great many of whom were Jewish), to apply for and be granted reparation funds from Germany ("Wiedergutmachung"). Recall that at time there was no diagnosis of "Post-Traumatic Stress Disorder" and the German authorities were, at first, questioning many claims on the basis of "pre-existing conditions". The sympathetic mental health community needed to arrive at a diagnostic entity that justified (to German authorities) the granting of indemnification for psychological harm and the concept and diagnostic term "survivor syndrome" was created during this time. While these social and economic conditions may have led to some conscious and unconscious excess in the report of symptoms by both survivors and their providers, and an exclusive emphasis on wounds, it would be erroneous to dismiss this diagnosis as fabricated. Indeed, the symptomatology was observed in many survivors of trauma beyond the Holocaust (e.g. Des Pres, 1976; Lifton, 1967). Richman does not seem to dispute the existence of postwar wounds; she is, however, providing an important inquiry into a pathologizing tilt in our literature – a corrective more emergent in the passage of time.

The other concern relates to the more general point that any categorical descriptions, including diagnoses, that are applied to a group, will never be descriptive of all members. In this regard, Sofia Richman's project of reminding us that all theories can be widely misused if they obscure the individuality of experience is laudible and, of course, correct. She reminds us of the subjectivity of all theorists, of the dangers of applying meta-psychological constructions to living beings, and of the tendency of theories to become reified as truths. Unfortunately, Richman puts forward the claim that all categorical descriptions of survivors (and their offspring) spring from theoretical perspectives influenced by subjective bias. The ironic aspect of this assertion is that it groups the overwhelming majority of clinicians and researchers of the traumatic residues of survivorhood into a biased group while somehow claiming objectivity for her own perspective. While Richman may find herself not adequately represented by the observations of clinicians who have accumulated enormous amounts of clinical data, this situation does not discredit the extensive literature of the past 50 years that documents the often searing and unremitting effects of surviving genocidal trauma. These personal and clinical accounts cannot be simply categorized as "metapsychological speculations".

In attempting to create space for post-war resilience, Richman's thesis ignores both the research findings and subjective accounts of second-generation children of survivors that poignantly document the difficult dynamic struggles encountered by the offspring of survivors (e.g. Bukiet, 2002; Eisenstein, 2006; Epstein, 1979; Hass, 1990; Hoffman, 2004; Kogan, 1995; Prince, 1985; Rosenbaum, 1999; Wardi, 1992; Weisel, 2000). It should also be noted that the memoirs and fiction of the second generation amply document how the creative spirit and resilience co-exist with, and do not obviate, the wrenching psychological challenges of the immediacy of first-hand learning about, and living with, the horrors of the Holocaust as transmitted by the surviving parent(s). A prime example of this is the work of Art Spiegelman, whose "Maus" (1993) was acclaimed as a creative tour-de-force even as it represented the emotional turmoil, conflict, and resilience faced by survivors and their children.

Dr. Richman directs the core of her critique at the work of Dori Laub – the preeminent researcher, scholar, and archivist of the psychological impact of the Holocaust, who was a founder of the Yale University archives and designed the testimonial interview which neglected Richman's post-war resilience. To Richman, the over emphasis on the enduring wounds of massive trauma derives from Laub's work and she decries its unquestioned assimilation in relational trauma theory. Richman asserts that the major formulations in Laub's work represent in essence no more than a set of assumptions that are "uncritically accepted and repeatedly quoted in the literature". Her argument relies, primarily, on the scholarly work of non-clinician academic scholars trained in political science and the history of science (Alford, 2008, 2009; Leys, 2000). The central focus of the critique that Richman and the aforementioned authors proffer concerns the notion put forth by Laub and other scholars that trauma interferes with representation and as such creates a psychic wound. Here, Richman and I have very different readings of Laub's meaning. Richman regards this idea in an absolute and concrete manner by correctly noting the great outpouring of memoirs and testimonials offered by survivors. For Richman, these memoirs and testimonials contradict Laub's thesis - indeed, the whole enterprise of archiving the experiences of survivors would be folly if not for the many, if not most, survivors' capacity to represent their trauma. To me, this capacity does not contradict Laub's position. It seems to me that the source of this confusion may reside in Richman's too literal interpretation of Laub and other trauma theorists' position about the representability of trauma – as if the question of "representation" consisted only in whether or not someone could recount the traumatic events that they experienced.

Richman's rendering of the concept of representation as simple recall leaves her perplexed that Laub, who writes so extensively about witnessing, could state about the Holocaust that ". . . the event produced no witnesses"; or that Hannah Arendt stated that "The only people who can write about the Holocaust are those who have not experienced it." – an idea that Richman refers to as a "bizarre conclusion". A careful and less literal reading of the work of Laub and Arendt indicates that their references to the absolute trauma of the Holocaust refers to the experience of those individuals who perished in its wanton and torturous methods. The absolute Holocaust trauma, the horror for which there is no witness and therefore no author, may be best captured in the moment when Holocaust victims realized that the showers were emitting gas and that there was no escape. For Laub and Arendt, the Holocaust is ultimately, I believe, the history of those who died and not of the survivors.

Herein lies a considerable difference between Richman's perspective and my own. I believe we have profoundly different readings of Laub, and also, a very different focus on time and subjectivity. Richman is focused here on the post-war adaptive experience of the survivor; and I (with Laub) am focused on the totalizing eclipse of mind and body *during* the genocide as well as its enduring residues over time. There is a similar confusion of perspectives between Richman and myself (Gerson, 2009) about the impact of the traumas of the Holocaust on survivors and their children that may account for our disparate reflections about resilience. Richman takes me to account for cautioning that: "valorizing the traits that might be associated with resilience and the creation of a new life is a grievous error as it obscures our contact with the deadliness that enveloped and destroyed their pre-genocide lives, shadows our present, and threatens the future (Gerson, IARPP Colloquium Series, No. 20; p. 20, May 10, 2012)." My words created some consternation among some participants in the IARPP Colloquium who understood me as somehow being opposed to the concept of resilience itself, or eschewing the importance of helping survivors develop and nurture adaptive modes of engaging post-war life with purpose and vigor. And apparently, Sofia Richman continues to believe that this is the case . . . so I shall repeat here my previous attempt at clarification – that I am problematizing the notion of resilience *in* the camps, rather than after liberation.

I have to clarify – of course, I am not at all opposed to recognizing the role of resilience, support, community and so on in adaptation to post-genocidal life. What I object to is claiming that any of these factors played a significant part in the survival of genocide. I am indebted to the scathingly honest work of Primo Levi in this regard – from the "Drowned and the Saved":

After my return from imprisonment I was visited by a friend older than myself . . . He told me that my having survived could not be the work of chance, of an accumulation of fortunate circumstances (as I did then and still do maintain) but rather of Providence. I bore the mark, I was an elect: I the nonbeliever, and even less of a believer after the season of Auschwitz, was a person touched by Grace, a saved man. And why me? It is impossible to know, he answered. Perhaps because I had to write, and by writing bear witness. Wasn't

I in fact then in 1946, writing a book about my imprisonment? Such an opinion seemed monstrous to me. It pained me as when one touches a raw nerve, and kindled the doubt I spoke of before: I might be alive in the place of another, at the expense of another . . . The 'saved' of the lager were not the best, those predestined to do good, the bearers of message: what I had seen and lived through proved the exact contrary. Preferably the worst survived, the selfish, the violent, the insensitive, the collaborators . . . I felt innocent, yes, but enrolled among the saved and therefore in permanent search of a justification in my own eyes and those of others. The worst survived, that is the fittest; the best all died . . . I must repeat: we, the survivors, are not the true witnesses. This is an uncomfortable notion of which I have become conscious little by little . . . We survivors are not only an exiguous but also anomalous minority; we are those who by their prevarications or abilities or good luck did not touch bottom.

As an addendum to Levi's admonition to not presume that it is a quality of the survivor that accounts for his survival, I wish to add the following statistics: There were an estimated 200,000 prisoners who survived Auschwitz, there were 70 who survived Treblinka, and there was only one who survived Belzec – the glaring disparity in the number of survivors of different concentration camps is accounted for by the fact that Auschwitz also housed "work" details whereas Treblinka and Belzec were only death camps. Resilience among the survivors of Auschwitz was, no doubt, of significant help – yet it must be acknowledged that had the war gone on for another year, or had the survivors of Auschwitz been sent to Belzec, even the most resilient would have perished. My request not to valorize traits associated with resilience must be seen in this context – it is a plea not to obscure the deadliness of the Holocaust, both in its reality and in its likely traces in the survivors and their descendents who come to us for help. This emphasis is not intended as a negation of survivors' postwar creativity and resilience, and it need not be reduced to a proposal for a singular and constraining guide for how to listen for, and respond to, the unique trials and triumphs of each and every survivor that one has the opportunity to be of therapeutic help to.

There is one other major area of Richman's essay that I believe requires commentary as it revolves around her strong thesis about the role of creativity in ameliorating the impact of the traumas of the Holocaust. I am referring to her analysis of Primo Levi's death as accidental as opposed to being a suicide. Primo Levi died by falling, or hurtling, over the stairwell barrier and down the elevator shaft in the home he had occupied his entire life. In my view, Richman's presentation of the "facts" is skewed to sustain her thesis – to support her conclusion of the accidental nature of Levi's death, Richman relies solely on a magazine article by Gambetta (1999/2005) who, based on the absence of a suicide note, questions Levi's suicidal intentions. She neglects the extensive research and reportage of Levi's three major biographers, each of whom having written extremely well-regarded and lengthy volumes (Angier, 2002; Anissimov, 2000; Thomson, 2002), have corroborated the police reports of suicide.

The evidence that Levi died by suicide are too voluminous to recount here, yet a few compelling pieces of evidence are warranted. First, as all three aforementioned biographers abundantly document, there is no doubt that Levi was suffering from severe depression in the months prior to his death. In a letter written two months before his death, in February 1987 to David Mendel, MD, a retired cardiologist in London, Levi said:

> I've fallen into a pretty serious state of depression, I've lost all interest in writing, as well as reading. I'm extremely dispirited and don't want to see anybody . . . My fear is that this will never end. Everything I do, even if it is banal, costs me strength, including for example writing this letter. I feel I need help, but I don't know what sort.
>
> (Thomson, 2002, p. 489)

Around the same time, on February 19, 1987, Levi wrote to Ruth Feldman, his translator in the U.S., that "I'm going through the worst time since Auschwitz: in certain respects it's even worse than Auschwitz, because I'm no longer young and I have scant resilience. My wife is exhausted. I beg you to forgive this outburst, I know you'll understand . . . *de profundis*" (Thomson, 2002 p. 491).

Levi's mental state grew increasingly despondent and full of despair, and at 9:30 AM on the Saturday of his fatal fall he called the chief rabbi of Rome and told him "I don't know how I can go on. My mother's ill with cancer – every time I look at her I remember the faces of those men stretched out on their plank-beds at Auschwitz" (Thomson, 2002, p. 499).

At 10:05 that morning, Levi went over the railing surrounding the staircase outside his third-floor apartment and hurtled head first to his death. His wife Lucia arrived home at 10:30, and in full hearing of the police, exclaimed "No! He's done what he'd always said he'd do."

A second realm for us to consider has to do with the anguished refusals to believe that Primo Levi, the most influential writer and witness about the Holocaust over two generations, could now take his own life. Richman is not alone in hoping that creativity can heal the wound. In the absence of an explicit suicide note, there immediately developed a controversy about whether or not Levi committed suicide – the police report and his wife's exclamation notwithstanding. Levi's funeral was scheduled for two days after his death and presented the rabbi with the dilemma of whether or not Levi could be buried in the Jewish cemetery, as tradition and Hebraic law has it that those who have committed suicide must be buried outside of the walled perimeter of the cemetery. The rabbi might, in light of the disbelief by many that Levi had taken his own life, have simply announced that Levi's death was accidental and therefore Levi could, of course be buried within the Jewish cemetery. Rabbi Artom chose truth over expediency and, moreover, created a profound and wise ruling. The rabbi created a 'theological exception" by claiming that Levi's was not a standard suicide, but rather he was a victim of "delayed homicide" since anyone who had been imprisoned in a concentration camp and then takes his own life was in essence murdered by the Nazis (Thomson, 2002).

As we consider the forces acting against Primo Levi's will to live, we should acknowledge that his despair may not have been primarily occasioned by his experiences at Auschwitz, but rather by his own compromised physical health, the illness of his mother, and perhaps most debilitating of all, his sense of failure in regard to his life's project of being an authorial witness combatting both denial of, and complicity in, genocide.

Yet in the face of all of these contributions to understanding Primo Levi's death, Richman even eclipses doubt, simply asserting that Levi's suicide was not very plausible. She has, in her other work, noted that the creative work of art can transform trauma; it provides a break with silence and, as such, creates a witness to both the adversities and to the enduring life force.

I am left with a combination of respect and disappointment with Richman's insistence on the transformative effects of creativity and witnessing. Respect, because she is able to so fiercely maintain this position of hope and transcendence – despite all the documented failures of creativity to ensure survivors', or creative individuals', psychological well-being. Certainly Laub's own work is an example of enormous creativity and resiliency in a survivor, and of the failure to remove memory's wound (see Laub, 2015). Nonetheless, her advocacy for the healing power of creativity (Richman, 2002; 2014) is, I believe, not only of a theoretical import, but also an inspiration for all of who are dedicated to reclaiming the vitality and humanity of those injured by massive trauma.

I am also, however, concerned about unrealistic hope, which can seem like an act of denial and even refusal by Richman to acknowledge how the grip of deadliness must itself be contacted and given a wide latitude of expression before a thorough healing transformative project can emerge (Grand, 2000; 2015). In trying to understand how Richman has arrived at her position, and taken such evident umbrage at the scholarly and clinical conclusions of many other respected workers with Holocaust survivors and their offspring, I find the best answer to be, ironically as she herself states, centering on the failure of having her own resilience witnessed.

It is regretful that the interviewers that day 25 years ago did not offer Richman the opportunity to give voice to the capacity for resilience that was, and remains, most essential in her own sense of her survival. In this failure, the powerful impact of a failure of witnessing is not only illustrated in terms of the moment of its occurrence, but also in its impact through the years.

And while I do, of course, disagree with how Richman has applied the "one size fits all" critique to my work, I must also claim that the potential healing power of acts of witnessing represents an essential "one size fits all" element in the relational healing of traumas whose size is too enormous for anyone to heal alone.

References

Alford, F. (2008). Why Holocaust testimony is important, and how psychoanalytic interpretation can help . . . but only to a point. *Psychoanalysis, Culture & Society*, 13, 221–239.

——, (2009). *The Holocaust Is Not Traumatic; The Holocaust Can Be Represented*. Paper presented at the 2009 Annual Meeting of the American Political Science Association, Toronto, Canada.

Angier, C. (2002). *The Double Bond: Primo Levi – A Biography*. New York: Farrar, Straus, & Giroux.

Anissimov, M. (2000). *Primo Levi: The Tragedy of an Optimist*. Woodstock, NY: Overlook Press.

Bukiet, M. (2002). *Nothing Makes You Free; Writings of Descendants of Jewish Holocaust Survivors*. New York: W.W. Norton.

Des Pres, T. (1976*). The Survivor: An Anatomy of Life in the Death Camps*. New York: Oxford University Press.

Eisenstein, B. (2006). *I Was a Child of Holocaust Survivors*. London: Riverhead Books.

Epstein, H. (1979). *Children of the Holocaust*. New York: G.P. Putnams's Son's.

Gambetta, D. (1999/2005). *Primo Levi's Last Moments: A New Look at the Italian Author's Tragic Death Twelve Years Ago*. http://bostonreview.net/archives/BR24.3/gambetta.html

Gerson, S. (2009). When the third is dead: Memory, mourning and witnessing in the aftermath of the Holocaust. *The International Journal of Psychoanalysis*, 90, 1341–1357.

——, (2012). IARPP Colloquium Series, No. 20.

Grand, S. (2000). *The Reproduction of Evil: A Clinical and Cultural Perspective*. Hillsdale, NJ: The Analytic Press.

——, (2015) Circles of witnessing. *Contemporary Psychoanalysis*, Vol 51, 2, 262–275.

Hass, A. (1990). *In the Shadow of the Holocaust: The Second Generation*. Cornell, NY: Cornell University Press.

Hoffman, E. (2004). *After Such Knowledge: Memory, History, and the Legacy of the Holocaust*. New York: Public Affairs.

Kogan, I. (1995). *The Cry of Mute Children: A Psychoanalytic Perspective of the Second Generation of the Holocaust*. London: Free Association Books.

Laub, D. (1992). An event without a witness: Truth, testimony, and survival. In: S. Felman & D. Laub, (Eds.), *Testimony: Crises of Witnessing in Literature, Psychoanalysis, and History*, (pp. 75–92). New York: Routledge.

——, (2015). Listening to my mother's testimony. *Contemporary Psychoanalysis*, Vol 51, 2, 192–215.

Lifton, R. J. (1967*). Death in life: Survivors of Hiroshima*. New York: Random House.

Leys, R. (2000). *Trauma: A Genealogy*. Chicago, IL: The University of Chicago Press.

Niederland, W.G. (1968). Clinical observations on the "survivor syndrome." *International Journal of Psychoanalysis*, 49, 313–315.

Prince, R. (1985). *The Legacy of the Holocaust: Psychohistorical Themes in the Second Generation*. New York: Other Press.

Richman, S. (2002). *A Wolf In The Attic: The Legacy Of A Hidden Child Of The Holocaust*. New York: The Haworth Press.

——, (2014). *Mended by the Muse: Creative Transformations of Trauma*. New York: Routledge.

Rosenbaum, T. (1999). *Second Hand Smoke*. New York: St. Martin's Griffin.

Spiegelman, A. (1993). *Maus: A Survivor's Tale*. New York: Pantheon.

Thomson, I. (2002). *Primo Levi: A Life*. New York: Metropolitan Books.

Wardi, D. (1992). *Memorial Candles: Children of the Holocaust*. New York: Routledge.

Weisel, M. (2000). *Daughters of Absence: Transforming a Legacy of Loss*. Herndon, VA: Capital Books.

Chapter 7

Don't throw out the baby!

External and internal, attachment, and sexuality

Galit Atlas

Beginnings

I would like to start with a confession. My first mother was a Kleinian. I guess that means that at least genetically, I am a Kleinian as well. Following her, I had other professional mothers too, relational clinicians and thinkers, and now being the middle generation, I am already having my own children and debating about how to raise them. I am worried about their education and their values, consciously and unconsciously comparing their experiences to mine, and I worry about their, our, future, as I am aware that we can't teach something that we are not. So I ask myself: who are we? What is it that we teach our students about psychoanalysis and about life? And I recognize that much has changed since I was a young student in Israel, more or less at the same time relational psychoanalysis was born.

Playing with the familial metaphor, it is not bewildering news that the new parent of our era is a different parent, but maybe it is surprising to realize that it is not only the parent that has changed, but also the baby. The baby that we meet in our clinical work and theory is a new and different baby.[1] Trying to differentiate the psychoanalytic role and image of the baby of the past from that of the present and future, in this chapter I will try to conceptualize the new relational baby, and therefore also the babies we lost in the wake of its creation and the impact of this new being on our psychoanalytic thinking, training, and clinical work with adults. I am raising questions that have bearing on infancy, sexuality, fantasy, relational observation, the tendency to look versus the ability to listen, and mysterious interior spaces that cannot be perceived within dialogue.

As we know, even as we rely these days on infant research, in fact it is never the actual baby that we are dealing with in our practice with adults. Daniel Stern (1985) differentiated the *clinical infant*, which is a theoretical conception of the infant created during an adult's psychoanalysis, and which is based on fantasy and inferences about the subjective experience of the infant, from the *observed infant*, which is the concept of the baby created by scientists in an experiential setting. He argues that both are providing important insights about the subjective life of the infant, and he calls for integration of those two perspectives.

The psychoanalytic vision of what a baby is[2] colors our view of fantasy, regression, access to different self-states and more. With our patients, we get in touch with elements of that baby; with our fantasy about that baby and about that baby's feelings, thoughts and fantasies, and with those young, babyish self-states.[3] In that sense, as Ghent (1992) suggests, that baby is both an object that the patient (from an adult position) fantasizes about, as well as a subject that he experiences and inquires. Ghent adds that the focus on the infantile, "the body language of breast and penis, and the worldlessness of affect memory" (1992, p. 139) all contribute to preserving a degree of irrationality and the untranslatable (see more on translation later), which tends to get lost in the purely interpersonal "mature" position, where the patient is required to be an adult. "Encountering the infantile in oneself affords another avenue of experiencing this quality of mix between one- and two-person psychologies," he adds (1992, p 139). Bromberg (1991) argues that:

> Certain patients will benefit from treatment only when they are allowed to reconnect with the "baby" as a reality that is lived with the therapist. . . . My clinical experience, similar to that of Ferenczi, is that speaking directly with the dissociated aspects of self (including, often, the preverbal aspects), is important for most patients but *vital* for some. For the latter, I have observed that if it does not take place, the therapy is simply one more exercise in pseudo-adulthood in the patient's life.
>
> (p. 417)

But who are those babies that we meet in the psychoanalytic room? We listen, we infer, we mirror, we experience, we question and we translate from one internal language to another. How we do all of this is based on our experience of the patient in the room, on our cultural and psycho-analytic generational perceptions of what a baby is, as we become in touch with the patient's fantasies about their history (see Aron, 2014, on Birth Fantasies) and our own ideas and fantasies. In contemporary rela-tional practice, as opposed to Ferenczi's view, we emphasize the mutual interactional processes between analyst and adult patient, while taking into account the clear asymmetry between them vis-à-vis the significant differences in their roles, function, and responsibility (Aron, 1992). In that analytic space, we are both babies and adults, aggressors and victims, sexual and sensual, and as I challenge those splits and related binaries between internal and external, I wonder about our ability to hold both in mind and speak more than one language. But first let's start from the beginning, back to the baby.

A different baby

I will begin by conceptualizing a few different babies that are part of the history of psychoanalytic theory and clinical work with adults and ask: who is this baby that we meet on the relational couch? Or maybe that baby sits on a chair? In what ways is she different from or similar to the Freudian baby, the Kleinian and other babies?[4] What did we gain and what did we lose as the result of her arrival?

Freud and Klein's models of infantile sexuality (as with Ferenczi, Speilrein and others) arose in an era in which infant life was radically under-observed and undertheorized. In the Hampstead Nurseries, during the Second World War, Anna Freud initiated careful and systematic observation of infants and children. Following the War, Ernst Kris developed a program of infant research in the United States. However, the revolution in understanding child mind, memory, affect states, symbolic and intersubjective capacity did not begin until the 1960s, and it's not until the eighties that Daniel Stern brings more modern infancy research into psychoanalysis. Our understanding of early development and the view of the baby have always served as an organizing metaphor for clinical data, which leads to different model of minds and technical consequences. We can see how that baby has changed and, accordingly, understand the implications for adult treatment.

The Freudian baby is the most primitive baby. This baby is riddled with drives and lacks internal structure, a baby whose drives either get frustrated or gratified. The Freudian baby is autoerotic and narcissistic and struggles with tension reduction. As Seligman (1999) describes this baby is motivated to reduce internal tension, and has little or no sense of the distinction between herself and other people. The Freudian baby is based on biological instincts with primary investment in the body, and later on randomly related to object for the purpose of gratification and discharge. She is dominated by hallucinatory wish fulfillment and the dominance of the pleasure principle. Discussing implications for adult treatment, Mitchell (1988) writes: "Freud's baby, and the analysand who is understood via Freud's baby as metaphor, are inevitably tormented" (p. 130).

Like the Freudian baby, the "Kleinian baby" is constructed along primitive and unorganized lines, but from the beginning, her instincts are related to an object, the mother. This first cathexis is to a part object, the breast, and gradually moves to a full, complex and distinct object. The Kleinian baby has a rich internal world—internal objects and her phantasized relationship with them and between them—and bodily based phantasies. This baby is connected to and her experiences are mediated by the object, the outside world, and the inside world. It is a baby with excessive affect and split experiences of love and hate, and with various levels of ability to tolerate her anxiety and frustration. While the Kleinian baby is known as flooded with aggressive and sadistic fantasies, many have not recognized that Kleinians view the baby as an active agent, curious, creative and reactive (Roth & Durban, 2013). In her unconscious phantasy, the baby isn't only being created by the object but also simultaneously creates the object. Roth and Durban describe how in Klein's writing she illustrates how the healthy baby charges the breast with aliveness and with love in order to motivate an appropriate treatment and then to re-internalize its goodness. Her perspective emphasized a world that the baby, and then the adult, creates and designs, and hence psychological work requires the development of an awareness of the ways our internal world creates the external one and therefore is responsible for it and can change it. Infant research supports the Kleinian assumption that the baby is active and an agent in the creation of her world, but at the same time research draws a picture of a new baby, the relational baby.

The relational baby is reality oriented, aware of others and essentially social from birth. That baby does not have a phantasy life, not until well after symbolic functioning, which consolidates by three years (B. Beebe, Personal communication. May, 2014). Her world of action sequences is procedural and includes spatial orientation toward and away from the partner, facial and vocal emotion (such as prosody, intensity, pitch), attention processes and touch (See Beebe & Lachmann, 2013). The relational baby is responding to the outside world from the beginning and as Beebe and Lachmann note, infant research assumes "an information-processing model in which the infant's perceptual abilities ensure a capacity for seeking out, perceiving and interacting with social partners from birth"[5] (Beebe & Lachmann, 2013, p. 25). The infant, they suggest, can translate between environmental stimuli and the other's inner states, as both infant and partner sense the state of the other, and sense whether the state is shared. The parent-baby dyad (note that the dyad transformed from mother-baby to parent-baby) is engaged in a constant correspondence, a process that they describe as enabling the infant to confine the quality of another's inner feeling state and to discriminate whether it is shared. Karlen Lyons-Ruth (1999), the Boston Change Process Study Group (CPSG) (1998), Lyons-Ruth and CPSG (2001), and Daniel Stern et al. (1998) all present findings that support the understanding that primary dyadic relations are co-created. These same processes, infant research suggests, organize adult personality and is ubiquitous in adult treatment as well. They write:

> In psychoanalysis the origin of mind has generally been based on reconstruction of what the adult patient might have experienced. The origin of mind has often been conceptualized within a one-person model, as an isolated mind (Stolorow & Atwood, 1992), an autistic mind (Mahler, 1968), or in other metaphors, a reflex arc (Freud, 1915) rather than a dyad in dialogue. Once a shared, dialogic mind is posited as the point of origin, the psychoanalytic theory of development shifts.
>
> (Beebe& Lachmann, 2013, p. 28)

Unlike the Freudian postulation, research assumes that normal infants are not disorganized or primitive, but just less organized and more dependent (Seligman, 1999). Knoblauch, following Stern, suggests that the term regression then is based on a misrepresentation of how development unfolds and how pathological patterns are catalyzed in later development (Knoblauch, May 2014, Personal communication). From that view, pathological patterns emerge as a complex interaction with context, rather than the previously understood linear backsliding to a primitive state.

The relational baby is an agent and a participant in the bidirectional co-creation of the interaction, but what radically differentiates this baby from the babies of the past is the fact that she doesn't have phantasy life and functions on the procedural level of interaction, what I call the Pragmatic[6] level (See more on Enigmatic and Pragmatic in Atlas, 2015), a level that is assumed to be observable and measurable.

That view has implications for psychoanalytic theory and technique, as we apply the Pragmatic level not only to the analytic dyad but to our understanding of the mind. The main critique of the traditional Kleinian perspective on unconscious phantasy is that it is too speculative and obscure, based on retrospective inferences and attributing abilities to the infant that are beyond his cognitive capacities. Green (1995) on the other hand harshly criticized observation as a tool for understanding the baby's mind. He argues that:

> at the beginning of life the encounters between the baby and its object take place in a very limited period of time of the day. There is no question about the richness of these experiences and the importance of that interchange through all kinds of contacts: skin, eyes, feelings etc. But is it possible to forget that the amount of these moments of encounter is very small compared to the period where the baby is by himself . . .
>
> (Green, p. 876)

His point is that by emphasizing the observations on what happens during moments of exchange, we might disregard that the baby's interaction with the outside world, especially in the first few months of life, is only a very small part of the baby's life and that there is hardly anything to observe at the other periods when the baby is by himself. Green argues that there is a tendency to minimize the importance of these other moments and to deny the world of solitude of the baby because it is unthinkable for us. He writes: "Observers prefer to see than to listen. To perceive is to be in connection with external reality. To listen is to be in contact with psychic reality" (Green 1995, p. 877).

Here we encounter a paradox. Infant research gives us much data about the baby's interaction, useful data that has an important and profound impact on our understanding of development, of the mind and of human interactions, but it leaves us with a question: How do we account for that which cannot be observed, measured, and known? And how can we work within the frame of that paradox? I argue that relational psychoanalysis, leaning on infant research, narrowed the scope to the Pragmatic levels in our understanding of the mind. It maintained the split between the internal fantasy world, privileging external reality, trauma, and observed interactions.[7] In the relational perspective, there is less space given to consideration of the unknown and unseen, to the Enigmatic, in both analyst and patient, and as I discuss later, sexuality is often described as derived only from a secondary precipitate of a desire for connection or as part of the mother-infant early sensual attachment, thus depriving sexuality of its mysterious dimension.

Internal and external

The tension between external and internal reality has been explicit in psychoanalysis ever since Freud abandoned the seduction theory. In 1897 in a private letter to Fliess, Freud addressed for the first time his doubt that the unconscious is able to distinguish fact from fiction, reality from fantasy. In other words, he suggests that what one assumes is external reality might in fact exist only internally. It was at that point that Freud began developing his new theory of infantile sexuality, arguing that neurotic symptoms are in fact not a result of real childhood sexual trauma, but rather an expression of internal conflicts, fantasies and impulses. Fletcher (2013) following Laplanche, shows how in Freud's earlier trauma theory there was no split between trauma and fantasy. Rather, in the earlier theory, fantasy was a way of dealing with, representing, and defending against trauma. Freud created the split binary between trauma and fantasy only later, when he abandoned his seduction theory. According to Fletcher, Freud's original view can best be seen in the work on creen memory, where ALL memory is a screen, hence there is no binary between reality and fantasy, memory and fantasy, and displacement and condensation operate in all memory of reality. Laplanche in an interview in 2001, explains that by privileging the internal world, Freud neglected the very dialectical theory and complex play between the external and the internal inherent in his original theory. For example, Freud's theory explained that trauma, in order to be psychic trauma, never comes simply from the outside. For him, trauma consists of two moments: the first is the implantation of something coming from outside. But that experience, or the memory of it, must be reinvested in a second moment, which is the internal reviviscence of this memory. It is the integration of the two moments, the internal and the external, that are traumatic. Laplanche (2001) adds that we can find this theory very carefully elaborated in the "Project for a Scientific Psychology," in Freud's famous case of Emma (410–413).

In abandoning the seduction theory, Freud dismissed external reality and childhood sexual trauma, and called for privileging the internal world of conflicts, fantasies and impulses. Ferenczi's *Confusion of Tongues* (1933), then, can be read as an argument with the notion of infantile sexuality, taking up the other side of the external–internal reality split by supporting the former. Ferenczi (1933) draws an important distinction between children's needs and adults' needs on the sexuality-relatedness axis, attributing exclusive responsibility for sexual exploitation to the adult, while claiming that sexual behavior in children is a symptom that attests to a rupture between the child and his surroundings. He points to the child's fantasy of playing within the domain of tenderness, while the adult, on the other hand, harbors sexual fantasies related to power, domination and aggression, and the abuser tends to project his unconscious desire, shame and guilt onto the child, thereby ignoring the child's actual needs for love and protection. Viewing children in this manner is especially important in that it paved the way for emphasis on the actual, reality basis for trauma, as well as caregivers' structural power and complete responsibility for abuse. Furthermore, it helped to develop the concept of identification with the aggressor. Just as significant to note, however, this view disregarded the child's agency, ability to impact reality, her own impulses and unconscious fantasies (Blum, 2004), as well as vulnerabilities and susceptibilities (Atlas-Koch, 2007). Applied to the therapeutic relationship, this perspective posits patients as potential innocent victims—perhaps in tandem with the way that Ferenczi experienced himself in the analytic community of the early Thirties, where he felt attacked and could not find the care, tenderness and support that he needed (Blum, 2004).

Following Ferenczi, and maybe in some similar ways as a reaction to the classical psychoanalytic environment, relational psychoanalysis emphasizes the importance of trauma, and canonizes attachment theory and infant research as meaningful ways to evaluate the impact of external "real" life on internal life and structures of the mind. Big and small T traumas often become the royal roads to the exploration of mental health situations, and sexuality is seen as another way of expressing residues of early intersubjective exchanges between mother and infant. As mentioned, the relational observed baby seems not to have phantasy, aggression, or sexuality. This is a baby that responds in highly complex ways to her environment, and the implication for adult life is that her sexuality is often described as derived only from early patterns of attachment or as a secondary precipitate of a desire for connection (see more in Dimen, 1999), as opposed to the infant sexuality of the Freudian baby.

It is interesting to realize that even as relational psychoanalysis developed in a post-modern era when people challenged the concept of absolute Truth, by focusing on the Pragmatic notions (of what we can see, measure, know) we too often privilege so-called truth and leave the Enigmatic levels of communication on the periphery. And while many relational thinkers who write about sexuality (See Goldner, Harris, Dimen, Saketopoulou, Corbet and more) believe that the mother–baby physical tie is only one aspect of sexuality, as Fonagy notes, a word search in the PEP archive shows that when the use of the term sexuality went down, relational terms went up. Here, I hope to illuminate the value of a both/and approach, where lines of development in regard to attachment and to sexuality are both separate and interdependent. I address the split between attachment and sexuality as it is related to other binaries, especially the one between intrapsychic and interpersonal, but also between the pre-Oedipal (sensuality) and the Oedipal (sexuality), innocence versus perverse, tenderness versus aggression and sexuality, and more. (For an extended treatment of these and other binaries, see Aron & Starr, 2013.) In the *Enigma of desire* (2015), I try to re-frame the theory of sexuality as a non-hierarchical mode, one that can maintain those dialectic tensions and the tension between the Pragmatic elements that can be observed, measured, and assessed, this is, the sensible, logical, operational, definable and practical on the one hand, and on the other hand those aspects which are Enigmatic and are opaque to observation, puzzling, riddled, polysemous, and hidden.

Attachment and sexuality

Sexual feelings are potentially overwhelming and touch upon suffering, which is the origin of the word passion in Latin. According to Kristeva (1999), passion always includes suffering, the suffering of pleasure, of the excess that the body and the mind cannot contain. "Lust," Dimen writes (1999), is "both the longing for pleasure and the pleasure itself" (p. 424). It simultaneously contains suffering and joy, the uncontainable and the unreachable. We know that people seek sexual experience for many different emotional reasons (Benjamin, 2004; Bollas, 1995; Kuchuck, 2012; Mitchell, 2002; J, Slavin, 2002; M. Slavin, 2006; Stein, 1998; Stoller, 1985 and others): as an attempt to charge their inner objects and self with excitement and realness and aliveness; to express their aggression and hostility, to hide or expose their vulnerability, to bolster the collapsing or fragmenting self; to heal trauma through the repetition of arousal; to achieve recognition and affirmation through the body of the other, and more. Sex can be an attempt to achieve emotional and physical regulation. It is a promise; a promise to be seen, to be known. It is a promise to fill for a moment the empty parts, to retrieve all of the losses, to find all the empty boxes. It is a promise that is fulfilled for a moment before collapsing back to square one, leaving the subject even more distressed and empty.

In the *Riddle of sex* (2004) Benjamin makes the clear connection between intersubjectivity and sexuality. Her rich theory is based on intersubjective developmental theory, which as mentioned, revised the notion of infancy with different implications for understanding sexuality. She adds to Laplanche and Stein the intersubjective view on sexuality, and writes that sexuality is bound to exceed what the relational dimension can contain (Benjamin, 2004). Later, we (Benjamin & Atlas, 2010, 2015) focused on aspects of the sexual that must be worked out intersubjectively in the arena of affective and bodily arousal for which the individual's earliest interaction already set the stage. Thus, as we discuss, the excess of sexuality can be seen as a more complex configuration of many relational issues that include efforts to regulate anxiety and stimulation, and manage aggression linked to disturbances in attachment on the mother's part as well as the infant's. In those clinical and theoretical discussions and others (Atlas, 2011, 2011b, 2013, 2014, 2015), we can see how sex connects us through the body to our early Pragmatic losses of the mother's body, her touch, her gaze, her holding and mirroring. We can often recognize patterns of excitement, distress, and regulation that are observed in current infant research (Beebe, Jaffe, & Lachmann, 1992; Beebe & Lachmann, 2002, 2003; Lyons-Ruth, 1999; Stern, 1985; Tronick, 1998) and emphasize a trajectory in development that sets the foundation for a person's capacity to soothe herself with touch, the capacity to receive adequate emotional responsiveness from the partner, to self-regulate and more. This is an area in which pragmatic theory and research are helpful in the consulting room, but we can recognize points at which there is a collapse of comprehension and clarity, where sexual self-states start with the mother-baby tie but lie somewhere beyond that attachment bond, outside of a connection to an other. This is where lust contains the unknown more than the known, and, therefore, where empirical research can't give us the complete answer. The mother–baby physical tie then is only one aspect of sexuality. Here I join those theorists who suggest that sexuality has its own existence, as a discrete phenomenon that connects us through the body with that which is Enigmatic and beyond our conscious knowledge of ourselves (Bataille, 1986; Frommer, 2006; Goldner, 2006; Mitchell, 1997; Stein, 1998, 2008; and more). Sex brings us in touch with a sensation beyond the body itself and beyond the object itself; with an Enigmatic loss that isn't about the actual object. Through the erotic, we encounter parts of ourselves and parts of life that may otherwise be inaccessible or too excessive in other ways, and the endless elusiveness and mystery of Otherness. The poignancy of sexuality then, as Stein (2008) writes, cannot derive solely from its specific sensual nature, but also has its own existence as a discrete phenomenon that connects us through the body with that which is beyond our conscious knowledge of ourselves. I wonder if this is one reason Freud always insisted that he was talking about psychosexuality and was not willing to limit his ideas to sensuality. I believe he repeatedly understood and ignored the pull to reduce the sexual to something less Enigmatic and foreign. And at the same time, while Enigmatic longing is powerful and has its own existence, I believe it cannot be differentiated from the Pragmatic intersubjective relationship. Can relational psycho-analysis include both? Internal and the external, known and unknown, Enigmatic and Pragmatic?

In my attempt for integration, I suggest that sexuality is always both Pragmatic and Enigmatic, which means that it is based on the longing for the original actual parent on the one hand, and the wish to connect with unknown parts of ourselves and of the world on the other hand. On the surface we are dealing with two different perspectives, models of the mind, and languages,[8] used by different theories that argue that sexuality is either an intersubjective or an intrapsychic event. But the Enigmatic and the Pragmatic always coexist and play a dual part in the "otherness" of lustful states of mind. The split between these languages then is only tentative since the two levels are interwoven and inseparable. The actual Pragmatic mother and her body always function as agents for the inaccessible parts of the Enigmatic elements. The body functions as the instrument by which all knowledge and information is received and pre-meaning generated. It is through the body (the "being-to-the-world," Grosz, 1994) that we all initially experience the presymbolic world, and through the body of the other that we experience our being. The body is a meaningful aspect of the connection to that which we otherwise cannot grasp, the unreachable parts of the mother, ourselves, and the world. In clinical work I find that as long as there is a real deficit—a longing for the absent, dysregulating primary caregiver—there is no access to other levels of existence and experience, there is no ability to think (in the Bionian sense), which means that feelings and experiences are limited. In those cases, patients and analysts are constantly encountering the zone of failure of recognition and regulation, arousal caused by inadequate or overwhelming responses, and absence of mentalization. Dysregulation in the original dyad is re-lived in the analytic dyad in ways that usually limit our view to the pragmatic original pieces of distress and dysregulation that the patient is trying to repeat and repair nonverbally. The ability to create a regulated analytic dyad promotes the growth and possibility for different erotic experiences to emerge, beyond concrete reparation of infancy ruptures. The mother's body hence is always a necessary foundation for the infant's existence—it is the container for her own body and mind. Originally it is the maternal function, the mother's real body, touch, gaze, voice and so on that is the actual representation of everything that can't be reached, including infinity and death. Kristeva (1982) notes that abjection is fundamentally related to death and to the place where meaning collapses, where "I am not." She differentiates the symbolic *meaning* or knowledge of death from the nonsymbolic *experience* of one's own death, and notes that abjection represents a revolt against that which gave us our own existence or state of being, and is therefore related to the mother's body. In that respect, the mother's body, the known physical pragmatic body, is the agent for the inaccessible unknown Enigmatic pieces, both in infancy and in adult sexual life. Therefore when approaching the Enigmatic level, although it's tempting to dismiss the real mother and connect exclusively with that which is beyond the physical, I believe we have to keep the Pragmatic mother in the picture too, since she and her body function as the container for the unrepresentable fragments. How can we recognize both—that which we can know and that which we cannot—in the consulting room? When is one a cover for the other? And can we actually think about what we know, what we don't know, what we wish we could know, as well as what we don't want to know?

Enigmatic and Pragmatic—translation and integration

This view proposes an integrative approach that brings back the Freudian, Kleinian and other pre-relational babies. It is based on the understanding that our patients are not only Pragmatic relational babies who have to repair their infancy and childhood traumas, but also beings who hold Enigmatic, unknown and unseen parts, fantasy, sexuality and aggression, that are internal, hidden and mysterious. Even when we don't see these parts, we can try to listen to, and as Laplanche suggests, translate and transform from one register to another. In other words, Laplanche suggests that a central piece of every treatment is the work of translation, which in my mind suggests focusing on unconscious and Enigmatic communication, and in our two-person model, assuming a bidirectional process (messages are transmitted simultaneously from patient to analyst and from analyst to patient). The main emphasis in translation is not on the words we hear and understand, but rather on the overall Enigmatic message that needs to be conveyed. Thus the translator, instead of paying attention to the verbal signs, concentrates more on the information that is being delivered.

Many of Laplanche's ideas were the beginning of an integrative approach, an attempt at bridging the internal and the external. Laplanche (1987; 1992, 1995) proposed a reformulation of Freud's seduction theory. He was interested in seduction as the origins of the repressed unconscious, rather than in Freud's etiological hypothesis about neurotic symptoms, and viewed seduction not as a traumatic experience that comes from the outside world, but as a "normal" complex concept that belongs simultaneously to external and internal worlds. Hence he opened up significant intersubjective implications, as he was seeking a solution to the problem of theoretical splitting between drive theory and object relations, between seduction understood as a concrete traumatic experience and as intrapsychic fantasy. Laplanche contends that Freud was too concrete in thinking seduction must either be real or imagined, and that he missed the category of the message; the transmission of affect and excitement without literal seduction. In his theory, Laplanche tried to hold that tension, and suggests that the Enigmatic message is the implicit communication, the transmission of enigmatic signifiers from the mother's unconscious into the baby's mind and body. The infant's mind, he believed, is invaded by the unconscious of the other, and those messages he receives are Enigmatic. The Enigmatic message, which according to Laplanche is packed with sexual significance, is in itself a seduction and a central part of the intersubjective dimension of communication, a mystifying implicit communication that is unconsciously transmitted from adult to child (Laplanche, 1992, 1995).

As mentioned, I believe that the next step in this integration is based on our ability to accept that the split between internal and external, Enigmatic and Pragmatic, is tentative much more than absolute. After all, states of consciousness always integrate different levels of existence and experience, the present and the absent, the known and the unknown, the pragmatic, procedural, representable, and the Enigmatic, mysterious, unknown and unrepresentable.[9] Since the body functions as the instrument by which all knowledge and information is received, our body and the mother's body are meaningful aspects of the connection to that which we cannot grasp, the unreachable parts of the mother, ourselves, and the world. The mother's body then serves as a container for the Enigmatic elements, and the early connection to the mother is a bridge to other levels of existence. In that sense, when this container is shaky, there can be no holding of the Enigmatic elements. In such cases, sexuality might be reduced to becoming a portal through which one tries to repair but instead, actually relives distress and over-arousal. This approach is related to the understanding that there are many levels of existence and that each level envelops another dimension within. Huston Smith (1976), a professor of comparative religion, claims that there is one thing in common to all traditions, and that is the belief in series of nests of being. That means that there is a universal view that each thing is interwoven with every other thing and all are ultimately enveloped with the Enigmatic inaccessible, unknown envelope of our existence. Wilber (1998) calls this scheme "transcend and include" (p. 7), and in his view, each level is a bridge to the other level and contains the other within.[10] For purposes of this discussion, I'm referring to the way the Enigmatic elements have to include the real body and real attachment to an Other, while the Pragmatic elements serve as a bridge to the unreachable parts of our being. Thus the unrepresentable, unknown elements, always include the Pragmatic in their nest. The Enigmatic and the Pragmatic, I suggest, are two aspects of one phenomenon, inseparable and dialectically related. Our sexual longing simultaneously connects us to the existential emptiness and to the lost parts of the real deficit. We connect with the mother's body and to the early mother-infant relationship, and bridge to another level of existence, touching the unknown of life and death. My main point then is not a claim that Enigmatic and Pragmatic mother are the same representation, but rather that there cannot be one without the other, and therefore I suggest considering them as inseparable.

The babies I meet on my relational couch dream. They love, they hate and they play with me. I try to listen to their phantasies and get in touch with their desires and the parts of them that I don't know and maybe never will, as I ask myself about the impact they have on me and about the ways we arouse and regulate each other. Beatrice Beebe taught me most of what I know about infants, my babies—actual and professional— taught me the rest, and I am sure that to some degree those who lay on my couch are unconsciously aware of that knowledge; an integral part of the way I listen. They also know that I trust my listening more than my vision. That I am interested in the caesuras between the lines. And that my Kleinian mother taught me to trust the mind to lead us to the most unknown truths and to believe that the ability to tolerate that truth allows us to live and to love.

Notes

1 The concept of the new baby was developed in my work with Adrienne Harris, and I would like to thank her for her contribution.
2 See discussion of the baby in psychoanalysis in Slochower, 2013.
3 Mitchell (1988) in his criticism on what he perceived as the *infantilism* of the patient, addressed the countertransferential use of psychoanalytic developmental theory in which the patient is regarded as a metaphorical baby while the therapist's perspective is assumed to be the adult one.
4 I demonstrate my thesis in this paper emphasizing the Fruedian and Kleinian babies, with the understanding that almost every theorist (Fairbairn, Wincicott, Balint, Kohut and others) have their own version of a baby.
5 For example, they add (2013) that research indicates infants' ability to imitate gestures of the experimenter as early as 42 minutes after birth (Meltzoff, 1990; 2007; Meltzoff & Moore, 1998; see Beebe et al., 2005 for a review).
6 The pragmatic is the actual interactive dimension of intersubjectivity, which is based on the mother–baby multi-model sensory interaction that includes patterns of arousal, regulation, touch, gaze, facial, vocal and rhythm, etc, and that can be observed and measured.
7 See discussion on Unconscious Phantasy and Relational Reality in Gerson, 2008.
8 I'm drawing on a variety of psychoanalytic traditions, some of which are rooted in Freud's energic hydraulic model, as well as in a psychological, intersubjective hermeneutic model.
9 Heidegger writes that what enables the jug to be a holding vessel is its emptiness, and that the emptiness, the void, is what actually does the vessel's holding. "The vessel's thingness does not lie at all in the material of which it consists, but in the void that holds" (Heidegger 1950, p. 169). The void, thus the emptiness, is the container for existing pragmatic material that is studied by science.
10 See the dialectic in mystical tradition of Kabbalah, with material containing spiritual and spiritual space containing materiality, both ways. Even physical sex is always for the purpose of bringing about God's unification—a cosmic spiritual primal scene.

References

Aron, L. (1992). Interpretation as an Expression of the Analyst's Subjectivity. *Psychoanalytic Dialogues*, 2:475–507.
Aron. L. (2014). "With you I'm Born Again": Themes and Fantasies of Birth and the Family Circumstances Surrounding Birth as These are

Mutually Evoked in Patient and Analyst. *Psychoanalytic Dialogues*, 24:341–357.

Aron, L. & Starr, K. (2013). *A Psychotherapy for the People: Toward a Progressive Psychoanalysis*. London and New York: Routledge.

Atlas. G. (2013). What's Love Got to Do With It? Sexuality, Shame and the Use of the Other. *Studies in Gender and Sexuality*, 14:51–58.

——, (2014). Touch me, Know Me: The Enigma of Erotic Longing. *Psychoanalytic Psychology*, 32, 1:123–139.

——, (2015). The Enigma of Desire: Sex, Longing and Belonging in Psychoanalysis. London and New York: Routledge.

Atlas, G. & Beebe, B. (2011). Disorganized Attachment: Infant Research Informs Adult Treatment. A panel with Beatrice Beebe, IPSS, NYC.

Atlas-Koch, G. (2007). *Toward an Assessment of Susceptibility to Sexual Abuse: An Expressive Psychoanalytic Perspective*. Ohio: Union Institute & University.

Atlas-Koch, G. (2010). Confusion of Tongues: Trauma and Playfulness. *Psychoanalytic Perspectives*. 6, 2:93–114.

Atlas-Koch, G. (2011a). Attachment Abandonment Murder. *Contemporary Psychoanalysis*. 47, 2:245–259.

Atlas-Koch, G. (2011b). The Bad Father, the Sinful Son and the Wild Ghost. *Psychoanalytic Perspectives*. 8, 2:238–251.

Atlas-Koch, G. & Benjamin, J. (2010). *The "Too Muchness" of Excitement and the Death of Desire: Theoretical and Clinical Perspectives*. San Francisco, CA: IARPP.

Bataille, G. (1986). *Eroticism: Death and Sensuality*. San Francisco, CA: City Light Books.

Beebe, B., Jaffe, J., & Lachmann, F. (1992). A Dyadic Systems view of Communication. In: N. Skolnick and S. Warshaw (Eds.), *Relational Perspectives in Psychoanalysis* (pp. 61–81). Hillsdale, NJ: The Analytic Press.

Beebe, B. & Lachmann, F. (2002). *Infant Research and Adult Treatment: Co-Constructing Interactions*. Hillsdale, NJ: The Analytic Press.

——, (2003). The Relational Turn in Psychoanalysis: A Dyadic Systems View from Infant Research. *Contemporary Psychoanalysis*, 39, 3:379–409.

——, (2013). *The Origins of Attachment: Infant Research and Adult Treatment*. London and New York: Routledge.

Benjamin, J. (2004). Revisiting the Riddle of Sex. In: Iréne Matthis (Ed.), *Dialogues on Sexuality, Gender and Psychoanalysis* (pp. 145–172). London: Karnac.

Benjamin, J. & Atlas, G. (2015). The "Too Muchness" of Excitement: Sexuality in Light of Excess, Attachment and Affect Regulation. *Intonations Journal for Psychoanalysis*, 1:39–63.

Blum, H. (2004). The Wise Baby and the Wild Analyst. *Psychoanalytic Psychology*, 21:3–15

Bollas, C. (1995). *Cracking Up: The World of Unconscious Experience.* London: Routledge.

Boston Change Process Study Group. (1998). Interventions that Effect Change in Psychotherapy: A Model Based on Infant Research. *Infant Mental Health Journal*, 19:277–353.

Bromberg, P. M. (1991). On Knowing One's Patient Inside Out: The Aesthetics of Unconscious Communication. *Psychoanalytic Dialogues*, 1:399–422.

Caruth, C. (2001). An Interview with Jean Laplanche. Emory University. http://pmc.iath.virginia.edu/text-only/issue.101/11.2caruth.txt

Dimen, M. (1999). Between Lust and Libido. *Psychoanalytic Dialogues*, 9:415–440.

Ferenczi, S. (1933). The Confusion of Tongues Between Adults and Children: The Language of Tenderness and Passion. In: M. Balint (Ed.), *Final Contributions to the Problems and Methods of Psycho-Analysis, Vol. 3*, (pp. 156–167). New York: Brunner/Mazel, 1980.

Fletcher. J. (2013). *Freud and The Scene of Trauma.* New York: Fordham University.

Freud, S. (1915). *Instincts and their Vicissitudes.* The Standard Edition of the Complete Psychological Works of Sigmund Freud, Volume XIV (1914–1916): On the History of the Psycho-Analytic Movement, Papers on Metapsychology and Other Works, pp. 109–140.

Frommer, M. S. (2006). On the Subjectivity of Lustful States of Mind. *Psychoanalytic Dialogues*, 16:639–664.

Gerson, S. (2008). Unconscious Phantasy and Relational Reality. *Psychoanalytic Inquiry*, 28:151–168.

Ghent, E. (1992). Paradox and Process. *Psychoanalytic Dialogues*, 2:135–159.

Goldner, V. (2006). "Let's do it again": Further reflection on Eros and attachment. *Psychoanalytic Dialogues*, 16, 61:619–537.

Green, A. (1995). Has Sexuality Anything To Do With Psychoanalysis?. *International Journal of Psychoanalysis*, 76:871–883.

Grosz, E. (1994). *Volatile Bodies: Towards a Corporeal Feminism.* London: Routledge.

Heidegger, M. (1975). The Thing. In: *Poetry, Language, Thought* (A. Hofstadter, Trans.) (pp.165–186). New York: Harper Colophon. (Original work published 1950).

Kristeva, J. (1999). *In De La Passion.* Ed: J. Andre Paris: Presses Universitaires de France.

Kuchuck, S. (2012). Please (Don't) Want Me: The Therapeutic Action of Male Sexual Desire in the Treatment of Heterosexual Men. *Contemporary Psychoanalysis*, 48:544–562.

Laplanche, J. (1987). *New Foundations for Psychoanalysis* (D. Macey, Trans.). Oxford: Blackwell, 1989.

——, (1992). *Seduction, Translation, Drives*. (J. Fletcher & M. Stanton, Eds.). Institute of Contemporary Arts, London, pp. 161–167.

——, (1995). Seduction, Persecution and Revelation. *International Journal of Psychoanalysis*, 76:663–682.

Lyons-Ruth, K. (1999). The Two-Person Unconscious: Intersubjective Dialogue, Enactive Relational Representation, and the Emergence of New Forms of Relational Organization. *Psychoanalytic Inquiry*, 19:576–617.

Lyons-Ruth, K. & Boston Change Process Study Group. (2001). The Emergence of New Experiences: Relational Improvisation, Recognition Process, and Nonlinear Change in Psychoanalytic Psychotherapy. *Psychologist/Psychoanalyst*, 21, 4:13–17.

Miller, J. P., Jr. (1990). Relational Concepts in Psychoanalysis. An Integration: By Stephen A. Mitchell. *International Journal of Psychoanalysis*, 71:727–731.

Mitchell, S. A. (1988). *Relational Concepts in Psychoanalysis: An Integration*. Cambridge, MA: Harvard University Press.

Mitchell, S. A. (1997). Psychoanalysis and the Degradation of Romance. *Psychoanalytic Dialogues*, 7:23–41.

Mitchell, S. A. (2002). *Can Love Last? The State of Romance over time*. New York: Basic Books.

Roth, M. & Durban. J. (2013). *Melanie Klein: Selected Writing 2*. Tel Aviv: Bookworm.

Seligman, S. (1999). Integrating Kleinian Theory and Intersubjective Infant Research: Observing Projective Identification. *Psychoanalytic Dialogues*, 9:129–159.

Slavin, J. H. (2002). The Innocence of Sexuality. *Psychoanal Quarterly*, 71:51–79.

Slavin, M. O. (2006). Tanya and the Adaptive Dialectic of Romantic Passion and Secure Attachment. *Psychoanalytic Dialogues*, 16:793–824.

Slochower, J. (2013). Psychoanalytic Mommies and Psychoanalytic Babies: A Long View. *Contemporary Psychoanalysis*, 49:606–628.

Smith, H. (1976). *Forgotten Truth*. New York: Harper & Row.

Stein, R. (1998). The Enigmatic Dimension of Sexual Experience: The "Otherness" of Sexuality and Primal Seduction. *Psychoanal Quarterly*, 67:594–625.

Stern. D. (1985). *The Interpersonal World of the Infant*. New York: Basic Books.

Stern, D. N., Sander, L. W., Nahum, J. P., Harrison, A. M., Lyons-Rith, K., Morgan, A. C. et al. (1998). Noninterpretive Mechanism in Psychoanalytic Psychotherapy: The "Something More" than Interpretation. *International Journal of Psychoanalysis*, 79:903–921.

Stoller, R. J. (1985). *Observing the Erotic Imagination*. New Haven, CT: Yale University Press.

Stolorow, R. & Atwood, G. (1992*). Contexts of Being: The Intersubjective Foundations of Psychological Life*. Hillsdale, NJ: The Analytic Press.

Tronick, E. (1998). Dyadically Expended States of Consciousness and the Problem of Therapeutic Change. *Infant Mental Health Journal*, 19:290–299.

Wilber, K. (1998*). The Marriage of Sense and Soul: Integrating Science and Religion*. Boston, MA: Shambhala.

Chapter 8

Multiplicity and integrity

Does an anti-development tilt still exist in Relational psychoanalysis?

Donna M. Orange

Nothing, Kurt Lewin loved to remind us, is so practical as a good theory. But our theories, as Charles Sanders Peirce taught relentlessly,[1] need holding lightly as they always need correcting. The "contrite fallibilism" in which the pragmatists believed serves us well as we study the history of psychoanalysis, including the shorter history of relational approaches. It comes with a robust optimism that we can always learn more, both from our patients and from each other, within a community of scholars that embraces those who speak many languages, and who teach in ways we may not initially appreciate, verbally and nonverbally. In our attempts to improve our theories, we may make false steps, but we can try again.

Introduction

Here I will describe related aspects of the theorizing of Stephen Mitchell and Philip Bromberg, mark where I believe residual problems lie, and suggest a tentative solution using resources from my two disciplines of philosophy and psychoanalysis.

When Stephen Mitchell died, he had just completed a decade of intensive study of the work of Hans Loewald, his favorite psychoanalytic writer. Their rereading of Freud shows not only in the first two chapters of *Relationality* (S. A. Mitchell, 2000) but in its entire developmental cast. Mitchell, author of the disparaging phrase "developmental tilt," had reversed himself, seeming no longer concerned about infantilizing patients, and now—with Loewald, Bowlby, and Winnicott—envisioned psychoanalysis itself as a developmental process. What has become of Mitchell's reversal since his death? Perhaps the clinical thinking of Jody Davies, with her receptivity to the younger voices of the patient, as well as the Winnicottian work of Slochower and Ogden, have taken up this reversal. The wildly popular turn to "multiple self-state" talk, however, I regard as ambiguous and problematic. While it advances our sense of the complexity of experience and replaces simple talk of regression, it may also occlude a developmental sensibility such as that possessed in common by Loewald, Winnicott, and Kohut, all voices needed within the relational chorus.

I will further suggest that this shared developmental sensibility, toward which Mitchell was firmly turning in his last years and which has faded again since we lost him, is a foundational element of the "ethical turn" in psychoanalysis, being written about by Cushman (2007), Layton (2009), Leary (2000), Baraitser (2008), and others. Psychoanalysis as process of mourning and integration relates closely to moral integrity and courage.

In this context I must mention the disdain for an ethic of care in some relational circles, as well as the exclusionary "not relational enough" and "that's not psychoanalysis" attitudes, that betray the anti-developmental tilt. By contrast, my essay will advocate compassion for the vulnerable and suffering child within our patients and ourselves, as well as toward the burning world within which we are all living and dying.

Mitchell: the influence of Loewald and the developmental turn

Like most analysts trained in the interpersonalist tradition, the young Stephen Mitchell lost no love on developmentalists such as Winnicott and Kohut. Though the critique began in his revolutionary book with Jay Greenberg (Greenberg & Mitchell, 1983), Mitchell published his now famous paper (1984) on "developmental tilt," making his objections much clearer, just a few months later. By "developmental tilt" he meant "accommodative strategy," (in the book "mixed-model"), that is, keeping drive theory and the Oedipus complex intact, but installing object relations earlier and deeper.[2] For him, primary practitioners of this approach now included Klein, Balint, Mahler, Guntrip, Winnicott, and Kohut. These theorists saw relational needs as infantile and regressive. Their practice, in the younger Mitchell's view, tended to see patients as passive victims of early deprivation, and analysts as all-good providers. In Mitchell's view, the more consistent theorists he preferred—Fairbairn, Sullivan, and Bowlby—understood relational needs—and even more mature dependency needs—as simply human. Unfortunately, he thought, their theorizing lost all the elegance and complexity of Freudian theory and tradition. In 1984, prior to the full development of his own relational perspective, Mitchell simply laid out this drawback with great clarity; he did not yet suggest his alternative concept.

In the next years, Mitchell's important books (1988, 1993, 1997) developed the *relational matrix* as the theoretical and clinical basis of what was coming to be called relational psychoanalysis. In 1987 he defined it thus:

> The relational model rests on the premise that the repetitive patterns within human experience are not derived, as in the drive model, from a pursuit of secret pleasures (nor, as in Freud's post 1920 understanding, from the automatic workings of the death instinct), but from a pervasive tendency to preserve the continuity, connections, familiarity of one's personal world. There is a powerful need to preserve an abiding sense of oneself as associated with, positioned in terms of, related to, a matrix of other people, both in terms of actual transactions as well as internal presences. The basic relational configurations have, by definition, three dimensions—the self, the other, and the space between them. There is no "object" in a psychologically meaningful sense without some particular sense of oneself in relation to it. There is no "self", in a psychologically meaningful sense, in isolation, outside a matrix of relations with others. Neither the self nor the object are meaningful dynamic concepts without presupposing some sense of psychical space in which they interact, in which they do things with or to each other. These dimensions are interwoven in a subtle fashion, knitting together the analysand's subjective experience and psychological world.
>
> (1987, p. 403)

The word matrix appears twice here: "a matrix of other people" and "a matrix of relations with others," as if the matrix were always contemporary.

But earlier, in discussions of Kohut, Mitchell had used the expression "maternal-child matrix" (S. A. Mitchell, 1979) and of Winnicott, "infant/ mother matrix" (S. A. Mitchell, 1983). So his capacity to absorb the profoundly developmental psychoanalysis of Hans Loewald, and to identify his relational matrix with Loewald's "primordial density" should not surprise us.

Arguably, what has developed since in contemporary psychoanalysis— whether it uses this language or not—stands in relation to this idea of the relational matrix.[3] Easy to reference is the work of those who write of thirdness in one form or another (Aron, 2006; Benjamin, 2004; Gerson, 2009; Knoblauch, 1999; Muller, 1999; T. H. Ogden, 1994), though clearly these authors differ widely in their use of the term. (None of these authors, however, to my ears, gives thirdness the profound developmental cast that Mitchell's matrix had by the end of his life). In addition, pervasive assumptions of mutual engagement, involvement, and responsibility in analysis owe their origin to Mitchell's relational matrix. His invisible influence may pervade us as insistently as does Freud's.

His pioneering voice, however, may mask his quieter path as a devoted and scholarly student of the history of psychoanalysis, one that emerged clearly in his *Relationality*, a book that appeared so close to his death that most of us never had the opportunity to engage him in conversation about the changes in his thinking that it signaled. He devoted the first two chapters of this book to the work of Hans Loewald, whose work he had been reading and rereading for more than a decade (S. Mitchell, 2004) with great "joy." He told us that Loewald had become "my favorite psychoanalytic writer." Who was this Loewald, and who was he to Mitchell?

Loewald gathered up the brilliant fragments of Freud's thinking— pieces Freud had left lying around as he inventively confronted new clinical and theoretical conundrums—and used what he learned from Heidegger to weave them into a whole.[4] Loewald saw us always trying to refind our original unitary experience, our "primordial density"—the same one Winnicott studied as "no such thing as an infant"—from which we later differentiate as we become ourselves in relation to others. (Balint would have called it the "harmonious interpenetrating mixup" (Balint, 1992)). Loewald reinterpreted drive theory much as contemporary evolutionary biology does, not as a theory of struggle, but as Eros (Lear, 1998), a striving to refind the original oneness. Instincts for him emerge from the integration of infant and environment. Basic concepts in psychoanalytic theory lose their strangeness in Loewald's hands—in part because he read and thought in Freud's German, and constantly attempted to escape what we might call the standardized edition. "Cathexis" becomes organizing activity, bonding, sometimes even love. "Primary process" becomes the richness of our ongoing access to our earliest and embodied mother-infant experience, constantly alternating with the differentiated, more organized and linguistic life. "Secondary" in Loewald's view gains the connotation of secondary as coming later in the process of psychological organization and integration of experience. "Primary process" completely loses its shamefulness and becomes the rich resource of imaginative, cultural, and even, perhaps, transcendent life. A close reader of Freud who never left the American Psychoanalytic and never founded a school of thought, Loewald recognized the baby-watchers and Winnicott as his kindred spirits.

No wonder. As a phenomenologist, Loewald had profoundly rethought temporality. Past, present, and future interpenetrate so much that he could welcome primary process as the source of our creativity and of religious life. (He repeatedly expressed regret that Freud could see so little constructive use for religion.)

How did Loewald accomplish all this rethinking? *Nachträglich*, that is, backwards. He took a late text of Freud, from *Civilization and its Discontents*, and used it to read everything that came before, as if to say, "Here is the deeper meaning in Freud that he would have developed, if he had had time." Freud wrote:

> An infant at the breast does not as yet distinguish his ego from the external world as the source of the sensations flowing in upon him. He gradually learns to do so, in response to various promptings. . . . In this way, then, the ego detaches itself from the external world. Or, to put it more correctly, originally the ego includes everything, later it separates off an external world from itself.
>
> (Freud & Strachey, 2005, pp. 66–68)

This text in hand, Loewald relationalized Freud and argued in his most famous paper (H. W. Loewald, 1960) that the therapeutic power of psychoanalysis resulted from the relational, that is, transferential, transformation of old miseries. The analyst, far from a detached and distant mirror, makes himself available to the patient for the ego-developmental process of transference, of which Loewald wrote:

> Without such transference—of the intensity of the unconscious, of the infantile ways of experiencing life which have no language and little organization, but the indestructibility and power of the origins of life—to the preconscious and to present-day life and contemporary objects—without such transference, or to the extent to which such transference miscarries, human life becomes sterile and an empty shell. On the other hand, the unconscious needs present-day external reality (objects) and present-day psychic reality (the preconscious) for its own continuity, lest it be condemned to live the shadow-life of ghosts or to destroy life.
>
> (Loewald, 2000, p. 250)

The most famous passage in this paper, so important to Mitchell that he named his paper on Loewald (S. A. Mitchell, 1998) after it, is always worth rereading:

> The transference neurosis, in the technical sense of the establishment and resolution of it in the analytic process, is due to the blood of recognition which the patient's unconscious is given to taste—so that the old ghosts may reawaken to life. Those who know ghosts tell us that they long to be released from their ghost-life and led to rest as ancestors. As ancestors they live forth in the present generation, while as ghosts they are compelled to haunt the present generation with their shadow-life. Transference is pathological in so far as the unconscious is a crowd of ghosts [my favorite definition of unconsciousness], and this is the beginning of the transference neurosis in analysis: ghosts of the unconscious, imprisoned by defenses but haunting the patient in the dark of his defenses and symptoms, are allowed to taste blood, are let loose. In the daylight of analysis the ghosts of the unconscious are laid and led to rest as ancestors whose power is taken over and transformed into the newer intensity of present life, of the secondary process and contemporary objects.
>
> (Loewald, 2000, pp. 248–249)

First, like the infant researchers, particularly Daniel Stern (1985) Loewald believed that we organize and heal ourselves through "internalization" especially in the areas that Freudians speak about in the region of superego development. No longer compelled like an automaton, the growing child or adult has made moral values her or his own: "A sense of self begins to emerge with increasing internalization, leading to the development of a sense of self-responsibility with the formation of the superego and the shouldering of guilt" (Loewald, 1985, p. 437). In analysis, he believed, the work of mourning indispensably linked up with resuming the processes of internalization:

> The relinquishment of external objects and their internalization involves a process of separation, of loss and of restitution in many ways similar to mourning. During analysis, problems of separation and mourning come to the fore in a specific way at times of interruption and most particularly in the terminal phases of treatment.
>
> (Loewald, 2007, p. 1114)

Mourning internalizes what must be relinquished, and integrates a personal life, a moral life, as he would later say.

Now, in the 1990s, in addition to Sullivan and Fairbairn, Mitchell had found a third proto-relational theorist, one who had become his "favorite psychoanalytic writer." Loewald had linked all the disparate experiences with which analysts and patients struggle with the original oneness, and understood the analytic process itself as linking. Mitchell elegantly condensed Loewald's account of psychopathology as the primal density lost:

> ... in Loewald's view, psychopathology, most broadly conceived, represents an imbalance between the centrifugal and centripetal forces of mind. In psychosis, the primal density undermines the capacity to make adaptive, normative distinctions between inside and outside, self and other, actuality and fantasy, past and present. In neurosis or, Loewald occasionally suggests, the normative adaptation to our scientistic, hypertechnologized world, the constituents of mind have drifted too far apart from their original dense unity: Inside and outside become separate, impermeable domains; self and other are experienced

in isolation from each other; actuality is disconnected from fantasy; and the past has become remote from a shallow, passionless present.

(S. A. Mitchell, 1998, p. 826)

Mitchell, restored to continuity with Freud by his immersion in Loewald, began to study attachment theory seriously, and to read Winnicott with an ear for "the core of the individual in a solitary privacy" (S. A. Mitchell, 2000, p. 87), for a similar sense of an individual's development, as well as for the differences regarding illusion and fantasy.

Bromberg on multiple self-states

Even before Greenberg and Mitchell shook the world for so many of us, or rather, gave us a way to think about our doubts and hopes, Bromberg was writing about regression (P. M. Bromberg, 1979)—a subversive activity for an interpersonalist, and a developmental question whether considered classically or from an object relations point of view—and corresponding, as we now know, with the radical Merton Gill (P. Bromberg, 2011). He also writes (P. Bromberg, 2013) of his affection for Mitchell, and we may assume, Mitchell's for him. At this early juncture, Bromberg seems to have seen regression as indicating almost precisely the developmental view of psychoanalysis that I am attributing to Loewald and to the later Mitchell:

> But regardless of how "deep" the regression is, I am suggesting that regression in the sense that I am using it here, is not a concept limited to analytic patients having severe ego impairment, but is a fundamental component to psychoanalysis in general, and the interpersonal approach in particular. The ego (or self) in order to grow, must voluntarily allow itself to become less than intact—to regress. Empirically, this is one way of defining regression in the service of the ego.
>
> (P. M. Bromberg, 1979, p. 653)[5]

Trained at the William Alanson White institute, Mitchell and Bromberg in the late 1970s and early 1980s were working their way toward integration of psychoanalytic perspectives from similar beginnings. Adrienne Harris writes of this period:

One of the fascinating puzzles for me has been the sea change in Mitchell in reapproaching problems of development and early experience, that is, his move away, at the end of his life, from the antidevelopmental tilt of his first relational work. I see now that Bromberg's work on regression was part of the preamble to those shifts in Mitchell. Certainly later on, the reemergence of Bowlby and attachment theory played a role in changes in Mitchell's preoccupations, but what Bromberg was doing, we can see, was crucial for his own work, but I also believe contributed to shifts in Mitchell's as well.

(Harris & Bass, 2011, p. 242)

Like most readers of Mitchell's last work, Harris here either misses or ignores his "favorite psychoanalytic writer" (Loewald).[6] Still, she makes a fascinating suggestion: the possibility that Bromberg planted something in his conversations with Mitchell, something that Mitchell early on could not take up but later did with a vengeance, and something that Bromberg himself later downplayed in favor of the less developmental concept of dissociation. Whether she would see in her own idea what I do, I cannot say, but nonetheless, I find it fruitful for tracing what seems to have occurred.

Beyond popular, multiple self-state theory (P. M. Bromberg, 1991, 1994, 1996) has become axiomatic in contemporary relational psychoanalysis, and in disciplines such as religious studies (Cooper-White, 2007). In an amazing metaphor, Bromberg imagines different, dissociated regions in the patient to which the analyst gains passports. The basic experience to which this theory refers, described originally by Harry Stack Sullivan, rejects particular emotions, motivations, actions, or traumatic residues as "not-me!" Bromberg explains the goal for such treatment:

Optimal mental functioning consists in a person's being able to access multiple self-states conflictually, and psychoanalytic treatment must provide a favorable context for facilitating internal communication between disjunctive states that are kept sequestered from each other dissociatively.

(P. Bromberg, 2009, p. 350)

Writers of clinical and applied psychoanalysis have used this concept routinely in recent years (e.g. G. Bass, 2002; Chefetz, 2003; J. M. Davies,

1996; Harris, 1996; Hirsch, 1997; Yerushalmi, 2001), without much attention to what may be lost, or to their corollary assumption that such talk implies that no central, organizing, or responsible personality exists. Yet Bromberg himself spoke, at least in the early years of this theory, quite otherwise:

> We count on the existence in the patient of a cohesive core personality that feels to us and to the patient more or less like the same person regardless of moment-to-moment shifts in self-state, alterations in mental functioning, or even the unanticipated emergence of dissociated phenomena that Sullivan (1953) calls "not-me" experience.
>
> (P. M. Bromberg, 1991, p. 403)

Matters become confusing, both phenomenologically and clinically, when extreme splits occur, with amnesia, as those who work clinically with survivors of torture and combat, extreme child abuse, genocides, and the like, can attest. Are we still speaking of the multiple self-states these writers so easily attribute to all of us? Where is the unifying personality when the spouse and children say "I don't know him anymore"? What about the patient who returns the next day and remembers nothing whatever of the previous day's session when she had relived a gang rape? Who is the patient, and who bears responsibility for what this patient promises, and does, and says? All these questions arise when we imagine that there exists, or does not exist, a central personality. In addition, of course, Bromberg and those he has inspired have developed extremely useful reflections on the intersubjective processes involved in many forms of dissociation, especially those we see in clinical work.

But we should note that these questions lie in different realms of discourse: (1) the philosophical and the ethical disputes about human identity that John Riker (2013) reviews for us, and that Charles Taylor laid out so masterfully in his *Sources of the Self* (1989); (2) the speculative (metapsychological) questions about what lies behind the clinical phenomena—a unitary totality or prime mover, a cluster of self-states, both, an emergent personality organization, and so on, and (3) the experiential clinical phenomena themselves, as describable from both sides. Our difficulties, I think, lie in our failure to distinguish these.

Distinctions, however, are the stock in trade of philosophers, so here we go. Let us look first at dissociation, a word used at least since Pierre Janet. In current psychoanalysis it has come to have a cluster of meanings that Ludwig Wittgenstein would have described as "family resemblance".[7] From full amnesia after an auto accident, to loss of memory while travelling because preoccupied with another problem, to rejection of aspects of one's emotional life as "not-me"—all these phenomena and more are being named dissociation. Multiple self-state theory, I would suggest, falls into a logical trap when it argues from a cluster of dissociative phenomena that have only a "family resemblance" with each other as if we could attribute this concept to everybody, and then reasons that humans cannot, *and should not*, strive for good-enough personality integration. This mode of clinical thinking tends to suggest that dialogue with ourselves cannot lead to some sense that "this is what *I* believe", and "these things are important to *me.*" We will return to the ethical problems generated by this "cannot."

Secondly, let us turn to the evidence adduced for multiple self-state theory. Bromberg writes:

> There is now abundant evidence that the psyche does not start as an integrated whole, but is nonunitary in origin—a mental structure that begins and continues as a multiplicity of self-states that maturationally attain a feeling of coherence which overrides the awareness of discontinuity (Bromberg, 1993, p. 162). This leads to the experience of a cohesive sense of personal identity and the necessary illusion of being "one self."
>
> (P. M. Bromberg, 1994, p. 521)

And what, exactly, is this "abundant evidence"? He continues:

> For psychoanalysts, this view of the mind has been supported by psychoanalytically oriented infant studies such as those by Emde, Gaensbaure, and Harmon (1976), Sander (1977), Stern (1985), Wolff (1987), and Beebe and Lachmann (1992), but the most direct support has come from nonanalytic empirical research into normal and pathological adult mental functioning—research representing a wide range of disciplines and research centers.
>
> (p. 521)

He then goes on to cite the studies by Frank Putnam (1988) of extreme dissociation that would now be diagnosed as Dissociative Identity Disorder and Complex Post-Traumatic Stress Disorders, and argues from these that mind is essentially multiple and self-experience illusory.

The argument for contemporaneous multiplicity persuades because it establishes continuity between extreme psychopathology and everyday human experiences, just as Freud did when he invented psychoanalysis. Dramatic and traumatic suffering draw closer to our ordinary struggles. "We are all more simply human than otherwise" (Sullivan & Mullahy, 1948, p. 16). But in this case we may need to hear the voice of Wittgenstein reminding us that the king in chess and the King of England function quite differently, though they share the same name. Not only dissociation may be a matter of family resemblances, but so may experiences of multiplicity generally.

Further, the "abundant evidence" from developmental studies for mind as multiple concurrent self-states, and mental health defined as the capacity to "stand in the spaces" between them, needs a close look. Unfortunately, Daniel Stern and Lou Sander are no longer with us, but we can consult their work. Stern's[8] classic work (1985) entirely concerns the human development of a sense of self, and to my reading, contains no hint that, at that time, he would have agreed that humans should give up on the project of personal integration. Yes, he differs with Winnicott and Loewald on the original oneness, but like them, pictures a human being always in search of integration. His later, more phenomenological work, on the developmental impact of the present-moment encounter and on the vitality affects, as well as his leadership of the attachment-focused Boston Process of Change Study Group, complexifies but does not abandon his earlier work.

Lou Sander, giant of infant research, worked, as does Bromberg, from the perspective of nonlinear self-organizing systems and complexity theories. For Sander, these theories best explained what he saw in development about identity emerging from recognition (Sander, 1995), and well accorded with what he had learned from Winnicott:

I know of no better description of a process of recognition than that of the process Winnicott (1972) describes. He describes, and illustrates with many case examples, the interactive process between therapist and child that goes on as each alternates drawings in the game he calls "squiggles." Winnicott details the drawings by which each embellishes the squiggle of the other, within the context of Winnicott's observations, to bring them both to a moment of shared awareness as the child becomes aware that another is aware of what the child is aware within. This is a moment of specificity in recognition that Winnicott called the "sacred moment"—a "moment of meeting" that involves a new coherence in the child's experiencing of both its inner and its outer worlds of awareness. The consultations Winnicott describes were often single diagnostic sessions, but if the "sacred moment" of being "known" was reached, there ensued a change in the child's self-regulatory organization that endured over many years, even from that single experience. Recurrence of such moments provides the conditions within which one comes to "know" oneself as one is "known." With recurrence and the brain's inherent construction of expectancy, it is a small step to Erikson's (1950) definition of identity as an "accrued confidence that inner sameness and continuity are matched by the sameness and continuity of one's meaning for others".

(p. 228)

Gradually, both Winnicott and Sander believed, in good-enough developmental conditions, a sense of a "true self"—as contrasted with the "false self" of compliance—would prevail.

Where Bromberg generalizes from his observations "the normal nonlinearity of the human mind" (P. M. Bromberg, 1996, p. 529), and believes that clinically "what is required is that the multiple realities being held by different self-states find opportunity for linkage" (p. 543), Sander finds a lifelong relational search for Eriksonian identity. It seems a stretch to cite his thinking as evidence for Bromberg's views.

Beebe and Lachmann's thinking, closely related to that of Stern and Sander, similarly describes the development of coherence and incoherence of self-experience depending on the infant's relational situation. In contrast to multiple self-state theory, Lachmann draws a clinical theory that presumes:

A process model of self as singular, striving for integration, and temporally continuous. This self is never static, but is constantly being updated in interactions that require the regulation of affects, arousal, and perceptions in a context, and with a background, of responsive, contingent, mutual regulation. Shifting in different contexts, the integrated self can prioritize experiences, embrace a range of conflicts, and tolerate disparate affect states.

(Lachmann, 1996, p. 610)

Clearly Lachmann, like Stern and Sander, finds in infant research "abundant evidence" for complex self-experience always in process of integration, but he would reject the uses to which Bromberg and other adherents of multiple self-state theory are putting his work. (Actually I believe Bromberg finds kinship with these infant researchers not because they provide evidence for multiple-self-state theory, but because he himself never really abandoned a developmental perspective [see for example Philip M. Bromberg, 1998, p. 90]).

Problems with multiple self-state theory

Beyond the weaknesses in the arguments adduced to support this theory, I believe it has serious inherent problems: 1) it returns relational psycho-analysis, even if unintentionally, to its early anti-developmental tilt; 2) it evades the problems of human finitude and mourning; and worst of all, 3) it fails to ground and support ethical subjectivity. These are serious charges, so let us fill them out.

1)

With important exceptions (A. Bass, 2009; J. Davies, 2009; Grand, 2010; D. M. Orange, 2011; Slochower, 2013)[9] it seems to me that relational analysis has largely returned to the anti-developmental tilt of the late 1980's, and forgotten the radical move of Mitchell's last years. Adopting a developmental perspective with Winnicott, Loewald, Kohut, Bowlby, Fairbairn, and the Mitchell of his last years, means seeing the analytic process itself as a developmental process. In the words of Heinrich Racker:

I close this section on the analyst's internal position by saying that the patient can only be expected to accept the re-experiencing of childhood if the analyst is prepared to accept fully his new paternity, to admit fully affection for his new children, and to struggle for a new and better childhood, 'calling upon all the available mental forces' (S. Freud, 1917). His task consists ideally in a constant and lively interest and continuous empathy—with the patient's psychological happenings, in a metapsychological analysis of every mental expression and movement, his principal attention and energy being directed towards understanding the transference (towards the always present 'new childhood') and over-coming its pathological aspects by means of adequate interpretations.

(Racker, 1968, p. 33)

It seems safe to say that contemporary psychoanalysis (Mitchell-inspired relationalists, relational self-psychologists, contemporary Freudians, and others) generally agrees with Racker, though developmentalists' attitudes may be diversely expressed. Analysts begin to write of "analytic love" (D. Shaw, 2003), and to remember Sandor Ferenczi not only for experi-ments in mutual analysis, but for his full-throated advocacy of the child in the adult patient (S. Ferenczi, 1931, 1949).

Multiple self-state theory, too, recognizes that many patients dissoci-ate[10], that is, split themselves, to cope with relational trauma, often of developmental origin, very often transgenerationally transmitted. Indeed, the theory intends to explain how patients and analysts evoke and catalyze each other's splits. The theory's official adherence to nonlinear temporality combined with the here-and-now doctrine inherited from interpersonalist psychoanalysis, however, makes it difficult to see the analytic process itself as developmental. If development requires a linear concept of time—as it does not for Stern, Sander, Beebe and Lachmann, or Loewald—this theory can aim at no more than standing in the spaces (P. M. Bromberg, 1996) between one's self-states.

Moreover, as Rich Chefetz asks (Chefetz & Bromberg, 2004), and I wonder, especially reading Sue Grand (Grand, 2000), whether such "standing between" takes the extreme traumatic states of the soul-murdered (Shengold, 1989) or the drowned (Levi, 1988) seriously. Whether we work with perpetrators as Grand and other colleagues do, or with victims of malignant narcissists (D. Shaw, 2014) who believe themselves benevolent but treat us cruelly, questions of responsibility arise that stretch multiple self-state theory.

But what if development, as Stern, Sander, Beebe and Lachmann all believed with Thelen and Smith's classic (1996) is itself nonlinear and complex? What if the *Nachträglichkeit* left to us by Freud, and so widely studied today (Birksted-Breen, 2003; Dahl, 2010) can now be understood as intersubjective *Nachträglichkeit*, without complete loss of the search for personal integration and ethical integrity that seems so fragile in today's world? This topic deserves more development than space allows here.

2)

Mourning and the recognition of finitude (Hoffman, 2000; Stolorow, 2007) require of each of us more integration than simply letting the self-states co-exist. Mourning means realizing that people and places and aspects of myself are actually and irretrievably lost, saving and treasuring what I can, and letting go of the rest. Freud began to teach us about this; Loewald and Mitchell continued. Accepting finitude, both death and vulnerability, means that someone knows that the many "not-me's", including those generated in early years (S. Ferenczi, 1949), belong to a someone who will not go on forever, and meanwhile has ever more limited capacities and future, even while expanding in other respects.

3)

How can one who stands in the spaces—the idealized outcome of much contemporary relational psychoanalysis—take an ethical stand against injustice? Even contemporary psychanalysts bear the legacy of those who claimed not to know what the Nazi regime or the Pinochet regime were doing. Likewise we psychoanalysts, like many of our fellow citizens, live in a comfortable bubble of "multiple self-states" that I call double-consciousness (D. Orange, 2016a), knowing and not knowing that we are destroying both our Earth and even sooner, our poorest brothers and sisters. A theory that valorizes maintaining split consciousness, and ridicules the search for personal integrity and integrated selfhood, just because we often feel "of two minds," may fail crucial tests of civic courage. I doubt that colleagues who speak glibly of multiple self-states have truly thought through the ethical and political implications of this theory.

Yet, ever more we hear voices within relational psychoanalysis crying for social justice: for those marginalized by gender and sexual orientation, by poverty and race, by exclusion of every kind. We feel more and more called to see and hear those others to whom our privileged position keeps us blind and deaf, and our own implication in their plight. Does preference for dissociation over developmental sensibility evade this ethical sensibility? If we cannot hear the voices of the children within ourselves and each other, to which developmental psychoanalysis attunes us, how will we hear the cries of the hungry and destitute? What does the struggle for development of personal ethics involve? Easily I can watch and listen as the parts of myself, called "self-states," debate the pros and cons of a political problem, and of my potential involvement. But when do I say: Here I stand, I can do no other? How does self-state theory account for the righteous gentiles, honored at Yad Vashem, who risked everything to protect their Jewish neighbors? How does it understand the clarity of a Nelson Mandela, who remained in prison for several extra years rather than compromise the full political equality of his people? How does it describe my activist neighbor, who goes to prison for protesting the U.S. government's treatment of undocumented immigrants, or the psychologist who confronts the involvement of other psychologists in torture?

No one would argue that one needs a fully unitary sense of self, much less a linear stage theory of development, to do these things; on the contrary, we define moral and civic courage by reference to the capacity to face down our fears for the sake of something that centrally matters to us. Now perhaps we come closer to the heart of the problem. "Self" eludes definition, as does "identity," many philosophers and psychologists would agree, though in daily life we Westerners use these concepts constantly and informally. Probably we need them for our implicit moral discourse.[11] When a patient tells me that he or she has no self, or no sense of self, I sometimes ask, "What really matters to you?" or "What do you most care about?" After some time, if the answers come out, I will say, well, that's what it is to be yourself, to be someone who has a strong sense of what matters to you. We can build on that, and see what else there is, and what else troubles you.

If, however, the answer comes that at times he seems to care for those in his life, and at other moments behaves as if they didn't exist or matter, and has no idea why, then do I conclude that he has multiple selves, or instead, that he (the speaker) is concerned about something seriously awry in his life for which he is seeking help? One of my first patients came to me because she found that someone was taking notes in her classes in her handwriting, but she had no memory of having attended these classes. I did not conclude that she had multiple selves, but understood that she (the patient) was someone seeking to live as one person. She did not want to be multiple selves, but an integrated person. She wanted to be sure that she could be responsible for everything that was done in her name.

Who is the patient in multiple self-state theory? Are there several, and several analysts? If an analyst holds the assumptions of this theory, what becomes of the patient who arrives seeking greater personal integration and ethical integrity? Will she be persuaded to abandon her search? To return to our earlier question, can great personal courage emerge from this kind of thinking and treatment? Am I, as patient or analyst, to be satisfied with standing in the spaces between my self-state in which I live in the entitlement of white privilege and one which hears the voices of Maya Angelou and Martin Luther King? Must I not struggle beyond standing in the spaces?

Let us consider, for example, Hans and Sophie Scholl. These student members of the White Rose resistance, killed in München in 1943, embodied the empathy and serenity that Heinz Kohut attributed to a fully integrated value system. A recent film, *Sophie Scholl: the Final Days*, based on newly discovered documents, convinced me of the rightness of Kohut's view of these students. Here is Sophie's last dream: After she had been aroused from her sleep to face the day of her execution, she told the following dream to her cellmate. In the dream, she said, "it was a sunny day, and I carried a child, dressed in a long white garment, to be baptized. The path to the church led up a steep mountain; but I held the child firmly and securely. Suddenly there was a crevasse gaping in front of me. I had barely enough time to deposit the child on the far side of it, which I managed to do safely—then I fell into the depth" (Kohut, 1985). "After Sophie had told her dream she immediately explained its meaning to her companion. The child, she said, is our leading idea. It will live on and make its way to fulfillment despite obstacles" (p. 21). Kohut reports further: "She went to her execution without a trace of fear" (p. 21). (Winnicott's description of the good-enough conditions necessary for the developmental capacity for concern (Winnicott, 1965) supports Kohut's views here, I think).

It seems to me that Kohut's emphasis on civil courage as manifestation of robust selfhood makes clear the ethical implications of my concern here. Without making any metaphysical claims for self or identity, it seems important to express concern for the evasive potential in a clinical theory that suggests giving up on personal integration and integrity. Oh well, I can always say, my other self-state did it, or didn't let me do it. Bromberg himself provides a wonderful personal example of this process in his story (P. M. Bromberg, 1996) about the homeless man outside his window and the two coffee cups. His inner dialogue, probably familiar to all of us who have lived in urban settings, includes a reflection on the clinical relevance of this situation, and like most such reflections, is cut short. "Saved by the buzz!" We are left with the decentered self, allowed to evade the ethical question. Courage waits for another day. Of course, one might object, clinicians need all their courage just to face another day of sessions. True, but do our theories support a belief in ultimate courage? Do they prepare us to act, as the pragmatists taught, or only to stand in the spaces between alternatives and self-states?

Bromberg's most recent published statement (P. Bromberg, 2013), in honor of Stephen Mitchell, actually expresses an integrated return to his earlier views of psychoanalysis as developmental process, toward cohesive selfhood. Using Winnicott, he writes of the transformation of fantasying into imagination:

> For a person who is "imagining," the state of affairs is different; the person is experiencing the self as it now exists, *projected into the future*. Because the self being imagined is the same self that is doing the imagining, the person as he is *now* has the capacity to act into a future that is real to him *because the future that is imagined in the here-and-now is itself real*.
>
> (pp. 2–13)

Here we have psychoanalysis as a developmental process, creating a continuous sense of self that acts, not content to stand in the spaces. We must earnestly hope that the many users and quoters of multiple self-state theory will hear Philip Bromberg now. Like him and and like Stephen Mitchell, we may find the courage to hold our theories lightly.

Notes

1 . . . no matter how far science goes, those inferences which are uppermost in the mind of the investigator are very uncertain. They are on probation. They must have a fair trial and not be condemned till proved false beyond all reasonable doubt; and the moment that proof is reached, the investigator must be ready to abandon them without the slightest tenderness toward them. Thus, the scientific inquirer has to be always ready at a moment to abandon summarily all the theories to the study of which he has been devoting perhaps many years" (Peirce, 1998, p. 25).

2 Here I borrow from my discussion of Greenberg and Mitchell's view of Kohut (D. Orange, 2013).

3 It would be more than unjust to ignore the use by Thomas Ogden (Thomas H. Ogden, 1986) of *matrix*. His use of it suggests its etymological reference to the mother, and particularly refers to Winnicott. I do not know whether Mitchell and Ogden arrived at their uses of this word independently, but suspect that their uses may have influenced each other.

4 This section expands paragraphs on Loewald in D. Orange (2016b).

5 A similar reverence for needed regressive process, of course, shows up in Ferenczi (Ferenczi, 1931; Ferenczi & Dupont, 1988), so is enormously influential in contemporary psychoanalysis (cf Aron & Bushra, 1998), as well as in the creative confrontations with evil in the work of Sue Grand (Grand, 2000, 2010) where perpetrators and sufferers re-engage, strangely.

6 Why Loewald himself has been so ignored is another question, addressed by Lawrence Friedman (2008). Harris and Suchet (2002) clearly note this influence in their review of S. A. Mitchell (2000) as does Harris (2011).

7 Replacing univocal concepts that apply in the same way to everything they cover, and replacing categories to which people or things simply belong or not, he reminded us that in families, some members have similar eyes, other have similar noses, chins or hair. These features, he thought, allow us to recognize people as related even when no two of them have all the same features in common. He thought concepts, whether of colors or of theories, similarly overlapped. "[W]e see a complicated network of similarities overlapping and criss-crossing: sometimes overall similarities, sometimes similarities of detail" (Wittgenstein, 1953/2001, §66).

8 Interesting to note is that the expression "self-state" became prominent in Heinz Kohut's work on self-state dreams, and was then picked up by Stern and Sander in their developmental studies. They considered the work of psychoanalysis to concern the transformation of self-states.

9 I ask forgiveness if I should have cited others; these are examples.

10 One of my most seriously "dissociative" patients repeatedly objected to me that 'dissociation' is a misnomer; one rather *associates*, under the right relational conditions, to the traumatic past.

11 Postmodernism has been in question, not to say demise, in recent years, precisely because of the ethical problems of its intellectual giants: Heidegger, Paul de Man, and perhaps even Derrida. So it is not surprising that a psychoanalysis dependent on postmodern ideas might also founder on ethical shoals. It may embrace difference, but not know how to stand up against totalitarians.

References

Aron, L. (2006). Analytic Impasse and the Third: Clinical Implications of Intersubjectivity Theory. *International Journal of Psychoanalysis*, 87, 349–368.

Aron, L., & Bushra, A. (1998). Mutual Regression: Altered States in the Psychoanalytic Situation. *Journal of the American Psychoanalytic Association*, 46(2), 389–412.

Balint, M. (1992). *The Basic Fault: Therapeutic Aspects of Regression*. Evanston, IL: Northwestern University Press.

Baraitser, L. (2008). Mum's the Word: Intersubjectivity, Alterity, and the Maternal Subject. *Studies in Gender and Sexuality*, 9, 86–110.

Bass, A. (2009). The As-If Patient and the As-If Analyst. *Psychanalytic Quarterly*, 76, 365–386.

Bass, G. (2002). Something Is Happening Here. *Psychoanalytic Dialogues*, 12(5), 809–826.

Benjamin, J. (2004). Beyond Doer and Done to: An Intersubjective View of Thirdness. *Psychoanalytic Quarterly*, 73, 5–46.

Birksted-Breen, D. (2003). Time and the après-coup. *International Journal of Psychoanalysis*, 84, 1501–1515.

Bromberg, P. (2009). Truth, Human Relatedness, and the Analytic Process: An Interpersonal/Relational Perspective. *International Journal of Psychoanalysis*, 90, 3347–3361.

——, (2011). The Gill/Bromberg Correspondence. *Psychoanalytic Dialogues*, 21, 243–252.

——, (2013). Hidden in Plain Sight: Thoughts on Imagination and the Lived Unconscious. *Psychoanalytic Dialogues*, 23, 1–14.

Bromberg, P. M. (1991). On Knowing One's Patient Inside Out: The Aesthetics of Unconscious Communication. *Psychoanalytic Dialogues*, 1(4), 399–422.

——, (1994). "Speak! That I May See You": Some Reflections on Dissociation, Reality, and Psychoanalytic Listening. *Psychoanalytic Dialogues*, 4(4), 517–547.

——, (1996). Standing in the Spaces: The Multiplicity Of Self And The Psychoanalytic Relationship. *Contemporary Psychoanalysis*, 32, 509–535.

——, (1998). *Standing in the Spaces: Essays on Clinical Process, Trauma, and Dissociation*. Hillsdale, NJ: Analytic Press.

Chefetz, R. (2003). Healing Haunted Hearts: Toward a Model for Integrating Subjectivity: Commentary on papers by Philip Bromberg and Gerald Stechler. *Psychoanalytic Dialogues*, 13, 727–742.

Chefetz, R., & Bromberg, P. (2004). Talking with "Me" and "Not-Me": A Dialogue. *Contemporary Psychoanalysis*, 40, 409–464.

Cooper-White, P. (2007). *Many Voices: Pastoral Psychotherapy in Relational and Theological Perspective*. Minneapolis, MN: Fortress Press.

Cushman, P. (2007). A Burning World, an Absent God: Midrash, Hermeneutics, and Relational Psychoanalysis. *Contemporary Psychoanalysis*, 43, 47–88.

Dahl, G. (2010). Nachträglichkeit, Wiederholungszwang, Symbolisierung: Zur psychoanalytischen Deutung von primärprozesshaften Szenen. *Psyche. Zeitung für Psychoanalyse*, 64, 385–407.

Davies, J. (2009). Love Never Ends Well: Termination as the Fate of an Illusion: Commentary on Papers by Jill Salberg and Sue Grand. *Psychoanalytic Dialogues*, 19, 734–743.

Davies, J. M. (1996). Linking the "Pre-Analytic" with the Postclassical: Integration, Dissociation, and the Multiplicity of Unconscious Process. *Contemporary Psychoanalysis*, 32, 553–576.

Ferenczi, S. (1931). Child-Analysis in the Analysis of Adults. *International Journal of Psychoanalysis*, 12, 468–482.

——, (1949). Confusion of the Tongues Between the Adults and the Child— (The Language of Tenderness and of Passion). *International Journal of Psychoanalysis*, 30, 225–230.

Ferenczi, S., & Dupont, J. (1988). *The Clinical Diary of Sándor Ferenczi*. Cambridge, MA: Harvard University Press.

Freud, S. (1917). Introductory Lectures on Psycho-Analysis: 27th and 28th Lectures. *Standard Edition* (Vol. 16–17).

Freud, S., & Strachey, J. (2005). *Civilization and its Discontents*. New York: Norton.

Friedman, L. (2008). Loewald. *Journal of the American Psychoanalytic Association*, 56, 1105–1115.

Gerson, S. (2009). When the Third is Dead: Memory, Mourning, and Witnessing in the Aftermath of the Holocaust. *International Journal of Psychoanalysis*, 90, 1341–1357.

Grand, S. (2000). *The Reproduction of Evil: A Clinical and Cultural Perpsective*. Hillsdale, NJ: Analytic Press.

Grand, S. (2010). *The Hero in the Mirror: From Fear to Fortitude*. New York: Routledge.

Greenberg, J. R., & Mitchell, S. A. (1983). *Object Relations in Psychoanalytic Theory*. Cambridge, MA: Harvard University Press.

Harris, A. (1996). The Conceptual Power of Multiplicity. *Contemporary Psychoanalysis*, 32, 537–552.

Harris, A. (2011). The Relational Tradition: Landscape and Canon. *Journal of the American Psychanalytic Association*, 59, 701–735.

Harris, A., & Bass, A. (2011). Nachträglichkeit. *Psychoanalytic Dialogues*, 21, 239–242.

Harris, A., & Suchet, M. (2002). Relationality: From Attachment to Inter-subjectivity. Stephen A. Mitchell. Hillsdale, NJ: Analytic Press, 2000. [Book review]. *American Imago*, 59, 102–111.

Hirsch, I. (1997). The Widening of the Concept of Dissociation. *Journal of the American Academy of Psychoanalysis*, 25(4), 603–615.

Hoffman, I. Z. (2000). At Death's Door. *Psychoanalytic Dialogues*, 10(6), 823–846.

Knoblauch, S. H. (1999). The Third, Minding and Affecting. *Psychoanalytic Dialogues*, 9(1), 41–51.

Kohut, H. (1985). On Courage. In: C. Strozier, & E. Kohut (Eds.), *Self Psychology and the Humanities* (pp. 5–50). New York: Norton.

Lachmann, F. M. (1996). How Many Selves Make a Person? *Contemporary Psychoanalysis*, 32, 595–614.

Layton, L. (2009). Who's Responsible? Our Mutual Implication in Each Other's Suffering. *Psychoanalytic Dialogues*, 19, 105–120.

Lear, J. (1998). *Love and its Place in Nature: A Philosophical Interpretation of Freudian Psychoanalysis*. New Haven, CT: Yale University Press.

Leary, K. (2000). Racial Enactments in Dynamic Treatment. *Psychoanalytic Dialogues*, 10(4), 639–653.

Levi, P. (1988). *The Drowned and the Saved*. New York: Summit Books.

Loewald, H. (2007). Internalization, Separation, Mourning, and the Superego. *Psychoanlytic Quarterly*, 76, 1113–1133.

Loewald, H. W. (1960). On the Therapeutic Action of Psycho-Analysis. *International Journal of Psychoanalysis*, 41, 16–33.

——, (1985). Oedipus Complex and Development of Self. *Psychoanalytic Quarterly*, 54, 435–443.

——, (2000). *The Essential Loewald: Collected Papers and Monographs*. Hagerstown, MD: University Pub. Group.

Mitchell, S. (2004). My Psychoanalytic Journey. *Psychoanalytic Inquiry*, 24, 531–541.

Mitchell, S. A. (1979). Twilight of the Idols: Change and Preservation in the Writings of Heinz Kohut. *Contemporary Psychoanalysis*, 15, 170–189.

Mitchell, S. A. (1983). Reflections. *Contemporary Psychoanalysis*, 19, 133–139.

Mitchell, S. A. (1984). Object Relations Theories and the Developmental Tilt. *Contemporary Psychoanalysis*, 20, 473–499.

Mitchell, S. A. (1987). Discussion. *Contemporary Psychoanaylsis*, 23, 400–409.

Mitchell, S. A. (1988). *Relational Concepts in Psychoanalysis: An Integration.* Cambridge, MA: Harvard University Press.

Mitchell, S. A. (1993). *Hope and Dread in Psychoanalysis.* New York: BasicBooks.

Mitchell, S. A. (1997). *Influence and Autonomy in Psychoanalysis.* Hillsdale, NJ: Analytic Press.

Mitchell, S. A. (1998). From Ghosts to Ancestors: The Psychoanalytic Vision of Hans Loewald. *Psychoanalytic Dialogues,* 8(6), 825–855.

Mitchell, S. A. (2000). *Relationality: From Attachment to Intersubjectivity.* Hillsdale, NJ: Analytic Press.

Muller, J. P. (1999). The Third as Holding the Dyad. *Psychoanalytic Dialogues,* 9(4), 471–480.

Ogden, T. H. (1986). *The Matrix of the Mind: Object Relations and the Psychoanalytic Dialogue.* Northvale, NJ: J. Aronson.

———, (1994). The Analytic Third: Working with Intersubjective Clinical Facts. *International Journal of Psychoanalysis,* 75, 3–19.

Orange, D. (2013). Those Old Wineskins: Greenberg and Mitchell on Heinz Kohut's "Mixed Model". *Contemporary Psychoanalysis,* 49, 103–112.

———, (2016a). *Climate Crisis, Psychoanalysis, and Radical Ethics.* London: Routledge.

———, (2016b). *Nourishing the Inner Life of Clinicians and Humanitarians: The Ethical Turn in Psychoanalysis.* London and New York: Routledge.

Orange, D. M. (2011). *The Suffering Stranger: Hermeneutics for Everyday Clinical Practice.* New York: Routledge.

Peirce, C. (1998). *The Essential Peirce* (Vol. 2). Bloomington, IN: Indiana University Press.

Putnam, F. W. (1988). The Switch Process in Multiple Personality Disorder and Other State-Change Disorders. *Dissociation,* 1, 24–32.

Racker, E. (1968). *Transference and Counter-Transference.* New York: International Universities Press.

Riker, J. H. (2013). The Philosophical Importance of Kohut's Notion of the Self. *International Journal of Psychoanalytic Self Psychology,* 8, 495–504.

Sander, L. W. (1995). Identity and the Experience of Specificity in a Process of Recognition: Commentary on Seligman and Shanok. *Psychoanalytic Dialogues,* 5(4), 579–593.

Shaw, D. (2003). On the Therapeutic Action of Analytic Love. *Contemporary Psychoanalysis,* 39, 251–278.

———, (2014). *Traumatic Narcissism: Relational Systems of Subjugation.* New York: Routledge.

Shengold, L. (1989). *Soul Murder: The Effects of Childhood Abuse and Deprivation.* New Haven, CT: Yale University Press.

Slochower, J. A. (2013). *Holding and Psychoanalysis: A Relational Perspective* (2nd edition). Hove, UK: Routledge.

Stern, D. N. (1985). *The Interpersonal World of the Infant: A View From Psychoanalysis and Developmental Psychology*. New York: Basic Books.

Stolorow, R. D. (2007). *Trauma and Human Existence: Autobiographical, Psychoanalytic, and Philosophical Reflections*. New York: Analytic Press.

Sullivan, H. S., & Mullahy, P. (1948). *Conceptions of Modern Psychiatry*. London: Tavistock.

Taylor, C. (1989). *Sources of the Self: The Making of the Modern Identity*. Cambridge, MA: Harvard University Press.

Thelen, E., & Smith, L. B. (1994). *A Dynamic Systems Approach to the Development of Cognition and Action*. Cambridge, MA: MIT Press.

Winnicott, D. W. (1965). *The Maturational Processes and the Facilitating Environment: Studies in the Theory of Emotional Development*. New York: International Universities Press.

Wittgenstein, L. (1953/2001). *Philosophical Investigations* (G. E. M. Anscombe, Trans. Third, with revised English translation ed.). Oxford: Blackwell.

Yerushalmi, H. (2001). Self-States and Personal Growth in Analysis. *Contemporary Psychoanalysis*, 37(3), 471–488.

Chapter 9

Reflections on relational psychoanalysis: a work in progress

Origins and evolutions

Anthony Bass and Adrienne Harris

Introduction: We have been talking together about relational psycho-analysis for thirty years. We met when we were candidates at the NYU Postdoctoral Program and have worked together on many projects since the earliest days in the development of relational psychoanalysis. We worked for the establishment of the Relational Track at NYU in the 1980s, where we were both on the faculty in its early days. We were founding members of the editorial group that started *Psychoanalytic Dialogues* in 1991, along with Stephen Mitchell and Lewis Aron, founding directors of IARPP and the Stephen Mitchell Center for Relational Studies, have co-led a discussion group together with Jody Davies on relational psychoanalysis at the meeting of the American Psychoanalytic Association each year for more than a decade, and have shared in many other projects and discussions throughout our long professional lives, which have unfolded along with the short history of relational psychoanalysis. We felt that it would be interesting in the context of this book of critical perspectives and as a chance to look back to where we began and where we are heading as relational analysts, to develop a dialogue in print in which we would compare and contrast some of our reflections on the history of relational psychoanalysis, and our own engagement with it. In the dialogue that follows, we begin to explore our respective visions of its unfolding over its first three decades, our recollections of how it began and our perspectives on the ways in which it has thus far evolved. We discuss the potentials it has thus far realized, the obstacles we face, and our sense of where relational psychoanalysis might go from here. Like relational psychoanalysis itself, the dialogue that follows is a work in progress, in which our own personal subjectivities and differing interests and perspectives are evident, a snapshot of the very heterogeneity and diversity of thought represented in relational psychoanalysis, about which we write. It is the beginning of a new phase of a longstanding conversation that we hope will continue to develop over time. – TB

TB: It has been almost thirty years since we began to think about relational psychoanalysis. That is, since there was something that we designated relational psychoanalysis as many of us were beginning to define and develop it. We were both among the group that christened it as such. Among those present were a first generation of relational analysts, including Stephen Mitchell, Emanuel Ghent, and Philip Bromberg as mentors, and Lewis Aron, Jody Davies, Neil Altman, Jessica Benjamin, Joyce Slochower, Muriel Dimen, Sue Grand and many others, recent graduates, or newly appointed faculty at the New York University Postdoctoral Program in the 1980s. Many of us were interested in the underlying links and complementarities among diverse perspectives that emphasized object relations, interpersonal relations, subject relations, self-other relations, and the various permutations and combinations of relations that populated lives and minds, external and internal. In preparing to establish a home for this evolving conceptualization of psychoanalytic therapy at the NYU Postdoctoral Program, an idea emerged: Let's call this approach, 'Relational' for short.

Appreciating the ways in which psychoanalysis informed by interpersonal, object relational, intersubjective and self-psychological theories were compatible, sharing common therapeutic values and sensibilities promised to open up a new, more capacious space for psychoanalytic conversation, fostering freer access to the wide range of clinical ideas that analysts of different persuasions emphasized. The inspiration for such a project was the publication of the 1983 Greenberg/Mitchell text, *Object Relations Theory in Psychoanalysis*, a penetrating work of comparative psychoanalytic theory that compared and contrasted a wide range of theories that did not rely on Freud's drive theory as the primary point of departure for their theorizing. A further forum for such excavation in comparative psychoanalytic ideas arrived with the first publication in 1991 of the new relational journal, led by Stephen Mitchell, *Psychoanalytic*

Dialogues, The Journal of Relational Perspectives, whose mission included the engagement of different theoretical and clinical approaches by sponsoring discussions of articles and responses to discussions by analysts of different persuasions.

From the start some of us held a distinction in mind between what we referred to as relational (small r) theory (denoting the diverse theories that were included in the mix of perspectives that placed some version of 'object seeking' rather than drive gratifying as a first principle), and Relational Theory (capital R) by which we meant a specific approach to clinical theory, its applications and a clinical sensibility that we believed was emerging from a creative synthesis of the diverse approaches mentioned above (Bass, 2009).

I believe that questions remain a quarter of a century later, about whether such a synthesis has taken place, giving shape to a recognizable unified relational approach, or whether relational psychoanalysis remains a loose confederacy of heterogeneous perspectives. We refer nowadays to a 'large tent' relationalism, loosely bound by a common set of therapeutic values, ethics, sensibilities, and theoretical assumptions regarding development in normal and disturbed variations, the nature of internal and interpersonal relations, the role and nature of drives and other motivational systems, yet with considerable diversity in the play of ideas, and the ways in which such ideas shape therapeutic engagement, understanding and intentions (Mitchell, 1997).

I believe that the range and heterogeneity of relational perspectives, including the considerable diversity of their applications, remains both a strength (in the breadth, creativity and generativity of its ideas) and a difficulty with which relational psychoanalysis continues to struggle in finding a cohesive identity of its own. I have found that the broad integrative nature of its project and the creativity that has sprung from its engagement with diverse ideas has widened the appeal of relational thinking among therapists of diverse perspectives, inside and outside psychoanalysis proper, while at the same time contributing to a lack of clarity in many quarters about just what relational psychoanalysis is, and is not. Relational emphases on intersubjectivity, including the unique contribution of each patient, each therapist and each dyad to the proceedings, is often challenging to new analysts in need of guidance when it comes to grasping and applying a theory of technique, and confusing to analysts trained in some traditions with more objectivistic perspectives, whose critique of relational psychoanalysis often includes the complaint that relational psychoanalysis doesn't have a theory of its own.

AH: I remember something from an early meeting, when Steve Mitchell described very precisely that position, wanting a theory that felt it belonged to you, was your tag. The whole project of *Dialogues* turns out to have emerged from contact Lewis Aron had with Larry Erlbaum and then he linked Steve with Erlbaum and *Dialogues* was birthed. I think Manny Ghent found the term 'relational' from Merton Gill. So it was inspired by Steve's genius but many people put the projects together and built a movement.

I always anchored things in the object relational wing of the inter-subjective sphere. What I and some others (Benjamin, Dimen, in the early groups) wanted to bring in, was the historical and socio-cultural dimensions of the two-person construction. We insisted on the *social* in social construction. For me, that came from a political history from the 60s but it has come to be linked to an older political history adjacent to and also inside psychoanalysis.

Very unfashionable now, tainted with the scourge of Stalinism, total-itarian regimes and other excesses, there was, from the 1920s on, in Europe and in North America, a lot of psychoanalytic work in which social critique, political analysis, class interests and the flourishing of radical theories of sexuality (Reich, 1930; Brown, 1959; Fromm, 1941, 1947) all thrived. Also we need to be mindful of the importance of the Progressive era for what came to be called first wave feminism, distinguishing it from the second wave feminism of the 1970s. I think of Joan Riviere's paper on 'Womanliness as Masquerade' (1929) (important to Lacanians and in a quiet way a radical critique of conventional psychoanalytic views of femininity) as well as a number of women analysts in the 1920s (Horney, 1950; Lampl-de Groot; Muller) who subtly undercut the binaries active/passive in thinking through female sexuality.

So once upon a time, it was Marx and Freud, and the Freudian left, which was then transmuted through identity politics, and post-struc-turalism. I think this tradition now lives in the current interest in inter-pellation, an old term from political theory now entering our considerations of how the individual is claimed by the state/culture/historical force. This tradition is also of some relational thinking about the importance of the 'other' in the emergence of psychic individuality (conscious and unconscious).

Back in the day, one described this as the story of how you come to want to do what you have to do. In all this, keeping exactly the right tension between unconscious and conscious, big history, little history, between and within intrapsychic and interpersonal was/is a huge preoccupation, an ongoing tension. Interest in intergenerational transmission of trauma is not exclusive to relational thinking, but it is a large part of relational analysts' interests in trauma and its leaks through the attachment system (Salberg & Grand, 2016). I think that there is a long tradition of which relational is only a part in which the state and the culture penetrate very deeply into psychic life, consciously and unconsciously.

But of course what I have just done is launch an origin myth, complete with its various primal scenes and inaugural launchings.

TB: Yes, and how apt that our preferred origin narratives, our constructions of histories, our fantasies, our understandings of how we (first-generation relationalists) came to our relational perspective, varies as much as it does. It reflects the diversity of our thought, of our backgrounds (personal and professional) and the paths which brought us to be relational analysts. Listening to your account of the streams of political and social phenomena that fueled a diaspora toward relational psychoanalysis enriches my sense of our shared history and fills in some of the gaps about how we found ourselves and each other in our shared experience of the relational movement.

AH: One thing I regret in the relational tradition is that we are not so well able to historicize our group or its projects. I think one particular precursor to relational thought was a group that developed in the late 70s in New York called The Group for Radical Human Science (GRHS). We had a radio show on WBAI called Reconstructing Psychology. We tried to launch a clinic. Briefly, we had a journal called *Psychcritique*. Because nobody had yet invented intersectional (the hybridic mix of gender, class, race, culture, sexuality, etc.) and for other reasons of course, our group came undone. Mitchell and the relational turn to the rescue. But that is just one birth narrative. There are here others.

I think considering the tensions you are describing and the ones I describe here, there is one underlying commonality: psychoanalytic work arises in conditions of uncertainty. One works both blindly and with insight. Increasingly, in the relational and intersubjective and the field theory worlds, the process of analytic work often exceeds the comprehension of its practitioners. This was one of Mitchell's early ideas: a revolution in what the analyst knows.

TB: 'It often exceeds the comprehension of its practitioners.' This is very well said. I would go so far as to say that when it comes to the process of psychoanalytic work, there are aspects of what we do, how we participate in the work with our patients, that *inevitably, always* exceed our understanding, and that this is indeed one of the hallmarks of our discipline. This is implicit, when not explicit, in the fundamental idea that both analyst and patient, being human, struggle ongoingly with the limits of their own awareness. Freud's (1912, 1958) original observation that psychoanalysis involves one unconscious (in the mind of the analyst) turning toward and receiving broadcasts from that of another (in the mind of the patient) left the impression that the analyst's unconscious functioned as a receiver, the patient's as a broadcaster. Ferenczi's (Dupont, 1988) critique of this position, in which he viewed analytic work as a 'dialogue of unconsciouses,' taking place on a two-way street, (Bass, 2001a), highlighted the limits of the analyst's awareness, when it came to the contributions of her or his own unconscious. This has been a fundamental feature of relational perspectives from Ferenczi forward. Given that our understandings (of the patient and of ourselves) are always limited, contextual and provisional, that one insight gives way to another, our insight and our blind spots are inextricably linked. Our recognition that our understanding will inevitably give way to new and revised understandings, and the enactment and discovery of new blind spots serves as a necessary bulwark against analytic hubris, highlighting our reliance on our patients for help in revising and updating our understandings. We try to work as much as possible with an awareness of our (the analyst's own) unconscious contribution to the patient's experience and the way the process unfolds. This is central to what I think is an important emphasis in relational psychoanalysis today.

You highlight something else which I think is important to understanding the heterogeneity of relational theory, and to some of its current challenges. Relational psychoanalysis has been a melting pot, a collection of 'immigrants,' as Jody Davies has suggested. Since the first generation of relational analysts in the 1980s, each of us had identified with another perspective before we came to identify as 'relational,' (interpersonal, object relational, self-psychological, Freudian, post-modern, constructivist, intersubjectivist, feminist, etc.). We became a group in designating ourselves relational analysts, but a group with many different origins and diverse identifications that influenced the way we thought and worked. This created a vibrant mix of perspectives and many spirited dialogues among us, but it also meant that it was challenging for those who were new to this conversation to grasp with clarity just what it meant to be relational.

This problem touches as well, I think, on your point about the challenges of 'historicizing our group or its projects.' As we have demonstrated here in a small way in what stands out to each of us about the origins of relational psychoanalysis, our views of our histories are extremely personal, derived from our own experiences, relationships and interests. Just as each sibling has different parents, a different family story, each of us carries a different history of the relational turn that we were part of.

Wherever I teach relational theory and technique, the questions arise: 'Well, just what is relational psychoanalysis? Is it different from Interpersonal Psychoanalysis? How is it different from Object Relations?' I know that many teachers of relational psychoanalysis answer these questions differently, with different nuances of emphasis about what is really important to the perspective, what makes a perspective 'relational'. This is true of how we work clinically as well. It is clear to me in reading accounts of clinical work, and in hearing it presented, that relational analysts do work quite differently from one another; not just in the sense that we each work differently with each patient, but in a systematic way, with different personal and theoretical emphases. Do you think that hearing a process recording of a session or two, that we could agree on whether the analyst at work would be identified or would identify her of himself as 'relational'?

AH: I actually don't think that this is a meaningful task/test. At this point in my career, listening to many case presentations claiming many different ancestors and authorities, I think that in a blind test, asked to judge the provenance of clinical material, we might be wrong a lot of the time. And sometimes the ground rules for judging clinical material make genuine differences hard to identify. Last year, I attended a group working on a process called Comparative Clinical Method and after a day of listening and interacting, I came to feel that the assumptions that set up certain activities – in this case the whole undergirding of the Comparative Clinical Methods – set up a grid for thinking and assessing that is already decided on the basic question of a one-person perspective. There was no theoretical space for a two-person perspective. You can listen to clinical material and pose a set of questions that entirely foreclose any consideration of an intersubjective approach. So many of these comparative clinical approaches have limited appeal from my point of view. And, as you say, there are so many kinds of self-described relational analysts, certainly with differing styles.

I wanted to say something about critique and difference. There is not a good history or track record in psychoanalysis for having differences without beheadings and exile. This ideal, I know, is one hope for this collection. I was struck recently in reading a book edited by Martin Bergmann (2004) on *Understanding Dissidence and Controversy*. It was pretty heavy handed. Particularly Andre Green. Green gives a paper in which he sounds like Homeland Security giving and lifting passports. A pass for Ferenczi maybe. Nothing doing for Fromm. Stern and the Boston Change group. Thumbs down. Debate and discussion are completely foreclosed. "It's not psychoanalytic" functioning as a kind of passport seizure which Green issues with complete confidence.

So one thing I have been thinking in light of the particular breadth and range of relational ideas is what really is the fate or utility of comparative psychoanalysis. Steven Cooper (2015) has a new term for thinking about metatheoretical interests. He uses the term 'bridge theory' to look at concepts that cross boundaries, become more and more theory-agnostic and more viable and visible across different orientations.

Would you agree with that? What makes a theory an identifiable perspective? Must it be monolithic. You have been particularly interested in a relational 'landscape'. Elizabeth Young Bruehl, at one point, talked about perspectives on gender and sexuality as situated within a 'plaza'.

Is it useful or actually restrictive for self-identified relational analysts to think about 'bedrock'? What would be there?

- Multiple self-states;
- Co-construction and social constructionism;
- A bi-personal field that will be conscious and unconscious;
- A divided self and an intersubjectivity.

Are there core of ideas about technique? What would they be?

I am interested in the work of Jean Laplanche (1999) at the moment, whose ideas about subjectivity are very intersubjective and deeply implicate the 'other,' including the other's unconscious, in the organization of individual psychic life. He thinks of his work as having no organizing effect on technique. Indeed, that many different ways of working might flow from his metapsychology.

To add the perspective of Haydee Faimberg in her model for clinical work, *Listening to Listening* (1996), perhaps we could cultivate moments of misunderstanding. Find in our theoretical discussions the place of incomprehension or struggle or disagreement and work within that tension. This is not to celebrate compromise or dilution of precise and important concepts in any approach. It is more an attempt to deepen – perhaps in a dialectical spiral of back and forth in discussion – the places where strong difference emerges.

In terms of wishing for something to change or grow, I would say that I would like to see a more elaborated discussion of the social and historical aspects of co-construction. But I don't require everyone to want or do that and I don't feel impeded from developing that approach more deeply.

Certainly, within the relational world there are distinct sub-sections, and some may be more powerful than others. I think it is still true that, as Jody Davies said of us a long time ago, we are a community of immigrants; I like to think of myself as hybridic. So what if we thought of ourselves as immigrants who made ourselves into citizens with all the strengths and weaknesses of a coherent or semi-coherent organization with all its governmental structures. Now perhaps, we can form some version of the EU where for certain experiences local identity fades.

For me, one bridge is field theory. It is so important to me because it crosses many borders: from cognition and general psychology to psychoanalysis, and it bridges a number of orientations within psychoanalysis. For some of us the diversity is important, for others the unifying force. Interpersonal, intersubjective, relational, neoBionian, object relational,

Lacanian. For some the border rules, screenings and passport monitoring is central. I want to make a plea for more anarchy, less government.

In the past year, I have found a new term to replace the idea of 'bridge' theories. It's from philosophy and the work of Gilles Deleuze. He talks about theories and concepts as 'nomads' or migrants moving across theoretical spaces. Less a mortgage or a debt and more a source of energy.

One thing that is interesting to me and crosses my mind a lot is the degree to which sexuality, gender, identity forms of various kinds have gotten ghettoized, often in their/our own journals. What would it mean to have a more integrated way of thinking of these phenomena as relational?

Intersectionality, by the way, I think is actually one of the potentially useful theoretical moves that could help liberate gender studies from its various ghettos/silos. A definition of intersectionality describes the study of overlapping or intersecting social identities and related systems of oppression, domination or discrimination. I think there is a pathway here in some of the newer conceptualizations outside psychoanalysis but in gender studies. The term 'intersectional' is being used to notice the unique and hybridic way gender intersects with culture, class, race and sexuality. We have some possible roadmaps out of the choking binaries.

There are things to talk about.

Also it occurs to me that all theories have a process of sorting out a new idea, overusing, pulling back, configuring how and when something is happening or needs to be happening.

Enactment seems to me to be such a term. I don't know whether it is overused. I would need to hear a specific example that seemed wrong. Maybe there is a spectrum of such events, mini scenes that pass unremarked and others that break into consciousness. One would think that there would be significantly more in a clinical dialogue than in everyday life. I think I am simply of the temperament that would rather say what I want to be doing and thinking rather than taking on the task of sanctioning people I don't agree with. I think that about Kleinians where I have lots of differences and many temptations to erect borders and passport control. So why not about relationalists?

TB: I agree with what you say about the appreciation of difference in what different analysts bring to our work and theory. And you rightly note that this has always been a great challenge in psychoanalysis, one with which we as a field have a poor track record. We, as a profession, haven't often risen to the occasion in this regard, and the tendency to banish those who see things differently was, of course, there from the start, with Freud's series of excommunications. As you point out, our history is filled with disturbing tales of apostasies, splits; even beheadings, as you have so vividly put it, though nowadays it is unfortunately necessary to specify that our use of the term is a metaphoric trope. Still, even shame sanctions are extremely damaging, and the excommunication of colleagues by wielding the banishing phrase, 'he is not a real analyst,' is an indignity that too many of us have been subject to. The damage to psyches and careers has been extreme at times. Ferenczi wondered if he had the physical and emotional fortitude to survive Freud's banishment of him following his presentation of 'The Confusion of Tongues between the Adults and the Child: The Language of Passion and the Language of Tenderness,' in which he sharply differed with Freud in matters of theory and technique (Ferenczi, 1932). And indeed, Ferenczi died soon after. It hasn't been a pretty picture.

One of the dark ironies of our discipline is that even as we recognize the ambiguity and 'uncertainty' at the heart of our work, our passions about what we do believe, about the way that we work, often leads us to make and enact assumptions that those who disagree with us are 'wrong.' We thus assert the very certainty about our ways of thinking, working and being with our patients that belies the very sensibility that lies at the heart of our perspective – that acknowledges and values the uncertainty at the heart of things. I think the tendency in our field to personalize differences as much as we do has something to do with our long gestation as analysts, and its unique form, in which long, close and transference-based relations with our analysts, our supervisors and others involved in our training generate powerful personal identifications and counteridentifications. We find that we are prone to internalize much of our psychoanalytic ancestry, consciously and/or unconsciously. This includes what we value (what has shaped and helped us), and what haunts us and stands as a kind of intergenerational transmission of family feuds and traumas. Your recent work on ghosts and hauntings is relevant to this process. I think that your appreciation of the ways in which we are all haunted, we all live with our own ghosts, contributes to the way you hold your 'live and let live' attitude.

Yet notwithstanding differences in our ways of being patients and analysts, psychoanalysts of all persuasions do similar work, and have more in common in their values, interests, and ways of being with patients than one would assume based on the passionate emphasis of difference which we highlight here. We find that psychoanalysts are more simply psychoanalysts than otherwise, a fact that one can lose track of in some of our more heated exchanges. I have found that in teaching on 'the clinical theory of relational technique' at classical institutes like the Columbia University Center for Psychoanalytic Training and Technique, and the New York Psychoanalytic Institute, students are often surprised once we get down to talking about working with patients themselves, rather than highlighting differences in theory, that the relational perspective seems less foreign, more accessible and clinically useful than would have been anticipating when reading theory dis-embodied from its clinical application. For that reason, I prefer to teach theory using a case method. Notwithstanding sharp metapsychological differences, when the conversation turns to what each analyst might think to do with a patient in a given moment, we usually find that we are speaking the same language, or at least that we can translate well enough from one to the other.

Your wish that we might hold difference while remaining interested in others, rather than disdainful or defensive in response to what others find important, seems central to the future development of psychoanalysis, as well, of course, to our survival as a species. As you show, when we can retain a focus on how we see things, how we work well to the benefit of our patients, as well as how and what we learn from our experience, we can be most creative – we can grow and change. The contemptuous contentious trope in psychoanalysis that takes the form of 'what they are doing is not analysis' on the other hand, fosters restrictive mutual defensiveness, mutual shame, and hardening of positions against reason.

Yet as we have matured as a perspective, I think we have come to take some of our shared sensibilities for granted, and have come to focus increasingly on differences in our thinking and in our clinical approaches. Still, in my view, relational psychoanalysis remains a big tent perspective (Bass, 2014), with different theoreticians and clinicians holding different aspects of our complex integration in the foreground or background. In this light, your use of Cooper's bridge theory is apt, along with your own theory-agnostic emphasis, by which we can perhaps help each other to hear what we are not currently listening to. A living, evolving theory cannot be monolithic. If it rigidifies, reaching a level of sclerosis that obstructs further growth, and evolution, it will soon be extinct. But notwithstanding increased flexibility and openness to new learning and experience, different ways of thinking and working do differentiate analysts of one persuasion from others, even when these are not simple differentiations to make, even for the analysts who hold different points of view.

As you noted, 'enactment' has been a slippery concept in relational psychoanalysis, notwithstanding its centrality as a frame of reference among most analysts informed by relational thought. Different authors do conceptualize it differently and make different uses of it clinically, even as most of us are striving to deepen our understanding of how patient and analyst become entangled in the work, reach impasses, and try to work our way out of such transference/countertransference binds in ways that include increasing recognition of their own contribution to it. This is certainly so in the variations of relational perspectives that are informed by intersubjectivity and field theories, in which we are much more likely to make use of ideas of enactment that include both participants in the trouble rather than one person constructs like 'acting out' ' or acting in,' where the analyst tends to assume that that the patient 'started it.'

You had said that in the case of enactment we might think about a spectrum of such events, mini scenes that pass unremarked and others that pass into consciousness. I have observed this as well. It is a distinction I made in my 2003 paper '"E" Enactments in Psychoanalysis: Another Medium, another Message,' in which I describe how those smaller, unremarked moments begin to gather steam, eventually breaking into consciousness in a way that can be disruptive, and move the analysis into new areas that had been inaccessible to that point. You also suggest that there would be significantly more of such moments in clinical dialogue than in everyday life. My own view is that 'enactments' themselves may be no more common in analysis than in other relationships; human relations in general are rife with moments in which states of mind are expressed not as much through words as action, and partners become entangled in ways that are not so dissimilar from what we call enactments or transference/countertransference interlocks (a phrase that Benjamin Wolstein might have coined). Rather, our careful way of listening, our ethically informed effort to 'work things out' with our patients, the attention we pay to the nuances of what is taking place between us, and what that has to do with 'the rest of the patient's story,' leads us to give much greater attention to moments in which 'enactments' are taking place so that we might find a way of giving words to experience. We are dedicated to understanding what is going wrong (and right) between therapist and patient, bringing to the surface sources of trouble that we might otherwise avoid in relationships in which we were not working so closely and carefully with the subtle movements of affect and energy. Enactments and impasses occurring in other more or less intimate relationships often lead to break-ups or transformations of relationships that might pass relatively unobserved and worked through, or that might be terribly upsetting and lead to breakups of couples, friendships or business partnerships. Those of us who do family and couples work or organizational consulting work with enactments in those spheres regularly. When we perform our rightful functions as analyst, attending to the frame, to our analytic intentions and the nuances of our inner experience in the service of the therapeutic work, we pursue communications taking place in the enacted dimension more assiduously than we typically do among friends and often sometimes between intimate partners and our children as well.

Regarding your list of important relational frames of reference (multiple self-states, bi-personal field, intersubjectivity, etc.), I agree that most relational analysts would recognize these as significant guideposts in analytic work. At the same time, as you also suggest, not all relational analysts use the same hierarchy of concepts in their way of orienting to clinical work. For some, relational thinkers (Slowchower, 1996) ideas and experiences of containment, holding, creation of transitional space (ideas prominent in Winnicott, Bion and the middle group in general) are more highlighted. For others, especially those who came out of or were strongly influenced by the Interpersonal tradition, greater emphasis might be put on expressive uses of countertransference and more transactional ways of working which emphasize 'what is going on' between therapist and patient (Bass, 1996; Levenson, 1985, 1989). I think most relational analysts are familiar with and utilize a range of ideas, such as those you mentioned: dissociation, multiplicity, mutuality, enactment, a dialogue of unconsciouses, postmodern perspectives related to gender, sexuality and culture, but each of us holds these ideas differently, and of course they are represented in our work differently with different patients, and with the same patient at different times. I think it is this complex mix of ideas and ways that we use ourselves with these ideas in mind that led Cooper to think of the relational perspective as a 'meta-theory.' How else, he wonders, to explain such a diversity of clinical perspectives under the rubric of a single theory? And how better to describe a perspective which analysts of so many different perspectives find useful and compatible with their own ways of working?

Our central emphasis on the intersubjective dimensions of psychoanalytic situations means that we are committed to recognizing and finding ways of taking into account in our theory and our practice the ways in which our individuality of thought, sensibility and personality affect our ways of working, and the experience of those we are working with. I think our dedication to the fullest possible awareness and acknowledgement of the effects of our own participation, our own impact, is part of an ethical dimension of our work. Our perspectives on intersubjective dimensions of development, human relations and difficulties in living that we experience have lead us to develop a psychoanalytic theory and ways of working that must make room for a multiplicity of ways of being and working with our patients. As we see, that is a very challenging task, but the complexity of this mission mirrors the complexity of our experience and that of the people we are trying to help.

AH : The history of thinking in these highly bifurcated terms seems to me to have had more to do with the social field and competitive world of analytic cultures and groups. The usual attempt to distinguish a psychoanalytic process from something that is not psychoanalytic seems more in the service of ideological warfare than enlightenment.

TB: I am sure that that is true.

AH: Comparative psychoanalysis is often seen as a kind of invention of Roy Schafer. He, himself is an interesting mix of in-law and outlaw. Maverick and mainstream. His impulse was to widen the scope in which psychoanalytic work, attitudes and sensibilities were imaginable. Mitchell and Greenberg had some of the same impulses and contradictions. I think, over time, this aspect of the comparative project has been more or less hijacked with old ideological and turf warfare, which is more likely to foster resentment and alienation than clarity. Too much energy spent telling how wrong and off the other guys are and not enough work to describe one's own process and commitments.

To me, the discussion between Donnel Stern, Ferro and Civitarese was both useful and irritating. The quarrel between shallow and deep and the tendency to see the intersubjective as less filled with unconscious process always makes me cross. But I think, it is always worth thinking that such critiques push self-defined intersubjective analysts towards trying to say more fully what is entailed in these two-person or systems approaches to analytic work that absolutely requires a concept of unconscious life. One way that I think of the renewed or new pull towards the archaic, the primitive, imperfectly evolving early states in patients or analysts is that this demand brings back the more object relational side of our landscape: Ferenczi, Winnicott, Fairbairn and their modern variants: Alvarez, etc. I think that is a preoccupation with a newer generation of relational analysts: Grossmark, Director, Reis, McGleughlin, Rozmarin, Guralnik (2010, 2011); Sakctopoulou (2014).

TB: Yes, I agree that object relations ideas are useful in creating a language and orientation to early, 'primitive' states in patient and analyst. And I think our emphasis on multiple and shifting states derives in no small part from object relational thinking. It has always seemed to me that this emphasis within object relations thinking was an important element in the original synthesis of American Interpersonal thinking with British Independent, Kleinian and Bionian thought. Many of us whose training had been primarily interpersonal in orientation, found the ideas, language and metaphors of object relations theory helpful in finding a way to talk about our own and our patients' deepest, most fraught inner experiences. It seemed to me that it was the need to find ways of representing this dimension of early, archaic experience that was part of the original motivation for a marriage between interpersonal and object relational ideas, in the form of relational psychoanalysis. In that sense, it has seemed to me that the return in our discussions to these uses of object relations theory may suggest that they had not been sustained in relational psychoanalysis in the way that the originators had intended. It seems that a number of the contemporary authors emphasizing object relations within the relational school must feel that those ideas that were fundamental to the original syntheses had become marginalized along the way. Or that the importance of what they emphasized had become diminished, and so is being reclaimed and emphasized anew.

AH: There is a NYC group calling themselves the *Unbehagen* – The discontented – a group that are tired of sectarian quarrels; their discontent is with our generation who behave too often like a seriously dysfunctional set of families and tribes too interested in warfare. People in that group and in others are launching a conference called 'Institute no Institute' to explore how and why and whether to centralize and institutionalize training.

Working beyond the project of comparative psychoanalysis might have some people wishing to self-describe in terms of an orientation. Other people may want a more generic account. We will differ in how trans-disciplinary we feel we need to be and certainly in how we think of the differing and overlapping 'responsibilities' of patient and analyst. The question of the analysand's duties are complicated by the problem of consent in general and by the complex responsibilities many patients bring to internal worlds and their own projects. Clinical impasses – for me and certainly for many others – usually entail some task of mourning and transformation in the analyst, whatever can and will alter in the analysand. Asymmetry and uncertainty are part of what makes the work so arduous.

I would also say, as a potential within any of the forms of psychoanalysis we have been talking of, that I think that the structure in us – the analyst – what the Barangers (2008) and others refer to as the 'bastion' (a structure of determined resistance to facing vulnerability or dread or despair) is often organized around omnipotence. This is, for me, our instrument and our Achilles heel, what makes us want to help and heal and what makes us too often opaque to shame and vulnerability.

People will differ in how variable their ways of working are, how idiomatic, how much immediate, intergenerational or social meaning enters the exploration and emerging map of meaning. How silent, how active, how creative, all vary. Here we would need something like Geertz' concept of thick description, as a full and intricate an account of what is happening.

TB: Yes, all these aspects of our work vary considerably. We are each the unique instruments of our work, and I think the unique qualities that we bring to our work become emphasized over time. We each become more and more ourselves over the years, and as we become increasingly unique in our own way of working, I hope we also become more accepting of others. I remember that one of my first supervisors, George Kaufer, at NYU, told me (personal communication) that an analyst doesn't typically get to have a self-sustaining practice until he or she has been practicing for about ten years. He explained that until an analyst finds his or her own voice, differentiated from his supervisors or his own analyst, any given patient could see that analyst or another. It is not until we find our own unique voice that it means something for a patient to want to see YOU, because of the unique qualities that you bring to the work. All that being said, I think the two-person model complicates the picture further by highlighting that an analyst is likely to work quite differently with different patients, depending on what arises with that patient, what is called forth, the countertransference that is evoked, the aspects of one's subjectivity that are engaged.

AH: I have one other point to add to our discussion of theoretical comparisons. Relationalists are often seen as disclosurers, breakers of the frame, analysts insensitive to the frame and analysts believing in the absolute symmetry of the analytic relationship. Personally, I don't think that is our perspective and positing analytic subjectivity does not make any scene symmetrical. The best discussion of this that I know is in Bleger's *The psychoanalysis of the psychoanalytic frame* (1966), in which he argues that the asymmetry of the relationship is bound up with the responsibility of the analyst to reset the frame. The structure of the project gets lost, disrupted, the analyst falters and the patient. Uncertainty and unconscious life floods out of the good enough structure of dialogue and action. The responsibility of the analyst is to be committed consciously (which won't always be in evidence) to resetting the frame.

I see this in the terms of Levinas' (1972) idea of responsibility: we are responsible for and to the other. That is inalienable. This demand has many implications. We will often fail of course, but, for example, I think we have to be responsible for the frame. It is one inalienable duty of the analyst.

I don't think ethics has been a strong enough focus for the relational group. It has taken too long for relational groups at the institutional level (journals and organizations) to take up diversity and to consider ethical matters deep in our field (boundary violations). It is interesting to me that it is not the founding generation that asks us these questions (Rozmarin,

McGleughlin, Suchet and White, 2007). It is newer voices and younger people who want relational psychoanalysis to address ethics and values always intertwined with analytic concerns at the level of metatheory and technique.

Judith Butler (1997, 2004, 2005, 2015) is an important figure here. I think we are getting to a point of being able to write and think this way because of the much more agreeable forms of conversation among groups and individuals. Also because in a new attention to Bion, we are getting more used to being stirred up to not always being the one that knows.

TB: You are raising here issues that have been important to me as well. I have thought and written for many years about the analytic frame, and the questions of symmetry, asymmetry and mutuality that are often implicated in thinking about it, including the relative and asymmetrical responsibilities of patient and therapist (Aron, 1992). I, too, believe that one of the fundamental areas in psychoanalytic work in which clear asymmetries of roles between patient and therapist obtain is in assuming the responsibility for setting, managing and resetting the frame of analysis: its guidelines and structure. That being said, I believe that the responsibility for managing the frame can include the therapist's responsible choice to hold the setting of the frame as part an elastic process, one that may vary in structure, and will often include negotiating a frame tailor made specifically for any given patient/analyst dyad. I don't believe that any one size frame fits all patients, and that there is a danger of creating a Procrustean couch which can leave parts of the patient out if constructed with too much rigidity. As I wrote about in a (2007) article, 'When the frame doesn't fit the picture', a frame is crucial in differentiating what is inside an analysis from what is not, and allowing the analyst to see with perspective through an analytic lens. But a frame that is adjustable and elastic, to fit the requirements of many different kinds of patients, is, I think, a necessary tool of analysis. It has also seemed to me that while the responsibility for setting and managing the frame lies with the therapist, and in that sense speaks to a fundamental asymmetry in analytic responsibility, that there are many aspects of a psychoanalytic process that are not so clearly asymmetrical in nature, and in which the mutuality of relations is especially prominent. In other words, while conscious role assignments (who is responsible for what in the analytic situation) are clearly delineated in an asymmetrical way (the therapist is responsible for the analysis in *this* way, the patient in *that* way) when we get beyond these conscious, intentional role-assigned identifications, the patient's and therapist's actual experience (of affect states including anxieties, longings, states of envy, anger or other forms of arousal) are likely to be more symmetrical, complementary and mutual than conscious role assignments and responsibilities would suggest (Bass, 2001b). To be aware of the latter forms of mutuality inherent to therapeutic work does not in my view compromise the former ethical commitment on the part of the analyst to manage the frame responsibly and with all the reflection on the process that one can bring to bear. As you said, the responsibilities for role based asymmetrical management of the therapeutic frame can only involve 'conscious' intentions, and we know that unconscious forms of engagement may also enter the fray of analysis in the form of enactment in these, as in all matters of analysis.

AH: While one important story of American psychoanalysis is inevitably an immigration story, with all the attendant psychic costs, I am also interested in the local context, culturally and politically. There is also the darkening mood in the United States beginning in the late 40s. Post-war McCarthyism is a period still not well metabolized in contemporary consciousness. The particular character and ambience of the Cold War in American is an under-described period of fear and constriction. The execution of the Rosenbergs in 1952 marks only the highly public and internationally felt experience of McCarthyism. But this terrifying event was accompanied and surrounded by hundreds of instances of consistent repression, secrecy, and attacks on livelihoods, and professional standing. The post-war period is one in which there are losses or inhibition of freedoms of many kinds. Ellen Schrecker, one of the main historians of the Cold War period, summarizes the effects of McCarthyism: Suppression was spread across distinct government agencies, some that identified dissidence and others punished and this made opposition difficult. There was almost no legal recourse, there was massive fear and insecurity, attacks on livelihoods and economic security. Primarily, there are job losses and intimidation but there are unnamed instances of exile, mental distress, alcoholism, stress related illness, suicides, and the deep sense of insecurity. Schrecker's primary source work is on the academy and public school teachers, but as she says in her introduction: "I could have written this book about doctors, social workers or movie stars" (Schrecker, 1986, p. xv; see also 1998).

Relational psychoanalysis and Mitchell's 'revolution' could only occur when that period of fearfulness was lifting. I think I am caught in some tangles, as part of the generation of the 60s trying to learn and connect to an earlier period of radicalism and struggles that was lost in the successful repressions of McCarthyism.

One must think of the great explosive reactions of the 1960s in the battles against racism, imperialism, and the oppression of women as arising after a long and frightening period of political repression. The continuities are complex and interesting: the moral ambiguities of lost causes, the mixture of regret and despair at lost ideals. Genealogy is important. We know this personally and clinically, I suggest it is so also institutionally.

TB: I always find your analyses of the cultural/political/social dimensions of our lives that have shaped our experience, psychoanalysis' place in it, and our place in psychoanalysis fascinating, and inspiring. Your account of the way political and social forces have provided a subtext for the warps and woofs of psychoanalysis must give us pause and lead us to reflection about how the current social and political turmoil in the United States will affect us, our patients and our work.

By the time this piece is published, the American presidential election will have taken place, and many of us are already in a state of dread about what a Trump presidency will bring, and what his election would reflect about the current social, political and cultural climate in which we are living and working. Your analysis of the ways in which wars have played such an important part in how our society functions, and what psychoanalysis has to offer, brought me back to my early training and first job as a psychotherapist, working in the VA hospital, and working with many patients whose psychoses seemed directly linked to their experience in Vietnam. As I write now, many of these patients come back to me in surprisingly vivid detail, given that my work with them took place almost forty years ago.

I have been intrigued by the ways in which your longstanding dedication and interests in the political/social/gender spheres have shaped your approach to clinical analysis. As you have highlighted, the development of relational thought per se was strongly influenced by developments in the 1960s, including the anti-war movement, the civil rights movement, the feminist wave, post-modern developments in the academy and in art, and the skepticism and distrust of authority that was part and parcel of these social/cultural movements. Mitchell was explicit in his linking of the relational in psychoanalysis to broader cultural and political developments, including the deconstruction and outright distrust of authority that pervaded the 1960s. Reconsiderations of the nature of the analyst's authority and knowledge followed directly from the cultural revolutions that preceded it. It seems clear that such emergent sensibilities were part of what fueled the turn away from classical ego psychology perspectives and other ways of practicing in which the authority of the analyst was a given. Interpretations were often given and received with a sense of the analysts as one who knew about the patient's unconscious and so had the authority to tell the patient about it. Intersubjective sensibilities in relational models suggest forms of participation in which the analyst offers a view from here, with an interest in what the patients' view might be from there.

Undoubtedly the current social/political/cultural forces that are shaping what our patients need and can make use of, and what we have to offer today, continue to play a major role in how psychoanalysis must evolve in order for it to stay relevant as an active, vital contribution to contemporary life, rather than a relic. For example, it was not so long ago that if a patient communicated with an analyst by e-mail or text, these forms of contact would have been regarded and interpreted as a kind of acting out of boundary diffusions. Nowadays, most referrals that I get come to me via e-mail, with a subject line that says referral, the body of the e-mail telling me who he or she got my name from, and asking if I have time for a consultation.

Mitchell and others began to think about a different kind of authority held by the analyst that had to do less with what was given as an assumption about what the analyst knew (Mitchell, 1993), and more to do with developing an openness to our patients' experience along with our own, in a way that made for more democratic, more mutual forms of practice in which trust was earned over time. For some of us, this led to picking up the strains of mutuality that Ferenczi had experimented with in the 1920s, when he took his experiments in working with radical mutuality all the way to a fully mutual analysis (Dupont, 1988). I have been interested in the ways that his efforts in that direction have evolved in the technique of contemporary relational therapies, where I believe we practice a form of mutual analysis in its own right, while maintaining the asymmetrical role identifications that Ferenczi played with sacrificing in his original experiments (Bass, 2015).

Aron (1992) and others, yourself included, of course, Harris, have emphasized the importance of sustaining more or less traditional asymmetries when it comes to the management of the setting (the frame), and holding firmly the responsibility for conducting the treatment, as we discussed above. I think that all analysts would agree that our responsibilities in the work are different from those of the patient. Mitchell referred to the analyst as the 'designated driver' of the analysis (personal communication), a role that was crucial in allowing the patient to loosen his or her controls and watchfulness, as a way of facilitating the freest possible access to unconscious experience, while relying on the analyst to remain sober, to keep things safe. The complexity and discipline of the analyst's job is reflected in the challenge that at the same time, the analyst has to keep a line open as much as possible to his own unconscious as a source of important data about the patient, and also because having an unconscious ourselves, it will inevitably make an ongoing contribution to the proceedings of analysis, whether we like it or not. So while I agree that such differentiation of roles is crucial to the enterprise of psychoanalysis, I have also suggested that such asymmetries apply most particularly in such areas as our conscious, role-oriented intentions, as you suggested in thinking about how we manage the analytic frame. But this is true, I think, not only in relation to managing the frame of the work. In carrying out our roles as analysts, we proceed from conscious intention (what we mean to be communicating when we make an interpretation, as another example) which may be different from what we enact or communicate, unconscious to unconscious. At the level of unconscious and dissociated dimensions of experience, the anxieties, internal self and object representations and relational configurations that shape our experience—I believe that here, as elsewhere, analysts and patients are more alike than otherwise. It is in the interaction between the inner world of the patient and that of the analyst that much of deep analytic work takes place. I think that it is the recognition of these forms of symmetry in analytic work that much interest in enactment and other forms of transaction in the transference/countertransference field of experience take place, and where I believe that much of what Ferenczi was attempting to explore in his efforts toward mutual analysis continue to evolve.

There is so much more I would like to say and hear from you in reflecting on our respective paths over the past thirty years as analysts, and relational analysts at that. The conversation we have had here has widened my frame of reference about what we have lived through in our respective journeys. I have learned a lot from it, and know that we will continue our conversation beyond what the space limits of this book chapter allow.

References

Aron, L. (1992). Interpretation as expression of the analyst's subjectivity. *Psychoanalytic Dialogues*, 2(4), 475–507.

Baranger, M. and Baranger, W. (2008). The analytic situation as a dynamic field. *International Journal of Psychoanalysis*, 89, 795–826.

Bass, A. (1996). Holding, holding back, and holding on commentary on paper by Joyce Slochower. *Psychoanalytic Dialogues*, 6(3), 361–378.

Bass, A. (2001a). It takes one to know one; or, whose unconscious is it anyway? *Psychoanalytic Dialogues*, 11, 683–702.

Bass, A. (2001b). Mental structure, psychic process, and analytic relations— How people change in analysis: Reply to commentaries. *Psychoanalytic Dialogues*, 11(5), 717–725.

Bass, A. (2003). "E" enactments in psychoanalysis: Another medium, another message. *Psychoanalytic Dialogues*, 13(5), 657–675.

Bass, A. (2007). When the frame doesn't fit the picture. *Psychoanalytic Dialogues*, 17(1), 1–27.

Bass, A. (2009). An Independent Theory of Clinical Technique Viewed Through a Relational Lens: Commentary on Paper by Michael Parsons. *Psychoanalytic Dialogues*, 19(3), 237–245.

Bass, A. (2014). Three pleas for a measure of uncertainty, reverie, and private contemplation in the chaotic, interactive, nonlinear dynamic field of interpersonal/intersubjective relational psychoanalysis. *Psychoanalytic Dialogues*, 24(6), 663–675.

Bass, A. (2015). The dialogue of unconsciouses, mutual analysis and the uses of the self in contemporary relational psychoanalysis. *Psychoanalytic Dialogues*, 25(1), 2–17.

Benjamin, J. (1988). *The bonds of love*. New York: Pantheon.

Benjamin, J. (1995). *Like objects, love subjects*. New Haven, CT: Yale University Press.

Bergmann, M.S. (Ed.). *Understanding dissidence and controversy in the history of psychoanalysis*. New York: Other Press.

Bleger, J. (1967). Psycho-analysis of the psycho-analytic frame. *The International Journal of Psychoanalysis*, 48(4), 511–519.

Brown, N.O. (2012). *Life against death: The psychoanalytical meaning of history*. Middletown, CT: Wesleyan University Press. (Originally published 1959).

Butler, J. (1997). *Excitable speech: A politics of the performative*. New York: Routledge.

Butler, J. (2004). *Precarious life: The powers of mourning and violence*. New York: Verso.

Butler, J. (2005). *Giving an account of oneself*. New York: Fordham University Press.

Butler, J. (2015). *Senses of the subject*. New York: Fordham University Press.

Chetrit-Vatine, V. (2004). Primal seduction, matricial space and asymmetry in the psychoanalytic encounter. *International Journal of Psychoanalysis*, 85, 841–856.

Civitarese, G. (2008). Caesura in Bion's discourse on method. *International Journal of Psychoanalysis*, 89, 1123–1150.

Cooper, S.H. (2015). Clinical Theory at the Border(s): Emerging and Unintended Crossings in the Development of Clinical Theory. *International Journal of Psychoanalysis*, 96, 273–292.

Corbett, K. (2009). *Rethinking masculinities*. New Haven, CT: Yale University Press.

Davies, J.M. (2004). Whose bad objects are we anyway? Repetition and our elusive love affair with evil. *Psychoanalytic Dialogues*, 14(6), 711–732.

Deleuze, G. (1994). *Difference and repetition*. New York: Columbia University Press.

Dimen, M. (2003). *Sexuality, intimacy, power*. Hillsdale, NJ: The Analytic Press.

Dimen, M. and Goldner, V. (2007). *Gender in psychoanalytic space*. New York: Other Press

Dupont, J. (1988). *The Clinical Diary of Sandor Ferenczi*. Cambridge, MA: Harvard University Press.

Harris, A. (2009). You must remember this. *Psychoanalytic Dialogues*, 19(1), 2–21.

Horney, K. (1950). The collected works of Karen Horney, volumes I and II. New York: W.W. Norton.

Faimberg, H. (1996). Listening to listening. *The International Journal of Psychoanalysis*, 77(4), 667.

Faimberg, H. (2003). *The telescoping of generations*. London: Karnac.

Ferenczi, S. (1933). The confusion of tongues between the adults and the child: The language of tenderness and of passion. In: M. Balint (Ed.). *Final contributions to the problems and methods of psycho-analysis* (Vol. 3), (pp. 156–167). New York: Brunner/Mazel, 1980.

Freud, S. (1958). *Recommendations to physicians practicing psychoanalysis.* Standard Edition, 12, 109–120. London: Hogarth Press. (Original work published 1912).

Fromm, E. (1941). *Escape from freedom.* New York; Avon.

Fromm, E. (1947). *Man for himself.* New York: Fawcett.

Greenberg, J. (1983). *Object relations in psychoanalytic theory.* Harvard University Press.

Guralnik, O. (2011). Interpellating grace. With culture in mind: Psychoanalytic stories. New York: Routledge.

Guralnik, O. and Simeon, D. (2010). Depersonalization: Standing in the spaces between recognition and interpellation. *Psychoanalytic Dialogues,* 20, 400–416.

Laplanche, J. (1999). *Essays on otherness.* London: Routledge.

Levenson, E. (1985). The interpersonal (Sullivanian model). In: A. Rothstein (Ed.). *Models of the mind and their relationship to clinical work* (pp. 49–67). New York: International Universities Press.

Levenson, E.A. (1989). Whatever Happened to the Cat?—Interpersonal Perspectives on the Self. *Contemporary Psychoanalysis,* 25, 537–553.

Levine, L. (2009). Transformative aspects of our own analyses and their resonance in our work with our patients. *Psychoanalytic Dialogues,* 19(4), 454–462.

Levine, L. (2016). Mutual vulnerability: Intimacy, psychic collisions, and the shards of trauma. *Psychoanalytic Dialogues,* 26(5), 571–579.

Mitchell, S. (1997). *The analyst's intentions in influence and autonomy in psychoanalysis.* Hillsdale, NJ: The Analytic Press.

Mitchell, S.A. (1993). *Hope and dread in psychoanalysis.* Basic Books.

Riviere, J. (1999). Womanliness as masquerade. *Female Sexuality: Contemporary Engagements,* 8, 127.

Rozmarin, E. (2007). An other in psychoanalysis: Emmanuel Levinas's critique of knowledge and analytic sense. *Journal of Contemporary Psychoanalysis,* 43, 327–360

Rozmarin, E. (2016). Discussion IARPP online Colloquium.

Saketopoulou, A. (2014). Mourning the body as bedrock: Developmental considerations in treating transsexual patients analytically. *Journal of the American Psychoanalytic Association,* 62(5), 773–806.

Salberg, J. and Grand, S. (Eds.). (2016). Wounds of history: Repair and resilience in the trans-generational transmission of trauma. Abingdon, UK: Taylor & Francis.

Schafer, R. (1981). *A new language for psychoanalysis.* New Haven, CT: Yale University Press.

Schrecker, E. (1999). *Many are the crimes: McCarthyism in America.* Princeton, NJ: Princeton University Press.

Slochower, J. (1996). Holding and the Fate of the Analyst's Subjectivity. *Psychoanalytic Dialogues*, 6(3), 323–353.

Stern, D.B. (2009). Partners in thought: A clinical process theory of narrative. *Psychoanalytic Quarterly*, 78, 701–731.

Wolstein, B. (1992). Resistance interlocked with countertransference. *Contemporary Psychoanalysis*, 28, 172–190.

Chapter 10

Beyond tolerance in psychoanalytic communities
Reflexive skepticism and critical pluralism[1]

Lewis Aron

> *The only good then is for a person to seek out honest friends who will*
> *enlighten his eyes to what he is blind and will rebuke him out of love,*
> *thus rescuing him from all evil. For what a man cannot see due to his*
> *inability to see fault with himself, they will see and understand and*
> *warn him, and he will be protected. On this scripture says: "in*
> *abundance of counselors there is salvation" (Mishlei 24:6).*
> (Rabbi Moshe Chayim Luzzato (1707–1746)
> Mesillas Yeshorim, The Path of the Just)

Psychoanalysis is widely known for its long history of splits and schisms among schools of thought. It has for this reason often been compared to religion, where schisms frequently involve mutual accusations of heresy. In the United States, for many decades, psychoanalysis was largely under the hegemony of American Ego Psychology, which dominated the psychoanalytic mainstream. The fall of this largely monistic psychoanalytic consensus coincided with the decades of the decline of the prestige of psychoanalysis as a male medical specialty, with the increasing feminization of the field, challenges from psychopharmacology, the health care industry, managed care, alternative therapies, the demand for empirically supported and evidence based medicine, the Freud Wars, and the new Freud Studies, a growing self-help movement, the critiques from feminists, gay, lesbian and queer studies, and the loss of the status and institutional bases of psychoanalysis in psychiatry and clinical psychology. (This history is reviewed in *A Psychotherapy for the People* (Aron & Starr, 2015)).

With this loss of status and prestige has come a newly-found and hard-won plurality of perspectives. Psychoanalysis is no longer psychoanalysis but rather many psychoanalyses. Multiplicity and pluralism is the state of the discipline today around the world. Many psychoanalytic institutes now teach multiple points of view, have various diverse tracks and orientations, and each school tends to support its own journals, assign different core texts, maintain separate canons of literature, speak its own idiom, and each school has its founding heroes or patron saints as well as its denigrated enemies.

For some observers and commentators our present state of multiplicity is a sign of the demise of psychoanalysis. Stepansky (2009) tells the story of a once cohesive discipline that has splintered into rivalrous "part-fields" and now struggles to survive under siege. He views our multiplicity as a fragmentation, the result of the inevitable marginalization of any profession that resists integration into the scientific mainstream of its time and place. Other scholars, notably Wallerstein (1992), have called for reestablishing common ground rooted in our shared clinical experience in consulting rooms where therapists relate comparably to the immediacy of the trans-ference and counter-transference interplay with their patients. Many other psychoanalytic leaders applaud and celebrate our multiplicity, not as a sign of disintegration and demise, but to the contrary as the mark of creativity, intellectual excitement, and generativity. Mitchell (1993), for example, described pluralism in psychoanalytic thought as essential and nourishing of growth. Cooper (2008), while welcoming this "pluralism" has made the point that it is unfortunately a multiplicity of authoritarian orthodoxies, multiple monistic views, each derived from a thinker and tradition. Cooper holds out the hope that empirical research might solve the problem. Some analysts, such as Govrin (2016), have even called for a future of psychoanalysis in which dogma and pluralism can coexist in what he refers to as "fascinated" and "disenchanted" communities.

In this chapter, I will argue that our multiplicity is not inherently good or bad, but what will determine its value is what we do with that diversity, how we view each other and make use of the range and variety of approaches now available. Until the 1970s there was hardly any discussion of "comparative psychoanalysis," a term associated with Schafer, who first used it in 1979. How could there have been a discipline of comparative psychoanalysis when analysts were convinced that any disagreement with the dominant view was heresy? In our own era, there have been passionate calls for a comparative and integrative approach (Willock, 2011). I will argue here that we need to move beyond "comparative psychoanalysis," and even beyond theoretical integration. In my view, informed by recent developments in the philosophy of science, the multiplicity and diversity of psychoanalysis, the many diverging psychoanalyses, may be best utilized when we focus in a balanced way on both common ground and difference, not for comparison and contrast alone, or to achieve integration, but to learn from each other's opposing views. We can gain the most, I believe, by moving beyond mutual respect and tolerance toward a genuine appreciation of the other, for what they can offer to us and what we can offer to them. The other, the other school, viewpoint or orientation, can provide a function that we cannot fulfil for ourselves nor they for themselves. In this view, the criticism of the other can become a unique gift, mutually exchanged among schools.

Critical pluralism

The ideas that I develop in what follows are derived from the work of the Israeli historian and philosopher of science, Menachem Fisch.[2] Trained in physics, philosophy, and the history and philosophy of science, Fisch has argued for a contemporary philosophy of science that steers a course between the Scylla of uncritical dogmatism and the Charybdis of radical relativism. His approach is influenced by Karl Popper's "critical rationalism," the contention that scientific knowledge grows not by accumulating supporting evidence but by subjecting our beliefs to the staunchest criticism we can gather. Although Popper himself dismissed psychoanalysis as a "pseudoscience" because he believed its propositions could not be "falsified," that is empirically tested and challenged, I will argue that, ironically, the post-Popperian approach articulated and applied by Fisch befits the current challenges of psychoanalysis. While it is beyond the scope of this essay to present in any detail, it is of interest that Fisch utilizes his philosophy of science not just to understand developments in the world of natural science but to facilitate interreligious dialogue and critique. That his approach lends itself to the study of religion as well as science may point to its relevance and suitability to psychoanalysis, which has affinities with both realms of discourse.

Fisch's "reflexive skepticism" suggests that self-doubt and self-criticism is our best attitude toward our own convictions because to assume that we are imperfect, limited or just plain wrong is the attitude that will most likely lead us to ongoing problem solving and improvement. If we allow ourselves to expose our vulnerabilities and our shortcomings, and remain open to criticism then we are in the best position to continually problem solve and improve. This is not a call for self-effacement or masochism, as Popper's theory was among the most optimistic and constructive of scientific philosophies; it is rather an appeal to the value of ongoing improvement and refinement that is gained by continuing dialogue and unending critique.

In today's psychoanalysis, we have improved our attitudes toward each other's communities greatly. In some societies and institutes today there is respectful dialogue across perspectives, and the various schools of thought have more often found ways to coexist. Our reading lists now refer to theories beyond our own schools and journals. But getting along and mutual respect, peaceful coexistence, is not sufficient. Fisch's reading of the history and philosophy of science calls on us to go beyond liberal tolerance. Tolerance is essentially the granting of the right for the other to be mistaken, but not in any way a recognition of their viewpoint being of value. In Fisch's model, the other is not seen as a threat but comes to be regarded as an asset, providing an essential benefit. This challenges our assumptions, raises questions that we might not think to ask, upsets our complacency.

The underlying assumption is that self-critique is always somewhat limited, or perhaps another way of stating it is that we are not as good at self-observation and self-criticism as we often like to imagine. Our beliefs, assumptions, and convictions are often egocentric, and we are so invested in these norms and suppositions that we take them for granted. As fish, we may not notice the water we swim in. It is only when our breathing is disturbed that we pay attention to the air. By focusing on our weaknesses and limitations, and by exposing these to analysis by those who have somewhat different beliefs, we gain a unique opportunity to improve.

Recent developments in psychoanalysis have, I believe, been overly influenced by an overly simplistic utilization of the excesses of post-modernism and associated trends in philosophy of science. Ludwig Flech's (1979, originally 1935) articulation of the idea of "Thought Communities,"

Thomas Kuhn's (1970) model of "Paradigm Shifts," and perhaps especially Rorty's (1979) "pragmatism" have been used to argue for the "incommensurability" of theories. Whether an intrinsic problem of Kuhn's or a result of a faulty misapplication, this has led to a form of radical relativism where it is argued that scientific developments do not proceed rationally, but are more like changes in taste or aesthetics. The problem, as I understand it, is this: If we believe with full conviction that our own views are correct or the most highly developed, the best, or absolutely true, then why would we bother talking to those with other, more "primitive" views? But if we cannot systematically compare our theories and argue rationally for the advantages of one or the other, then why should we bother talking to each other? We might agree to live together, respectfully, with liberal tolerance, but if our theories are incommensurable, if we cannot agree on any shared norms, then on what basis could I expect that you could ever convince me of the rightness or wrongness of your views? Whether monists or relativists, absolutists or pragmatists, there is no need to talk with or learn from those others who have different beliefs. We might liberally tolerate them, but we have no need for them in their very otherness. For reflexive skeptics, the other is not merely tolerated but is regarded as essential in and for their very otherness.

The framework problem

Now we must ask, how could the other ever convince us that we are wrong. If they persuade us that we are incorrect on one level, isn't it because they have appealed to our norms, to our framework of understanding, on a higher level? If they persuade me that my theory of mind does not capture the complexity that another theory reveals, it is because they can appeal to my wider frame of belief regarding the psychical. If not, then on what basis could I conclude that I had been mistaken? But then, how can they convince me that these background assumptions are themselves limited? Only by appealing to a yet higher level of assumptions. But this model would lead to an infinite regress in which there would always be a need for yet some higher level of norms and assumptions that would serve as the basis for challenging one's beliefs and convictions. This is what is called in philosophy of science, "the framework problem."

Fisch and his colleagues have proposed a solution to the framework problem along the following lines. Essentially, Fisch argues that while we cannot be convinced by others, because of the framework problem, we can be "ambivalated" by critics. By ambivalated he means that our convictions may become destabilized, some hesitation or unease is introduced, and then we can promulgate these doubts within our own communities. To become so ambivalated, however, we must have sufficient "trust" in these outside critics. Often this comes in the trading zones of ideas outside our immediate scientific communities, in teaching to non-specialized audiences or at conferences where we meet people in related disciplines or associated schools of thought. In the process of this trading and conversing outside of our immediate like-thinking colleagues we may be open enough to destabilizing and ambivalating forces of external criticism.

Why do we need criticism from the other? Why isn't self-criticism sufficient? We are simply too close to our own ideas, and even if we can challenge our own ideas, it is even harder to challenge the norms and values upon which these ideas rest. And even if can challenge those values, it is even harder yet to challenge the underlying norms upon which those values themselves rest, and on and on. The respectful challenges, criticisms, questions of the other are essential in our efforts to improve.

The Chimera and like-enough subjects

It is here that I think psychoanalysis itself may make a small contribution to Fisch's thought. I would suggest that Bach's (2016) symbol of the Chimera is a useful metaphor for understanding Fisch's solution to the framework problem. Here is how I understand it. We are all egocentric, especially about newly-acquired ideas and theories, but also about all our beliefs and convictions. Decentering is always a challenge. In Bach's terms, we tend toward a narcissistic state of consciousness, a state of being, heavily leaning toward subjective self-awareness. In this state of being, the other is perceived as a threat to our very existence. Why would we risk trusting our own mind to that of a stranger? Our narcissistic defenses are designed to deal with the other's strangeness and to gradually allow the other to be recognized, affirmed, and slowly metabolized. The immune system classifies a foreign body as distinct from the self, and therefore as dangerous, but this must change to take in a foreign body. The other must become the self, or like-enough to the self to pass. It is this process that Bach calls "chimerization".

This process is also reminiscent of the affect regulation literature when developmentalists such as Gergeley and Watson (1996) show how mothers teach infants to define and evaluate their feelings by "marked" matching responses. Human caregivers provide "marked" affective mirroring signals, expressions that are altered displays of the responses that the caregiver would normally use to express affect states. In other words, the parental mirroring is not like a real mirror, but rather it mirrors with a difference. It is close to the child's affective experience but not the same, and it is precisely in its commonality and yet difference that it is taken in as a marked response.

I translate the above to mean that to take in the other, we must generally make them "like-enough subjects," to paraphrase and condense Winnicott (1965) and Benjamin (1995), or transform them into chimeras, with mixed or shared DNA, such that we take them in as parts of ourselves. Their criticisms of our theories, of our assumptions, norms, and values, must share enough commonality so that we are fooled into thinking that they are us. We can then take in their criticism as if it were our own without our antibodies attacking their criticism. In short, we identify with their criticism, which is what allows their ideas to penetrate our defensive narcissistic barriers and destabilize us, "ambivalate" us from the inside-out. This is meant as a slight contribution to Fisch's solution to the framework problem.

There is an additional understanding of this change process that psychoanalysis may contribute to Fisch's model. Contemporary psychoanalysis, and especially relational theory places central importance on mutuality, mutual influence and mutual regulation. In a major contribution to our understanding of the therapeutic action of psychoanalysis, Slavin and Kriegman (1998) demonstrated that it is the patient's experience of the analyst's changing that provides the crucial knowledge that there is a genuine working negotiation occurring. It is the patient's observation of real changes in the analyst that provides the crucial experience for patients being willing to risk opening themselves up to reorganization. I would suggest that similarly, in Fisch's model, we would be much more likely to open ourselves up to becoming "ambivalated," if we saw that our interlocutors, our other, was also being affected by our criticisms of them. If we saw that our ideas were taken seriously enough by the other to cause them to become ambivalated, that would support our own willingness to open ourselves up to the input of the other. The experience of mutuality, intersubjectivity, facilitates change.

One might object that I am inviting us to return to the schisms, battles and even holy wars of earlier psychoanalytic generations. In my view, this concern does not consider the possibility of transforming "doer-done to," sado-masochistic, polarized interactions, beyond opposition and simple reversals, into the structure of "thirdness." The structural position of thirdness represents a move beyond subject-object, us/them, with us or against us, kill or be killed thinking (Aron, 2006). Benjamin (2018) suggests that protest can be given a positive function. If we embrace the centrality of learning from rupture and repair, of acknowledging our vulnerability and imperfection, then the other's protest can be turned into an asset and advantage. She writes that thirdness "transforms the potential meaning of such challenges: not a dangerous power struggle but an occasion for mutual exploration and working through together" (p. 62). What I am adding and highlighting in this chapter is that this approach to protest and criticism is useful clinically and socially but is also valuable in inter-school psychoanalytic dialogue and debate.

The question for psychoanalytic communities is the following: Do we want only to sustain, protect, and perpetuate our schools, our approaches? Or do we want to continually test them, challenge and improve them? Is preservation alone a recipe for stagnation? Are we best off maintaining that our own school of thought, (Contemporary Freudian, Kleinian, Kohutian, Relational, Lacanian, or whatever) is the most advanced, deepest, most sophisticated, most comprehensive, answering all the problems with which we deal? Or are we better off assuming our theories and approaches are limited, problematic, incomplete, and in need of constant improvement to be brought about only by being challenged and criticized? Reflexive skepticism is the neo-Popperian attitude that respects the other precisely for the challenge that they provide, stimulating our own questioning and self-examination.

Freud as reflexive-skeptic

In this regard, I want to argue for a view of Freud's achievement somewhat different from the way he is often imagined and presented. Especially with the rise of the New Freud Studies, Freud's embattlement, and his excommunication of dissenters have been highlighted. It is thought that Freud had little use for anyone who disagreed with the shibboleths that he enumerated (the unique importance of sex, Oedipus, dreams, and the unconscious). But I want to suggest that while Freud politically may have exiled his dissenters, nevertheless, he took their criticism seriously and often in fact made their criticisms his own – even while he disavowed such influence. An example of this is his 1914 paper "On Narcissism." The paper is unfortunately read as part of teaching Freud's work, without reading the works of Adler and Jung that had led up to it. It is essential in my view that one reads these works, and especially Jung (1972), who also criticizes Adler for his over emphasis on the psychology of the self, and criticizes Freud for not having a self-psychology. When one reads "On Narcissism" in this context, not only does one understand Freud's paper differently, that is as a response to and attempt to integrate the criticisms of Adler and Jung, but one sees that Freud spent years struggling with his critics' arguments. It is not simply that Freud was trying to persuade his followers that his views were superior to Adler's and Jung's – that is not the only or superordinate concern. Freud may have denigrated their theories and contributions, he may have split them off politically and socially from the psychoanalytic profession, but he took their criticism seriously and spent years struggling with their perspectives, even if he often took their arguments and ideas and made them his own. I am not suggesting that this is proper personal conduct or good ethics but rather that Freud did use others' criticism to bolster his own theory. In his *Interpretation of Dreams,* he had written that: "My emotional life has always insisted that I should have an intimate friend and a hated enemy" (1900, p. 483), and Freud made excellent use of these many enemies to criticize, challenge, and improve his own theories.

One can readily see that despite his polemic writing style, which often made him seem so certain about his contributions, there is another Freud, perhaps an altered and dissociated self-state, a second state of consciousness, a Freud who was very much a reflexive skeptic! To add one illustration, consider how Freud made use of the challenges of critics to reconsider his wish fulfillment theory of dreaming when confronted with traumatic dreams. Even concerning such a favored and hyper-valued contribution as his own theory of dreams, Freud in fact maintained a reflexive skepticism that allowed him to revise his theories. I understand that this may be considered a very generous reading of Freud, and I acknowledge that it is not the only Freud we are familiar with, but it is one of his multiple selves.

Freud seems to have used the criticism of others (external criticism), to facilitate his self-criticism (internal criticism). Self-criticism and self-examination are essential, but they are weak tools. While Mitchell (1993) described self-reflection as the distinguishing characteristic of the analytic function, it should not be forgotten that this analytic self-reflection takes place in the relationship with another, that is with the patient, who as Bion (1980) describes, is the analyst's "best colleague." Try as hard as we may, as sincerely as we might, we are egocentric beings who take many of our assumptions for granted and it is hard for the eye to see itself (Stern, 2014). Stern argues that the eye can see itself, that we can begin to self-observe using our multiplicity. But that multiplicity is itself discovered through enactments with others who hold and embody other versions of ourselves. I would suggest that what Stern calls "snags" and "chafing" (p. 208), which he describes as some tension, a sense of something wrong, contradictory, or uncomfortable, is quite like what Fisch describes as becoming "ambivalated." Self-criticism and self-examination need to be supplemented and amplified by criticism from significant and like-enough others, so that we can take in their criticism in the form of chimeras, we can identify with their criticisms and make them our own.

The relational tradition: internal and external criticism

Relational Psychoanalysis was arguably the first American school of psychoanalysis to emerge following the decline of the dominance of Ego Psychology and the resulting proliferation of multiple schools of psychoanalytic thought (Aron, 1996). Its initial formulation was the result of a comparative psychoanalytic project (Greenberg & Mitchell, 1983). Mitchell once spoke to me of relational psychoanalysis as a form of "critical eclecticism."[3] Certainly, it became a big tent, an overarching perspective, which is why Mitchell and I (1999) referred to our first collection of relational articles as "the emergence of a tradition" rather than a school.

It was also, undoubtedly, offered as a corrective to what were perceived to be excesses in what had previously been viewed as the "mainstream." Important as well, its rise coincided with the development of the Division of Psychoanalysis (39) of the American Psychological Association, and therefore offered a new perspective to a national audience of psychologist-psychoanalysts, many of whom had been excluded for decades from the mainstream. It was a broad and unifying theoretical framework that was fresh, contemporary, post-women's movement, post-classical, post-gay rights, and perhaps most importantly, uniquely its own and not that of the heretofore medical association.[4] This is not to reduce important theoretical developments to politics and professional factors alone, but rather to emphasize that there was a socio-political context within which the relational tradition could burgeon.

That efflorescence of the relational tradition occurred in the 1980s and it has now been almost 30 years since its institutionalization. It went from being an intimate and local movement in New York City to quickly become a national movement and eventually an international force in psychoanalysis.

These two volumes, *De-Idealizing Relational Theory: A Critique from Within* and *Decentering Relational Theory: A Comparative Critique* mark a new turning point for the relational tradition. As captured in the two titles, Sue Grand, Joyce Slochower, and myself, as editors, set out to bring together both internal and comparative critique. It is typical among psycho-analytic schools to argue for the advantages of one school over another, for leaders to point to the deficiencies of other schools and to champion their own. This can be part of a healthy development. The competitiveness of the schools for students and adherents can be constructive and may stir a sharpening of conceptualization and formulation. As I have argued throughout this essay, external critique, when respectful and based on sufficient common ground and shared values, can be useful and even essential to growth.

In these volumes, we see how the seemingly dualistic opposition of "internal" and "external" critique fails to capture the richness of the critical process, and instead I suggest that we view internal and external critique as a dialectic rather than a binary (see Aron & Starr, 2015). The authors in these volumes are engaged in self-critique; as editors, we invited authors who are at the center of developments in relational psychoanalysis, broadly defined. Many would be regarded as quintessential "insiders." We selected insiders precisely because we wanted to provide a forum for evaluation of the state of relational psychoanalysis that would not be perceived as looking in "from the outside." However, it should be clear that all of the authors make use of the other in some ways. They may draw on other schools or theories to formulate their analysis. They may evaluate developments in another variety of relational theory, other than their own. They may reflect on the work of supervisees or junior colleagues and discuss the work from the point of view of the supervisor. They may compare two different relational theorists or approaches, or even compare their own work at two different periods of their development. They may compare the thinking on the relational "left wing" – closer to Interpersonal Theory – with the "right wing" – closer to Object Relations Theory. In sum, even when attempting an internal critique there is ongoing use of an other's perspective.

The point is that the very distinction between internal and external critique is simplistic precisely because of the arguments made in this chapter. Internal critique would be weak indeed without the benefit of a viewpoint outside of one's own perspective. We need more than one vertex to decenter. Luckily, we each have multiple self-states and we have identifications in multiple directions that allow us to feel some snags and chafing such that the eye can come to see itself. The chapters in these two volumes represent an exercise in self-critique aided by numerous external perspectives. Internal and external create, sustain, and define each other dialectically.

What is required for generativity is that each school be receptive to learning from these critiques and not just defending against them. We know of no other books where a school of psychoanalysis has openly and publicly engaged in self-critique (critique by insiders) of the kind published here. In retrospect, this is surprising. After all, doesn't every doctoral dissertation and published research always include a section on the study's limitations and inadequacies? Why wouldn't we expect that psychoanalytic texts would also be willing to expose their limits, restrictions, and biases? As I argued above, this is not a call for masochistic submission to the other, nor does it require us to be overly hesitant or modest in our formulations. We can and should argue for and persuade others of our convictions as much as any school of thought. We can speak and write strongly, and yet remain open, vulnerable, responsive to criticism and to corrective feedback. This is a strength and not a weakness.

To reiterate what we wrote in the Editors' Introduction, we do not attribute our openness to any personally positive or admirable character traits among relational analysts. Relationalists may be as dogmatic, doctrinaire, narrow-minded, and defensive as any other psychoanalyst! We all know that personal analysis has its limits. We view the emergence of this book as the result of theoretical advancement, not personal development. Relational psychoanalysis was based on conceptualizing the nature of transference and countertransference not as distortion, displacement, and false-connection but as a personal, idiosyncratic but plausible construction. This shift in our understanding of transference phenomena led the relational clinician to respond to so-called negative transference as based on plausible perceptions of the analyst's participation with the patient, rather than dismissing the observations as distortions and displacements from past objects.

Why would relational writers reject theoretical criticism as based on misunderstanding, mis-readings, distortions of relational theory, when these same analysts listen to criticism from patients and strive to understand the plausibility of the criticism? We no more believe that our patient is always "right," than we assume that our critics are always right. What we do believe is that when external criticism seems to be accompanied by good will and an effort to understand and respect our point of view it may offer us valuable insight that we would and could not achieve as readily on our own. What we see in these two volumes are relational analysts who are making use of internal and external criticism dialectically, each informing the other. Criticism that may have been rejected when it came from outsiders may have nevertheless been sufficiently internalized such that it led to some "destabilization," and this slight shaking up of perspective may then spread among insiders.

When we acknowledge the contributions of others, this in turn may make them more likely to accept our own reciprocal feedback about their approach. Psychoanalysts have increasingly been promoting an ethos of "mutual vulnerability" (Aron, 2016). Such an attitude among the "schools" might prove valuable as well. As in any transitional phenomena (Winnicott, 1953), it may become impossible to say whether the criticism came from inside or outside. This is the chimera (Bach, 2016), with its mixed DNA, a self-object that allows us to internalize otherness, without fearing for our lives because we have metabolized the other's feedback, and the other has become us. This chimera may then save our lives.

For our approaches to grow, thrive, remain alive and vibrant we need the dialectic of internal and external criticism and we need to allow ourselves ongoing ambivalating. To facilitate its occurrence, psychoanalytic educators need to make space for students and practitioners to "practice ambivalating," that is, to practice being responsive to the snags and chafing that inform us of limits and contradictions and allows us to awake from our dissociations. As editors, it is our hope that these books provide such potential space.

Perhaps you will disagree with these arguments. You may point out the limitations of my thesis and contradictions in my propositions. As a reflexive skeptic, I hope to have argued strongly and stated my proposal with conviction. I do after all wish to persuade and convince and promote my own ideas as much as monists and relativists do. If you have reasoned objections and can prove me wrong, well then – that would certainly make my point, wouldn't it?

Notes

1   This chapter first published as Aron, L. (2017), Beyond Tolerance in Psychoanalytic Communities: Reflexive Skepticism & Critical Pluralism? *Psychoanalytic Perspectives*, 14(3): 271–282. Reprinted by permission of National Institute for the Psychotherapies.

2   Menachem Fisch is a prolific author and a good select bibliography of his work may be found in: Tirosh-Samuelson and Hughes (2016), which also includes several representative articles, an editorial overview, and an intellectual overview. I am not a historian or philosopher of science and have no expert competence in evaluating Fisch's professional contributions. I have been influenced by his work, but the responsibility for any misuse or misunderstanding of his theory is mine alone. Other books of his that I have studied are included in the reference section: Fisch and Benbaji (2011); Fisch (1997). Special thanks to Daniel Marom for introducing me to the philosophical writings of M. Fisch. Marom is responsible for curricular and pedagogical development at the Mandel School for Educational Leadership in Jerusalem, where we have been collaborating in an ongoing study of psychoanalytic education.

3   Unfortunately, I have not been able to find a published reference to his using this phrase to describe his own form of theorizing, but there are several times when he did speak against "uncritical eclecticism" or

"muddled eclecticism," and this usage does support my memory that he considered his own approach a form of "critical eclecticism."
4   It is significant that Greenberg and Mitchell's (1983) book coincided with the first annual meetings of Division 39, and that the establishment of the Relational Orientation at NYU's Postdoctoral Program in Psychotherapy and Psychoanalysis in 1988, and the establishment of *Psychoanalytic Dialogues* in 1990, immediately followed the lawsuit against the American and International Psychoanalytic Associations which was settled in November 1988, with the institutes promising not to discriminate against psychologists or other "nonmedical candidates" (see Wallerstein, 2013).

References

Aron, L. (1996). *A Meeting of Minds*. Hillsdale, NJ: The Analytic Press.
——, (2006). Analytic Impasse and the Third. *Int. J. Psycho-Anal.*, 87: 344–368.
——, (2016). Mutual Vulnerability: An Ethic of Clinical Practice. In: D. M. Goodman & E. R. Severson (Eds.) *The Ethical Turn*. London & New York: Routledge.
Aron, L. & Starr, K. (2015). *A Psychotherapy for the People*. London & New York: Routledge.
Bach. S. (2016). *Chimeras and Other Writings*. Astoria, NY: International Psychoanalytic Books.
Benjamin, J. (1995). Sameness and Difference: Toward an "Overinclusive" Model of Gender Development. *Psychoanal. Inq.*, 15(1):125–142.
——, (2018). *Beyond Doer and Done To*. London & New York: Routledge.
Bion, M. (1980). *Bion in New York and São Paulo*. Perthshire, UK: Clunie Press.
Cooper, A. M. (2008). American Psychoanalysis Today: A Plurality of Orthodoxies. *J. Am. Acad. Psychoanal. Dyn. Psychiatry.*, 36:235–53.
Fisch, M. (1997). *Rational Rabbis: Science and Talmudic Culture*. Bloomington, IN: Indiana University Press.
Fisch, M. & Benbaji, Y. (2011). *The View from Within: Normativity and the Limits of Self-Criticism*. Indiana, IN: University of Notre Dame Press.
Fleck, L. (1981). *The Genesis and Development of a Scientific Fact* (edited by T. J. Trenn and R. K. Merton, foreword by Thomas Kuhn), Chicago, IL: University of Chicago Press.
Freud, S. (1900). The Interpretation of Dreams. *The Standard Edition of the Complete Psychological Works of Sigmund Freud, Volume IV (1900): The Interpretation of Dreams (First Part)*, ix–627.
——, (1914). On Narcissism. *The Standard Edition of the Complete Psychological Works of Sigmund Freud, Volume XIV (1914–1916): On the*

History of the Psycho-Analytic Movement, Papers on Metapsychology and Other Works, 67–102.

Gergeley, G., & Watson, J. S. (1996). The Social Biofeedback Theory of Parental Affect-Mirroring: The Development of Emotional Self-Awareness and Self-Control in Infancy. *Int. J. Psycho-Anal.*. 77:1181–1212.

Govrin, A. (2016). *Conservative and Radical Perspectives on Psychoanalytic Knowledge*. London & New York: Routledge.

Greenberg, J. & Mitchell, S. A. (1983). *Object Relations in Psychoanalytic Theory*. Cambridge, MA: Harvard.

Jung, C. G. (1972). *C. G. Jung's Two Essays on Analytical Psychology*. Collected Works of C. G. Jung (Book 7), Princeton, NJ: Princeton University Press.

Kuhn, T. S. (1970). *The Structure of Scientific Revolutions*. Chicago, IL and London: University of Chicago Press (Second Edition).

Mitchell, S. A. (1993). Reply to Bachant and Richards. *Psychoanal. Dial.*, 3(3):461–480.

Mitchell, S. & Aron, L. (1999). *Relational Psychoanalysis: The Emergence of a Tradition*. Hillsdale, NJ: The Analytic Press.

Rorty, R. (1979). *Philosophy and the Mirror of Nature*. Princeton, NJ: Princeton University Press.

Schafer, R. (1979). On Becoming a Psychoanalyst of One Persuasion or Another. *Contemp. Psychoanal.*, 15:345–360.

Slavin, M. O. & Kriegman, D. (1998). Why the Analyst Needs to Change: Toward a Theory of Conflict, Negotiation, and Mutual Influence in the Therapeutic Process. *Psychoanal. Dial.*, 8(2):247–284.

Stepansky, P. E. (2009). *Psychoanalysis at the Margins*. New York: Other Press.

Stern, D. B. (2004). The Eye Sees Itself. *Contemp. Psychoanal.*, 40(2): 197–237.

Tirosh-Samuelson, H. & Hughes, A. W. (2016). *Menachem Fisch: The Rationality of Religious Dispute*. Leiden, Netherlands & Boston, MA: Brill.

Wallerstein, R. S. (1992). *The Common Ground of Psychoanalysis*. New York: Aronson.

——, (2013). *Lay Analysis: Life Inside the Controversy*. London and New York: Routledge.

Willock, B. (2011). *Comparative-Integrative Psychoanalysis: A Relational Perspective for the Discipline's Second Century*. London and New York: Routledge.

Winnicott, D. W. (1953). Transitional Objects and Transitional Phenomena— A Study of the First Not-Me Possession. *Int. J. Psych-Anal.*, 34:89–97.

——, (1965). The Maturational Processes and the Facilitating Environment. *Int. Psycho-Anal. Lib.*, 64:1–276. London: The Hogarth Press and the Institute of Psycho-Analysis.

Index